Derivatives Markets and Investment Management

Derivatives Markets and Investment Management

Mark Fox-Andrews
Nicola Meaden

PRENTICE HALL
WOODHEAD-FAULKNER

London　　New York　　Toronto　　Sydney　　Tokyo　　Singapore
　　　　　Madrid　　Mexico City　　Munich

First published 1995 by
Prentice Hall/Woodhead-Faulkner (Publishers) Limited
Campus 400, Maylands Avenue
Hemel Hempstead
Hertfordshire, HP2 7EZ
A division of
Simon & Schuster International Group

© Mark Fox-Andrews, Nicola Meaden 1995

All rights reserved. No part of this publication may be reproduced, stored in a retrieval system, or transmitted, in any form, or by any means, electronic, mechanical, photocopying, recording or otherwise, without prior permission, in writing, from the publisher.

Typeset in 10/12pt Times
by Dorwyn Ltd, Rowlands Castle, Hants

Printed and bound in Great Britain by
Hartnolls Limited, Bodmin, Cornwall.

Library of Congress Cataloging-in-Publication Data

Fox-Andrews, Mark.
    Derivatives markets & investment management/Mark Fox-Andrews, Nicola Meaden.
    p. cm.
    Includes index.
    ISBN 0-13-343013-8
    1. Derivatives securities–Marketing.   2. Portfolio management.
I. Meaden, Nicola.   II. Title.   III. Title: Derivatives markets and investment management.
HG6024.A3F69 1994
332.63'228–dc20   94–35312
                                                                                   CIP

British Library Cataloguing in Publication Data

A catalogue record for this book is available from the British Library

ISBN 0 13 343013 8

1 2 3 4 5   98 97 96 95

Contents

Preface	vii
Acknowledgements	ix
1. Introduction	1
2. Derivatives funds – regulation and distribution	19
3. Taxation issues and derivatives	39
4. Performance indices and benchmarks	64
5. Traders and investment managers	82
6. Fund products	109
7. OTC derivatives and investment management	125
8. Investor considerations and fund selection	136
9. Where to from here?	153
Appendices	159
Postscript	176
Index	184

Preface

The use of derivatives markets and instruments continues to be one of the fastest growing, and controversial, areas in the financial world. Investment products using these tools are pushing back the limits of new techniques and systems and are challenging global regulators. Investors seek reassurance and opportunity, as well as understanding and information. Litigation is on the increase.

The collapse of Baring Brothers Bank in March 1995 has caused new storms about these markets. The full facts are still unclear, but the information available so far suggests either the complete failure of internal procedures and/or a trading strategy which got completely out of control.

We are not academics and this is not an academic book. We have tried to present a reasonably comprehensive overview of the current situation in this field. The early chapters summarise the historical development of the markets, the legal position in general terms, and the accounting and taxation position. After giving the infrastructure, we move on to benchmark and performance issues and information. We report on some specific products in the international markets, cover current issues, such as systemic risk, convergence and switcher fund developments.

We then provide an analysis of the buy and the sell side of the product, before trying to look into the future. Following from comments on our first book *Futures Fund Management* published in 1991, we have also put in some appendices with some quite basic general information about this industry. Hopefully this will help make the book of interest to both 'professional' and 'amateur' readers.

Acknowledgements

We have been helped by a large number of friends, associates, professional sources and references. We would first like to thank the following for their specific written contributions: Eric Bettleheim and Ed Black from the London Office of Rogers and Wells, for the legal information; Emma Lubbock, Richard Clarke and Kathy Ryan from the London Office of Price Waterhouse, for the accounting and taxation information; and Antony Belchambers from the Futures and Options Association in the United Kingdom for most of the introductory overview and for an early review of the manuscript.

We would like to recognise some specific press and journalistic sources: *Managed Derivatives*, *Derivatives in Fund Management*, *Managed Account Reports*, *Hedge* magazine, *Risk* magazine, *Futures and Options World* and the specialists at the *Financial Times*.

We have used public source material from Citibank, Merrill Lynch, Hypo Foreign and Colonial, Swiss Bank Corporation, the Japanese Commodity Association and ISDA.

We have used information provided by the Futures Industry Association, the main futures exchanges, and Powers and Dubin.

Any use of material without acknowledgement or recognition is unintentional.

Finally we would generally like to thank our colleagues at TASS Management and the Mees Pierson group – in particular Carrie Dodd-Noble and Emma Maloney for their help with the manuscript.

Nicola Meaden
Mark Fox-Andrews

1
Introduction

Whilst 1994 set new records for volumes in derivatives instruments, whether traded through exchanges or over the counter, the results from investment managers specialising in using these markets made a less impressive and often more controversial story.

Whilst derivatives-related funds showed average returns in 1993 in excess of 20 per cent, the provisional results for 1994 suggest losses in the region of 10 per cent. Even those funds which had shown positive returns made very low percentage increases. Funds specialising in the commodity markets were amongst the few to reward investors satisfactorily.

Whilst investors may have been happy to see the end of the year, activity in the world futures and options exchanges significantly increased worldwide. The average increase was 25 per cent, with contracts traded exceeding

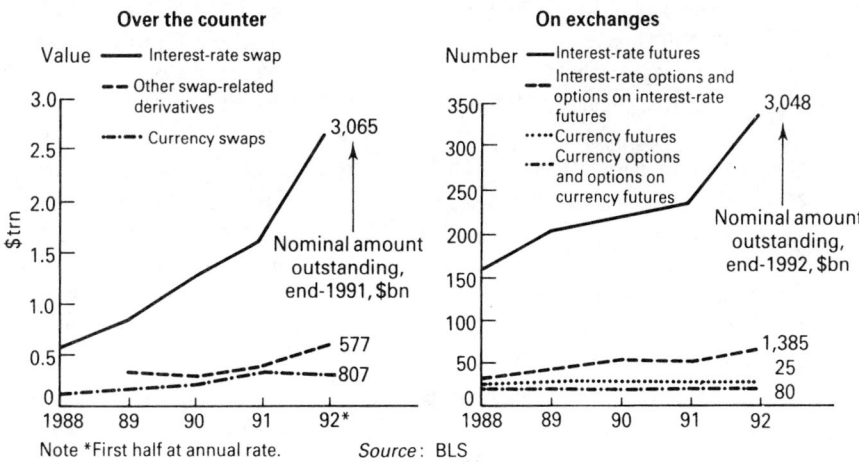

Figure 1.1 Derivatives contracts traded.

Table 1.1

'94 Rank	'93 Rank	Exchange	1993	1994	Percent change
1	1	Chicago Board of Trade	178,773,105	219,504,074	22.8%
2	2	Chicago Mercantile Exchange	146,746,990	205,185,603	39.8%
3	3	LIFFE, U.K.	97,108,712	148,726,421	53.2%
4	4	Chicago Board Options Exchange	81,927,411	114,952,472	40.3%
5	7	BM&F, Brazil	52,213,672	102,981,783	97.2%
6	6	MATIF, France	72,263,961	93,438,671	29.3%
7	5	New York Mercantile Exchange	74,266,549	78,661,383	5.9%
8	8	DTB, Germany	37,924,127	49,323,237	30.1%
9	9	London Metal Exchange	35,289,932	47,687,717	35.1%
10	10	TIFFE, Japan	24,126,147	38,034,953	57.7%
11	17	MEFF RENTA VARIABLE, Spain	14,419,497	34,562,437	139.7%
12	12	Sydney Futures Exchange, Australia	21,481,096	31,556,584	46.9%
13	11	Tokyo Commodity Exchange for Industry	21,557,795	30,481,313	41.4%
14	15	SIMEX, Singapore	15,729,787	24,060,274	53.0%
15	14	OM Stockholm	15,973,443	21,741,415	36.1%
16	22	MEFF RENTA FIJA, Spain	8,147,332	19,735,329	142.2%
17	13	Tokyo Stock Exchange	18,979,492	17,453,621	(8.0%)
18	16	Osaka Securities Exchange	14,551,833	14,935,942	2.6%
19	19	International Petroleum Exchange, U.K.	13,769,978	14,534,403	5.6%
20	21	Coffee, Sugar and Cocoa Exchange	11,304,823	12,664,052	12.0%
21	18	Philadelphia Stock Exchange	14,246,794	12,612,020	(11.5%)
22	20	Tokyo Grain Exchange	13,687,746	12,122,483	(11.4%)
23	23	SOFFEX, Switzerland	6,808,963	9,372,445	37.6%
24	26	South African Futures Exchange	4,484,973	7,377,937	64.5%
25	29	MONEP, France	4,212,275	5,751,470	36.5%
26	24	Kansai Agricultural Commodity Exchange	6,299,702	4,960,772	(21.3%)
27	33	Hong Kong Futures Exchange	2,698,994	4,799,738	77.8%
28	31	New York Cotton Exchange	3,437,664	4,680,278	36.1%
29	27	Marcato Italiano Dei Futures, Italy	4,414,248	4,369,917	(1.0%)
30	25	European Options Exchange	4,508,182	4,318,154	(4.2%)
31	30	London Commodity Exchange, U.K.	3,704,315	3,867,400	4.4%
32	28	AMEX	4,365,512	3,613,651	(17.2%)
33	38	Montreal Exchange	1,714,701	3,514,766	105.0%
34	36	Osaka Textile Exchange	1,753,624	3,107,228	77.2%
35	37	Manila International Futures Exchange	1,749,650	3,091,894	76.7%
36	32	Mid-America Commodity Exchange	3,002,480	3,074,562	2.4%
37	43	Kobe Rubber Exchange	1,275,051	2,933,883	130.1%
38	34	Kanmon Commodity Exchange	2,145,245	2,416,245	12.6%
39	40	Winnipeg Commodity Exchange	1,516,044	1,759,525	16.1%

Table 1.1 *Continued*

'94 Rank	'93 Rank	Exchange	1993	1994	Percent change
40	50	Austrian Futures and Options Exchange	890,490	1,734,220	94.7%
41	39	Kansas City Board of Trade	1,523,979	1,697,866	11.4%
42	45	BELFOX, Belgium	1,133,697	1,635,346	44.2%
43	44	Guarantee Fund Danish Options and Futures	1,156,425	1,335,293	15.5%
44	49	Nagoya Textile Exchange	920,076	1,200,742	30.5%
45	48	Financial Futures Market, Amsterdam	963,855	1,121,252	16.3%
46	42	Nagoya Grain and Sugar Exchange	1,507,871	1,098,721	(27.1%)
47	41	Yokohama Raw Silk Exchange	1,512,132	998,686	(34.0%)
48	47	New York Futures Exchange	976,829	873,359	(10.6%)
49	51	Minneapolis Grain Exchange	876,776	805,919	(8.1%)
50	53	New Zealand Futures Exchange	624,304	772,783	23.8%
51	52	Kobe Raw Silk Exchange	687,723	695,172	1.1%
52	54	Oslo Stock Exchange	430,435	637,139	48.0%
53	55	Kuala Lumpur Commodity Exchange	362,958	568,132	56.5%
54	46	Toyahashi Dried Cocoon Exchange	1,066,374	488,558	(54.2%)
55	35	Maebashi Dried Cocoon Exchange	1,782,394	475,978	(73.3%)
56	56	Toronto Futures Exchange	294,873	384,010	30.2%
57	57	Hokkaido Grain Exchange	288,835	331,525	14.8%
58	58	Agricultural Futures Markets, Amsterdam	204,307	273,870	34.0%
59	59	Pacific Stock Exchange	153,007	73,678	(51.8%)
60	61	Philadelphia Board of Trade	25,103	42,346	68.7%
61	60	New York Stock Exchange	41,745	31,004	(25.7%)
62	62	Irish Futures and Options Exchange	13,807	16,362	18.5%
63	63	MERFOX, Argentina	12,554	52	(99.6%)

1.4 billion. The strongest growth continued to be in the non-US markets with options growth especially notable.

The International Swaps and Derivatives Association estimates the total notional principal amount of new swaps business in 1993 at US$5,518 billion. Most (US$4,100 billion) were in interest rate swaps – where the actual capital value risked is 2 to 3 per cent of the notional principal value. Interest rate swap options were the fastest single growth segment, mainly denominated in US dollars.

In the first half of 1994 volume in privately negotiated swaps and related derivatives transactions represented a notional principal value of US$4,200 billion. Second half numbers will probably be lower.

In 1994 it was estimated that the combined total value of derivatives traded on the futures and options exchanges and the over the counter products in

4 Derivatives Markets and Investment Management

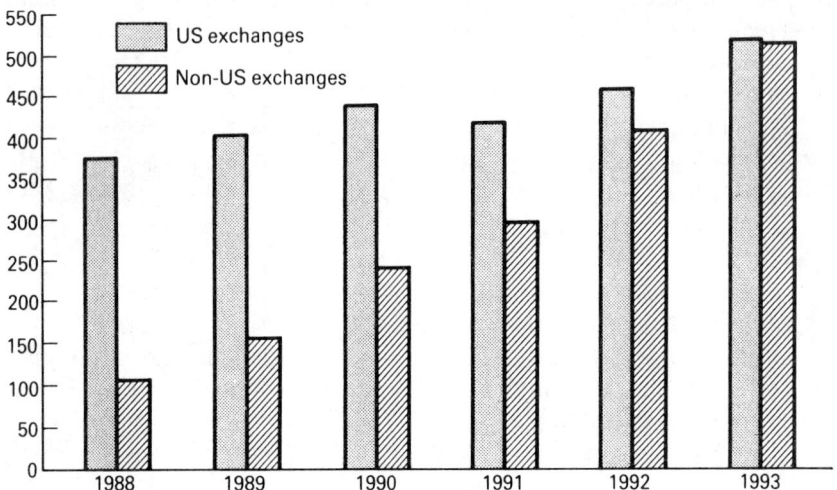

Figure 1.2 Global futures volumes.

notional terms was US$16 trillion. Gross domestic product (GDP) in the United States is approximately US$6.5 trillion.

1993 ended on a strong note in the Investment Management side of the Industry with positive performance and further increases in funds under management to US$100 billion. This number includes most so-called hedge-fund managers and a lot of specialist in-house investment by the major investment banks. 1994 did not produce such positive results.

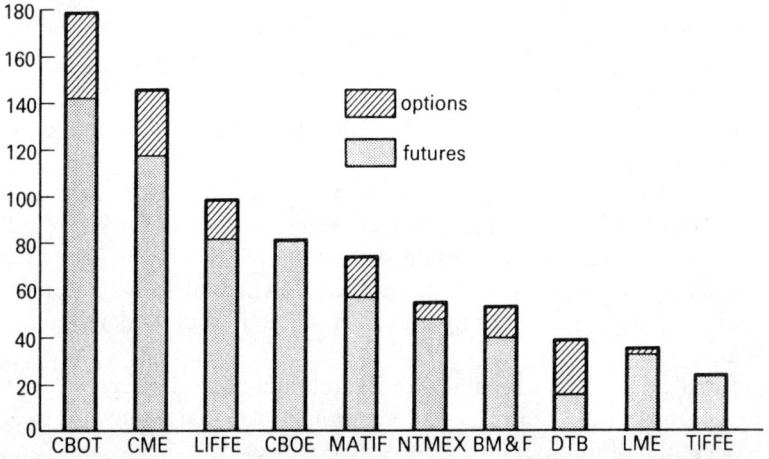

Figure 1.3 Futures and options trading volume: top ten international exchanges.

Against this general euphoria must be put the continued concern amongst central bankers and regulators about the perceived risk that financial systems could collapse as a result of any upsets in the trading of derivatives. Moves are afoot in the United States to set up a Federal Derivatives Commission to establish standards for Capital Accounting disclosure and suitability for Institutions dealing in Derivatives. The provisional legislation has the rather wonderful name 'The Derivatives Safety and Soundness Supervision Act of 1995'.

Recent history

There has been no slowdown in the growth of the derivatives industry. Global futures volumes of 886.4 million in 1992 became 1 billion in 1993 and 1.4 billion in 1994. The turn in the global bond markets in 1994 meant that the derivatives markets offered one of the best escape routes for the stale bulls from 1993.

Details of the major exchange volumes in 1994 are listed below:

Exchange	No. of contracts (m)
CME	226
Chicago Board of Trade	219
Chicago Board Options Exchange	184
LIFFE	153
MATIF	93.4
NYMEX/COMEX	78.7
DTB	59.2
LME	43.8
TIFFE	38.0
SOFFEX	28.0
SYMEX	24.1
IPE	14.5
NYCSCE	12.7
MONEP	8.8
NY Cotton Exchange	4.7
LCE	3.8

Political and economic volatility remained dramatic with even the emerging markets' optimism deteriorating severely at the end of the year. Orange County in the US did no favours to the industry, although the collapse has not yet led to the broader systemic ripples which have been a matter of media and regulatory concern in recent years.

Interest-rate markets are the main areas both of growth and activity, although the commodity markets have been more active in 1994 than in recent years. The gold and the grains markets both had large rallies, and rising interest rates led to inflation expectations. The coffee market exploded upwards assisted by an old fashioned frost scare! In the European context, there are now over twenty exchanges, providing domestic markets hedging opportunities for local interest rates and stock indices. A number of the exchanges have joint working arrangements and are operated on screen based systems, unlike the major United States and UK exchanges which work primarily through open outcry.

As far as the futures fund industry is concerned, the expansion in opportunity and acceptability of international markets has been very helpful, and contributed to the recent growth in activity and investment. In particular, Europe's geographical location has assisted the process.

Why derivatives fund management?

As experience of using futures and options markets has expanded in the last 20 years an increasing number of traders have established successful reputations for themselves as profitable participants on the investment and money-management front. Since the performance of investments using these instruments should be uncorrelated and is judged on an absolute as opposed to a benchmark basis the approach has been becoming more attractive. Attention to Hedge Funds increased with their extraordinary results in 1993. High potential returns, market and geographic variety and flexibility and premium fee pricing have been a potent melting pot for the development of the use of derivatives for fund-management purposes. Increasingly sophisticated data analysis and pricing power promoted OTC activity.

Futures and options – a brief history

Futures and options are the ideal mechanism for managing risk and they have been used for this purpose for centuries. While it is true that the modern futures contract emerged to overcome supply problems in government pork during the American Civil War, the commercial practice of trading forward in order to secure price stability is even older, going back to the Middle Ages – even to the Roman occupation of Britain! Indeed, the forward selling of Japanese rice in the sixteenth century exhibited many of the features that are present in futures today (e.g. standardisation of contract terms, payment of deposit). Some argue that a very rudimentary form of commodity future was first traded in the Liverpool cotton trade in the eighteenth century. Others point to the trading of tea and rubber in and around London's coffee houses at around the same time; while yet others point to the forward dealing of Dutch tulips in the early seventeenth century.

In reality, the need for standardisation in the endless variety of individually tailored contracts only became of real commercial importance in the nineteenth century, with the internationalisation of markets and the move from trade protectionism to a new free trade philosophy; and it was the Chicago Board of Trade which, in 1865, introduced the first exchange-traded contract by which all contract variables (e.g. quality, quantity and delivery) were standardised.

Financial futures and options, on the other hand, are a comparatively new product and did not emerge until the lifting of the Bretton Woods Agreement in 1972. Institutions suddenly found themselves contending with the 'boom and bust' economics of fluctuating exchange rates, double-digit inflation and interest rates, and a succession of international and economic crises. Only then was it realised that money was just another raw material and that its value could fluctuate like any other commodity. Once again, it was the United States exchanges which developed the first financial futures contract. The new contract became an instant success and resulted in a proliferation of new risk-management products (many of which are traded over the counter) and a new generation of financial futures and options contracts and exchanges. Today, futures and options are tradable in respect of all the world's most traded commodities and in relation to every primary market and enjoy full international, regulatory and commercial acceptability in all the world's major financial centres.

It is perhaps not surprising therefore that futures and options have become the fastest growing financial service sector, with global volumes outstripping significantly volumes in securities. Since 1987, they have grown by a factor of about 8 and, at the end of 1992, the total notional amount outstanding has been estimated at exceeding 9 trillion dollars, two-thirds of which are attributable to trading in over-the-counter (OTC) derivatives. Internationally, Europe has seen the highest rate of growth, enlarging its share in this business from 7 per cent of the world's total in 1988 to nearly 30 per cent at the end of 1992. In that same year, London's futures and options exchanges traded over 120 million contracts, giving London 65 per cent of total European business and representing a volume increase of over 40 per cent from 1991. Today, there are over twenty exchanges in Europe trading over a hundred financial and commodity futures and options contracts (excluding equity options).

This growth in institutional awareness of futures and options as a mechanism for hedging against price and money rate risk is less noticeable when it comes to using futures and options as an alternative asset class for investment purposes (i.e. managed futures).

The emergence of managed futures

Futures and options funds have been in existence since 1949. However, money under management in such funds remained comparatively insignificant

– at least until the 1980s. Then, in 1983, the role of managed futures as a perceived alternative asset class was given academic recognition when the late Professor Lintner of Harvard University established:

first, that there was a low correlation between returns on managed futures and options move at different times and according to different economic and market criteria than, for example, transferable securities (e.g. a rise in commodity prices can have an adverse effect on inflation and lead to a firming of interest rates which, in turn, may generally generate a fall in equity prices);
second, that as a result of that correlation, the inclusion of managed futures in the traditional investment portfolio could reduce volatility and enhance investor return;
and third, that portfolios which included managed futures reflected substantially lower risks at all levels of return than portfolios which did not include managed futures.

These findings were confirmed graphically at the time of the stock-market crash in October 1987 (i.e. Black Monday) when the S&P 500 fell by 23 per cent, yet managed futures made an average net return of 12 per cent – proving that futures funds tend to perform better than equity funds during periods of financial instability. This soon led to a significant increase in the number and sophistication of commodity trading advisors (CTAs) and managed futures funds, the latter of which grew from 14 in 1979 to over 400 in 1992. Indeed, CTAs have since expanded their trading activities and experience into currency, interbank, cash and forward markets. Perhaps even more significantly, growing numbers of banks are now launching or considering launching their own managed futures funds.

The futures-fund industry is developing at such a pace that even the term 'managed futures' is today regarded by some as *passé*. The word 'derivatives', loosely incorporating both exchange traded futures and options, OTC derivatives and interbank forwards, is increasingly superseding the word 'futures'. In the United Kingdom, specialist investment managers dealing in futures, options and other derivatives are not called CTAs, but are classified as derivative fund managers (DFMs).

European institutional investors, unlike their United States counterparts, while recognising the value of futures and options as risk-management tools, still regarded them as too risky and preferred to invest in cash, bonds and equities. For them, risk management continued to remain a low-priority discipline. Institutional recognition of the value of futures for investment purposes has been consistently hampered by fragmented, inappropriate and obstructive regulation, and the disincentive of high management charges. Fortunately, all that is in the process of changing. More to the point, increasing volatility in the world stock markets and continuing financial crises (e.g. in

1988, sterling interest rates jumped by 4.5 per cent points within three months; in 1990 the dollar slumped by nearly one fifth against sterling; and, in 1992 and 1993, the notorious currency crises which nearly broke the exchange rate mechanism (ERM)) resulted in European interest in futures going on a sudden and upward curve. Investors soon realised that portfolio protection through diversification could not be secured by domestic or international stock selection, but only by investing in liquid alternative assets of known and recognised quality which have little or no correlation with mainstream investment instruments. At the same time, investment strategy itself shifted from maximising profits to minimising risk. Growing numbers of Europeans began to attend international conferences on futures money management and, in 1991, the European Managed Futures Association was established. More significantly, while global money under management in futures funds has grown from US$600 million in 1982 to over US$26 billion in 1994 (equivalent to a total fund exposure, even at a conservative level of gearing of US$400 billion), a small but growing proportion of that investment money has been raised from European investors and by the end of 1994 this was estimated to be 30 per cent.

The role of futures in fund management

In the context of fund management, futures and options have three fundamentally important roles:

efficient portfolio management: that is, the protection of investment portfolios against adverse movement in the value of the instruments in which the portfolio is invested and/or as a hedge against fluctuations in money rates (e.g. interest rate or exchange rates) or as a means of reducing relevant costs (e.g. more efficient cash flow management);
tactical asset allocation: that is, generating additional growth by taking immediate and short-term positions in other sectors, products or instruments without disturbing the underlying core holdings of the fund;
direct investment: that is, use of futures and options as an alternative investment medium thereby enabling fund managers to diversify across a much wider range of instruments and commodities and, because of the liquidity of most markets, to do so more easily (and at lower cost) than might otherwise be the case.

As far as efficient portfolio management is concerned, the argument is that if you take out insurance to protect the physical assets of your company, why not take out a hedged position to protect the financial assets on your balance sheet or, indeed, in equities and other investments in your portfolio? There are, of course, stories of corporate treasurers who have taken positions in derivatives and incurred unexpected and sometimes severe losses. However, these are nearly always in sophisticated over-the-counter products, rather than through positions taken in futures exchanges. On the other hand, and even more importantly, there are many more stories of companies that have incurred substantial losses by failing to insure themselves against unexpected movements in interest and exchange rates. In many respects, it is they, rather than the users of futures markets, that are the risk-takers. Put simply, hedging through the use of futures (or using futures as a means of efficient portfolio management) is similar to casualty insurance. You may not always need it, but when you do, you really need it!

Few private investors have the time or the skill to trade futures successfully, but for those who wish to take advantage of the prospect of above-average returns (and run the risk also of above average loss) which may be obtained through taking positions in geared contracts, there are distinct advantages in investing in a futures fund. These include:

professional management (not otherwise available to the small private investor), which is of particular value in such sophisticated and fast-moving markets as futures and options;
limited liability, so that potential losses are limited to the sums invested and, in some cases, could even be protected through the provision of a guarantee (i.e. thereby restricting the risk of loss to the return on capital itself);
diversification, which reduces investment risk by investment in a widespread of instruments and products;
greater choice, in so far as funds range from high-risk/high-return to low-risk guaranteed funds, from fully diversified funds to, for example, specialist 'currency only' funds;
greater flexibility, in that profits may be made in falling, as well as rising, markets;
greater independence of price movement because, first, constituent positions in a futures portfolio may move more independently than constituent equity positions in a stock portfolio; and, second, individual futures markets do not exhibit the 'herd' instinct of stock markets (i.e. a downward move in one equity exchange often generates comparable movements on other equity exchanges).

A further and significant advantage is that futures and options can replicate the capital growth (loss) and achieve the same economic effect as direct investment in underlying instruments/assets. In other words, stock and bond exposure may be obtained through futures and options funds, but more efficiently, at less cost, even same-day settlement and no withholding tax problems and with the benefit of a higher income return. The last-mentioned benefit is achievable because, by having only to pay margin in order to secure the required positions, most of the fund can be applied to producing higher income without disturbing the underlying instruments. The two most common types of futures funds which seek or have the effect of replicating direct investment in the underlying instruments are synthetic index funds, which seek to better the performance of a particular share or sector index, and '90:10 funds', which invest up to 90 per cent in, for example, zero coupon bonds or fixed-interest stocks and up to 10 per cent in futures and options.

It should be noted that, while there is a significant range of products and markets in which positions may be taken, trading styles vary between technical traders (who base their trading decisions on analysis of the historic price and other data in different markets), fundamentalists (whose trading decisions are based on anticipated market movement generated by such fundamental factors as political events, supply and demand, agricultural and mineral reports and changes in interest rates and taxation, etc.) and discretionary traders (who might use a mixture of both fundamental and technical analysis).

It is apparent from the foregoing that futures funds constitute an alternative investment medium which may not be correlated with stocks and bonds; provide a more efficient means of being invested in stocks and bonds; and have a capability of providing the investor with better performance during periods of financial stress.

Developments in Europe

Mention has already been made of growing European interest and involvement in futures. Indeed, the increasing depth and liquidity of the major European exchanges; the lack of correlation between United States domestic contracts and European contracts; and the lack of position and price limits on European exchanges are all helping to generate increasing business from the United States. United States CTAs are beginning to look at the benefits of establishing a European base to manage the European futures business of United States funds and, at the same time, extend their own client base to include European fund managers. Unfortunately, the European growth curve in managed futures (unlike in the United States or Japan) continues to be hampered by the failure of the regulatory authorities to accord managed futures adequate recognition either at European Community (EC) level or, in the case of some member states, through domestic regulation.

One of the objectives of the establishment of the single European market was to unify the European Community's financial markets in such a way as to create a single EC financial centre in which customers would be able to raise finance, invest, trade and hedge positions and deposit funds with or through any duly authorised institution in any member state substantially free of inter-state restrictions.

This single market in financial services (due to take effect on 1 January 1996) is founded on two basic freedoms, namely, the freedom of financial service institutions authorised in one member state to carry on their activities and set up branches wherever they wish within the Community without having to be established in any other member state; and the freedom of their capital and that of their customers to flow across member-state frontiers without restriction.

The method by which these objectives are to be achieved is the harmonisation of standards for prudential supervision and for investor protection; mutual recognition by and between the regulatory authorities of each member state; and by what is called 'home country control and supervision' (i.e. by the member state in which the financial institution is based).

The question is whether such a single market has been or is even intended to be created in relation to collective investment in futures and options. At present, there is only one directive which seeks to passport funds across all the member states of Europe and to establish common regulations for their authorisation, supervision, structure and investment activities. Unfortunately, this directive (the Undertakings for Collective Investment in Transferable Securities Directive (or UCITS)), does not extend to closed-ended funds or funds invested in instruments other than transferable securities. In other words, it does not cover futures and options funds. However, Article 21 of the directive provides that member states may authorise a UCITS fund to use derivatives but only for purposes of either 'efficient portfolio management' or 'provide protection against exchange rates in the context of the management of their assets and liabilities'.

The present position is that the European Commission is working on a proposal to extend the UCITS directive to include money-market funds and fund of funds. In addition, Article 21 is to be amended to further define 'efficient portfolio management', first, because member states are adopting their own competitive interpretations of the term; and, second, to include a limited form of 'tactical asset allocation'. However, this enlargement of the permitted use of futures and options by UCITS funds has not been matched by the extension of UCITS to cover futures funds. Unfortunately, comparatively few futures funds have been established in Europe and they are therefore seen as insignificant when compared with, for example, money-market funds, even by those member states which have actually authorised various forms of futures funds.

The enlargement of UCITS to include futures and options funds would be entirely consistent with, and would further the establishment of, an internal market in financial services; would further the cause of investor protection through the development of a common regulatory framework; would enhance the competitiveness of European Community futures firms and exchanges; and would provide greater choice for investors. Until UCITS is so extended, fund mangers will continue to be bedevilled by the complexity of disparate rules across the EC Member States; and the principle of investor protection will continue to be ill-served by the withholding of the EC passport from collective investment in futures and options (but not from direct-position trading). There are a number of directives which cover other sectors. For example, the insurance directives and the proposed funds directive accommodate the use of futures and options for efficient portfolio-management purposes, so that if the definition of efficient portfolio management is enlarged as indicated by the Commission, this will impact beneficially on those other sector directives.

A number of reports have predicted significant (and sometimes over-enthusiastic) benefits for financial-service providers and institutional and private customers through the establishment of a single European market. However, even the more realistic expectations will not be realised if the process of harmonisation results in inappropriate or unnecessarily costly or onerous regulatory requirements. This will only have the effect of impeding the very sectors of industry which are in the process of being liberalised and their ability to compete with non-EC financial-service providers and exchanges. It is important therefore that EC negotiations designed to liberalise markets and agree minimum regulatory requirements should not become a vehicle for stunting their development or sustaining protectionism.

In the absence of effective framework for harmonisation, it is necessary to consider the very different regulatory requirements of each member state which actually permit managed futures (only one of which, namely the United Kingdom, has developed a special licensing and regulatory requirements for CTAs, locally called 'derivative fund managers' (DFMs)).

France

Futures and options funds have been permitted since 1989, but only as mutual investment funds or *fonds commun de placement* (FCPs). These are open-ended mutual funds where the assets are jointly owned by the investors, each of whom has an undivided proportional interest in them, but which are required to be held by a French depository. The FCP is one of two open-ended structures, the other of which is the SICAV or variable capital investment company. Closed-ended futures funds are not permitted under French laws.

An FCP futures fund must be registered with the Commission des Operations de Bourse (COB) and may invest only in contracts invested in authorised markets; must hold at all times 'liquid assets' (e.g. cash deposits; treasury bonds; short-term negotiable-debt instruments) in an amount at least equal to 50 per cent of its assets or such higher amounts as the fund's internal regulations may provide. Further, the fund may not invest more than 10 per cent of the securities in the same class issued by any one class of that issuer's securities. Cash or security borrowings may not exceed 10 per cent of fund assets. Finally, the FCP may only commence trading after it has raised a minimum of US$500,000 within 30 days.

Such funds are subject to highly prohibitive marketing restrictions with the result that all advertising and public solicitation is prohibited and no distinction is drawn between professional and private investors or between private placements and public offerings. FCPs may, of course, advertise themselves by way of image advertisements, use seminars for promotion, respond to requests for information from potential investors and, in the case of certain institutions, may engage in limited marketing to existing customers.

Offshore futures funds must first seek authorisation from the Ministry of Finance and, in the case of a public offer, approval of the prospectus by COB.

Belgium

Managed futures funds were first introduced in 1991 and may constitute open-ended or closed-ended structures and may be in contractual (FCP) or corporate (SICAV) form, but they must invest in either commodity futures and options or financial futures and options. Managed futures funds are regulated by the Banking and Finance Commission.

Offshore funds may be offered for sale in Belgium, provided they obtain prior regulatory approval from the Banking and Finance Commission, but they must maintain the same distinction between commodity or financial futures and options funds.

Ireland

Futures funds are authorised and regulated by the Central Bank and may take the form of unit trusts under the Unit Trusts Act (1990) or open-ended investment companies pursuant to the Companies Act (1991). There are a number of diversification requirements. The funds may invest only in exchange-traded contracts (and, in certain circumstances, OTC options). They are divided into capital-protected (or guaranteed) funds and leveraged funds. As might be expected, the latter category of funds is subject to more stringent marketing rules.

Offshore funds may be marketed in Ireland with the prior approval of the Central Bank.

Luxemburg

Since 1984, futures funds have been able to operate as either mutual investment funds or open-ended investment companies. New rules permit 70 per cent of net assets to be invested in margin and premium (thereby accommodating a high level of gearing), but assets may not be invested in OTC instruments and, for example, a fund may not maintain an open position in a single futures contract if the margin is 5 per cent or more of the fund's total net assets. Further, no open position may be held in futures contracts relating to a single commodity or a single category of futures contract if the margin payable exceeds 20 per cent of the fund's total assets. A minimum subscription requirement of LFr500,000 is imposed per investor.

It has been argued, somewhat tenuously, that the rules governing the right of funds to use derivatives for efficient portfolio-management purposes are sufficiently flexible as to enable such a fund to operate as a low-geared futures fund, yet maintain its uses or 'EC Passportable' status.

Offshore funds may be marketed in Luxemburg provided that they are established in a properly regulated jurisdiction and have obtained the prior approval of the Luxemburg Monetary Institute (IML).

The Netherlands

Futures funds became permissible in 1990 and may take the form of an investment company or a mutual fund and may be open-ended or close-ended. They must be registered with the Dutch Securities Board and with the Central Bank and are regulated pursuant to the Supervision of Investment Institutions Act (1990). There are few investment restrictions imposed on such funds and funds offered only to professional investors do not require prior authorisation.

United Kingdom

Until the United Kingdom introduces legislation to accommodate open-ended investment companies (OEICs), which is currently the subject of consultation by government with practitioners, the only authorised vehicle is the unit trust. This was introduced in 1991 and permits managed futures funds to take the form of low-geared or 'covered' futures and options (FOFs) and geared futures and options (GFOFs). Both funds may invest in exchange traded derivatives and in OTC options. GFOFs may invest up to 20 per cent of fund assets in initial margins and premiums (together with an additional 10 per cent of bought options), whereas exposure must be fully covered in FOFs. Both may be invested at any time in up to 100 per cent in securities, cash or near cash. There are no specific spread requirements, although there is an obligation to exercise 'reasonable prudence'. While both categories of the fund may be marketed to the general public, GFOFs are subject to a more stringent marketing regime.

Managed futures funds may also be established as unregulated collective-investment schemes. While they are not subject to investment- and borrowing-powers regulations (although they still fall within the general UK regulatory framework), they are subject to even more limited marketing restrictions than GFOFs (although they may be promoted to authorised institutions and firms and certain categories of corporate, sophisticated or existing customers).

Offshore futures funds may be marketed in the United Kingdom, but they must be authorised in a country recognised by the UK Securities and Investment Board or recognised individually by them as providing a comparable

16 Derivatives Markets and Investment Management

level of investor protection and meeting the general standards set by UK authorised unit trusts.

Germany

Until very recently, all futures transactions were null and void under section 764 of the German Civil Code (passed as a result of the major losses sustained by wheat farmers in the last century). The first relaxation was made in the Stock Exchange Act which allowed certain exchange-traded futures and options transactions to take place between 'consenting' businessmen. In August 1989, a further amendment designed to accommodate the establishment of the Deutsche Termin Bourse (DTB) provided that all financial futures and options transactions between registered businessmen became valid and binding and, further, that private investors could deal with duly-authorised firms. However, this relaxation did not extend to cover commodity futures and options other than in precious metals.

As for managed futures funds, German domestic-investment funds are regulated by the Capital Investment Companies Act 1957 which, while permitting funds to invest in futures and options to a limited extent (i.e. currency deriva-

Figure 1.4 Getting it wrong.

tives), makes no allowance for domestic futures and options funds. On the other hand, offshore futures funds may be marketed without restriction in Germany, save that if they are part-invested in securities (e.g. for the purposes of providing a guarantee or for any other reason), the Foreign Investment Act (1969) provides that they must be registered with the Federal Banking Supervision Authority. It is advisable to obtain prior clearance from this authority for all funds, whether or not they fall within the Foreign Investment Act (1969).

Other EC jurisdictions

Domestic futures funds are not permitted in other EC jurisdictions, nor in a number of other European countries (apart from Switzerland) although a Spanish government order passed in July 1992 permits funds to use futures and options as an investment medium provided they are authorised by the Comisión Nacional de Valores (CNMV).

Other non-EC jurisdictions

For a detailed overview of the regulatory requirements of, for example, the United States and Japan, reference should be made to Chapter 3.

The perceived dangers of getting it wrong are well summarised in Figure 1.4.

Conclusion

While it is clear that Europe is comparatively new to futures and options funds, there is no doubt that it has a sophisticated and credible client base of almost limitless potential.

Whilst the collapse of Baring Brothers Bank arose from its extraordinary market exposures to Far Eastern equity index positions, the relative robustness and liquidity of the markets was shown in the success of the relatively orderly liquidation of the outstanding positions. The value of the clearing house settlement system and the skills and depth of the market participants prevented the feared contagion of systemic risk.

There can be no doubt, however, that the long term consequences of this collapse will be much greater internal management of derivatives departments, whether using OTC contracts or exchange traded instruments, as well as greater regulatory reporting and risk management controls.

At the risk of stating the obvious, it was not the markets themselves which caused the downfall, but the use to which they were put by Barings and its staff. Failures of this type serve to reinforce market discipline.

Institutional distrust of futures and derivatives continues and there are a number of problems both educational and regulatory which have yet to be overcome. For example:

most fund managers use derivatives for tactical asset allocation and efficient portfolio management, rather than as a vehicle for investment;

continuing uncertainty and problems in valuation and accounting for futures and options contracts;

the absence of a harmonised EC regulatory framework and, in some member states, continuing regulatory distrust of managed futures;

the absence of lengthy track records (because managed futures are a comparatively new investment product) and harmonisation of performance data, both of which make it difficult for investors to compare products;

the need for greater focus on the investment needs of customers;

more and better education on the benefits and advantages of managed derivatives.

Careful note should also be paid to the structure and level of management charges, performance fees and commissions, all of which can reduce significantly the rate of return for the investor. Indeed, it could be argued that substantially more money could have been raised in earlier years if the fee structures included in many of the funds had been less excessive, the divergence between projections and results rather less wide and the regulators rather more commercially aware.

On the other hand, the academic findings of Lintner and others, the deepening liquidity of Europe's futures and options exchanges, the investment experiences of recent years, reductions in fees and more realistic performance projections are all helping futures funds gain increasing credibility. Of course, academic findings and expectations on performance can be undermined significantly by poor quality fund managers and trading advisors, and a lack of trading discipline. It is important therefore for private and institutional investors to choose carefully when selecting DFMs and funds, looking in particular at those funds and DFMs which have performed consistently well over a period of years and have the benefit of a reputable and well-established management. Particular attention should be paid to the level of commissions and charges which are levied on the fund or account and how a firm's track record has been compiled.

The potential of Europe as a new entrant to managed futures is almost limitless and now that many futures and options funds have proved their worth, particularly in times of financial stress, the outlook for such funds is optimistic – providing that the regulatory authorities in some (but fortunately not in all) of the member states become rather more sensitive to the investment needs of investors and the commercial needs of EC firms.

2
Derivatives funds – regulation and distribution

Futures and derivative funds, like all categories of managed money, are based on the assumption that the investments handled by others are more likely to yield positive returns. In short, that someone else's advice is likely to be better than your own. Futures funds are, as described elsewhere in this book, relative newcomers to the field of managed products. Like financial futures, which now dominate the world's exchanges, they first emerged in the United States. It was there that the ethos of open-outcry trading nurtured the culture of the floor traders. And it was in United States investment banks and other companies that the proprietary trader emerged as a major contributor to a business's profit and loss (P&L).

Commodity Training Advisors (CTAs) or Derivatives Fund Managers (DFMs), which are the foundation of futures funds, were originally often ex-floor traders with an ambition to become fund managers.

Recently, and particularly in Europe where open-outcry trading failed to reach the critical mass it did in the United States, in-house 'upstairs' traders of fixed income and other proprietary trading activities of banks and brokers have provided recruits to the futures fund management community. Floor trading and increasingly proprietary 'desk' trading are two of the natural entry points to the managed-derivatives industry. Floor traders who survive the intense competition of the markets long enough and make some money for themselves or for their employers, usually try to determine what they have been doing right and what they have been doing wrong. If a rationale of their behaviour emerges, and it usually does, they try to exploit it more or less systematically. Physicists, mathematicians and engineers recently entered the fund management industry through the development of computerised and mechanical trading strategies developed by studying the historic price and other related data of various futures markets. If the approach makes profits, through luck, skill or both, the rationale becomes a trading system. At this point they try to find a way to trade more money than they have themselves, that is, to trade other people's money for a fee and a share of the profits. It is also at this point that they really feel the pinch of the world's regulatory systems for the first time.

United States requirements

Unless they trade only for family and friends or, in the United States, less than fifteen investors whose total funds do not exceed $200,000, advisors have to register as CTAs in the United States and in other categories elsewhere. Most importantly of all, they have to put down in writing who they are, how they trade, and their performance history, and do so in a way which allows comparison with other advisors. In the United States this must be set out in a uniform format, in a document known as a 'disclosure document'. The disclosure document, together with an account agreement form and risk disclosure statements, must be given to every person approached by a CTA for money to trade using his methodology. In recent years, the methodologies have come to include computer-driven, market-based 'technical' systems, as well as more traditional intuitive, economy-based 'fundamental' styles of trading. The mathematics has become increasingly complex, particularly as the use of options has increased. The principle, however, is the same: the CTA must inform each prospective investor how the money will be traded, where (on what markets) it will be traded, some of the risks involved in such trading, and the CTAs personal and trading, or 'performance', history.

Given their origins, CTAs typically do not have access to high net worth or institutional investors. In order to solicit such perspective customers, CTAs ordinarily need a futures broker (in United States regulatory terms a futures commission merchant or 'FCM') or professional organiser of pooled investments: in the United States a commodity pool operator or 'CPO'. FCMs and CPOs, which are often combined operations, must also register with a United States regulatory authority, the Commodity Futures Trading Commission ('CFTC') and with the self-regulatory body, the National Futures Authority ('NFA'), to carry on their businesses. CTAs must also be members of the NFA and register with the CFTC. Such registration includes background checks and passing standardised examinations. CPOs, in addition, must meet higher standards of disclosure and comply with detailed rules in the handling of client money. FCMs, which have a variety of business functions, must meet even higher standards, including minimum paid in capital (at present the greater of $250,000 or 4 per cent of customer segregated funds) in the United States.

The essential function of a CTA is to make trading decisions on behalf of discretionary account customers of FCMs (all futures customers in the United States must deal through an FCM (Future Commission Merchant) – maintained account) or on behalf of pools of investors (i.e. funds) assembled by CPOs. The CTAs are not allowed to handle customer funds or to set margin requirements. They operate under an agreement with the customer or pool, which grants them a limited power of attorney to make trading decisions for them and which can be terminated by either side. The agreement also will provide for the CTAs fees which typically include a management fee based on total funds under management and a performance fee based on net trading profits. Although formulae vary, the performance fee is usually charged net of brokerage commissions, management fees, and customary exchange, clearing house and regulatory fees. In 1992 the CFTC issued rules which reduced the disclosure requirements for CTAs and CPOs who limit their solicitation to high net-worth individual and institutional customers. The requirements as to risk disclosure and disclosure of the past and current performance in particular have been sharply reduced on the basis that such customers are sophisticated enough to make their own enquiries, that is, undertake their own due diligence, in determining whether or not to allow particular CTAs and CPOs to handle their money. The changes parallel changes to SEC (Securities and Exchange Commission) rules which allow the private placement of securities to comparably equipped customers. Such qualified eligible participants ('QEPs') must be (1) investment professionals (including other CTAs and CPOs provided they managed $5,000,000 or more of QEP funds); (2) accredited investors (those with either investments of $2,000,000 or $200,000 deposited as margin and option premiums); and (3) non-United States citizens. All other futures-fund investors must be provided with the full disclosure of materials.

Non-United States operations

Futures funds which raise money from United States residents, wherever the fund may be organised, must comply with the CFTC rules, and their promoters must be registered as CPOs. Trading advisers to the funds must be registered as CTAs. There are no special exemptions from CPO registration for CPOs located outside the United States if they transact business directly with or for United States customers in contracts traded on United States exchanges. A CPO located outside the United States but trading United States futures and options markets is exempt from CFTC registration as a CPO if it ensures that none of the participants is a United States resident or citizen and no money is contributed from United States sources. A non-United States CPO operating a fund which trades solely in futures and options traded on non-United States exchanges ('foreign futures and options') may transact business with or for United States customers without CFTC registration (1) if it does not have a United States office, by appointing an authorised agent in the United States for service of process; or (2) if it has a United States office, and is a member of one of the UK, French, Canadian, Australian or Singapore regulatory authorities which have reached exemption agreements with the CFTC, by appointing a United States agent for service of process.

In principle, foreign advisors and pool operators can handle United States clients, as United States regulations recognise foreign systems of regulation with comparable categories of financial businesses; but to date no other regulatory system has established comparable CTA or CPO criteria acceptable to the CFTC with respect to handling funds of US clients traded in US exchanges.

Offshore funds can, in certain limited circumstances, be made available to United States customers, but this invariably involves the use of a United States-registered entity, such as an FCM, CPO or SEC-registered broker/dealer.

SEC requirements

The range of permitted investments or futures funds is quite broad and has recently been expanded to include over-the-counter, or 'off-exchange', derivative instruments such as swaps and OTC options. If, however, the fund invests in securities in any significant way (as investments *per se*, rather than instruments held as margin), registration of the funds with the SEC and compliance with additional Securities Act regulations are necessary. Ordinarily, such mixed-investment vehicles will also need to register as investment companies, and advisors to such funds as investment advisors, under the Investment Companies Act and the Investment Advisers Act. While efforts are under way in the United States to modernise these detailed rules and bring them into greater conformity with the CFTC rules as to commodity pools, they still present significant obstacles to foreign-based funds and promoters. Even United States funds, which mix securities and commodities, futures or options, must comply with both the CFTC and the SEC rules as to registration, disclosure and solicitation. This can be particularly awkward, as the securities regulations do not permit the payment of performance fees to advisers in the way that CFTC regulations do.

United States public offers

In order for 'securities' to be sold to the general public in the United States by means of interstate commerce (broadly speaking, any mailing, telephoning or travelling across state lines or into the United States from abroad) a Securities Act registration statement, including a prospectus, must be filed with the SEC. The issuer of registered securities typically becomes subject to continuing reporting requirements under the Securities Exchange Act.

The forms to be filed as part of such a registration require detailed disclosure of information concerning the fund vehicle and its proposed investment programme and the performance of the CPO and CTAs. These requirements are designed to enable United States investors to make an informed decision about the merits of the fund as an investment. The SEC has a broad discretion to require the inclusion of any information it regards as necessary to ensure that the registration statement and prospectus are not misleading. After the filing has been made, interests in a fund may be offered to potential buyers orally or through the use of a preliminary prospectus which forms part of the initial filing. However, no sales may be made until the registration statement is approved ('declared effective') by the SEC. A copy of the prospectus in final form must also be delivered to each purchaser no later than the time the sale is finalised.

The securities of any issuer having over 300 United States shareholders (500 world-wide) and over $5 million in total assets must also be registered if they are publicly offered in the United States. Once an issuer's securities are registered, it must thereafter file information with the SEC in the form of annual and other periodic reports, which are designed to keep current the business and financial information initially provided.

In addition to compliance with the federal securities laws, the public offering of interests in futures funds requires separate registration under state securities laws for every state in which they are offered for sale. In many states the SEC filings may be used to achieve registration in routine fashion. In certain states, regulators require additional information. In some cases a state securities administrator can prohibit sales of a particular security in that state if he or she considers that the terms of the security or the type of offering contemplated would not be 'fair' to investors. These 'fairness' standards place a great deal of discretion in the hands of state administrators.

Offshore funds

Offshore funds which are offered to the United States public are generally subject to SEC regulation. SEC Regulation S gives a limited exemption. It permits offshore funds to be sold to United States citizens not residing in the United States and to be sold to United States citizens provided that no 'directed selling efforts' occur in the United States and the offer and sale are made in an 'offshore transaction'. Directed selling efforts are those which are aimed at producing United States sales. An 'offshore transaction' is one in which the seller does not make an offer to sell to a person in the United States and the buyer is outside the United States or the sale is conducted through a non-United States exchange.

Private placements

The exemption which is most likely to be useful in avoiding the need for Securities Act registration of a futures fund, on- or offshore, is the 'private placement exemption'. A 'private placement' or offering of securities to a limited number of sophisticated investors is exempt from the Securities Act registration requirements. The Securities Act does not define a 'private placement'. Court cases, in determining whether an offer is private or public, have focused on factors such as the number of investors, their sophistication, their relationship to the issuer and the information available to them. Regulation D under the Securities Act provides a 'safe harbour' from registration. This means that an offering made according to the detailed rules in Regulation D is deemed to be 'private' by the SEC. Providing the rules regarding qualification of investors and disclosure are met, securities can be sold to non-institutional investors under Regulation D. Sales to a limited number of institutional investors may also be structured as private placements. A private placement typically utilises an offering memorandum which provides a description of the fund and is similar in purpose but considerably less technical and detailed than a full prospectus.

UK requirements

Although the FSA (Financial Services Act) and certain of the rules governing futures funds, such as those providing for use of derivatives in efficient portfolio management and tactical asset allocation, are based on United States precedents, most of the United States regulatory infrastructure has not been replicated in the United Kingdom. Pressure has recently been brought to bear on the UK regulators to bring their rules on presentation of track records, performance fees and capital requirements into line with the United States, but it remains to be seen how far they will actually go.

All fund promoters and advisors who carry on business in the United Kingdom must become members of one or more of the self-regulatory organisations (SROs) and comply with their rules and those of the Securities and Investments Board (SIB), as well as the provision of the FSA. Registration is possible with the Securities and Futures Authority (SFA), either as a 'broad-scope' firm (equivalent to United States broker/dealer or FCM) or as an arranger or advisor equivalent to an introducing broker (which does not handle client money). The SFA category of DFM is simply a sub-category of arranger or advisor with a reduced capital requirement of £10,000. Advisors who restrict their activities to institutional clients can become members of the Investment Managers Regulatory Organisation (IMRO) and those operating or marketing unit trusts are able to become members of a new body, the Personal Investments Authority (PIA), formed by a merger of the Life Assurance and Unit Trusts Regulatory Organisation (LAUTRO) and the Financial Intermediaries Managers and Brokers Regulatory Association (FIMBRA). None of the available categories of registration is focused on futures and options or futures and options funds. There is however, now a particular examination for those dealing with such products as opposed to securities. The examination is now mandatory except for those who are exempt by reason of their previous experience in the industry or equivalent examinations elsewhere.

One important result of the lack of specific categories of futures advisor or fund promoter (with the exception the UK DFM), and the same is true throughout Europe, is that a wide variety of people and firms call themselves 'CTAs' when they are not registered as such. The temptation to turn the phrase CTA into one of general usage as opposed to precise regulatory standing, is likely to mislead investors who may assume that someone calling him- or herself a CTA is in fact registered and regulated under United States law. Similarly, investors in what are generically called 'futures funds' may not appreciate the significant differences between a fund complying with UK or US regulations and one established offshore in an unregulated jurisdiction. The differences, in particular in respect to rights of compensation and avenues of complaint and redress, are great. While a risk-disclosure statement goes some of the distance in attempting to explain this, all too often the meaningful distinctions are lost in the solicitation process.

Public funds

In the United Kingdom, futures funds, like all managed investments, are now subject to regulation under the Financial Services Act. The FSA, together with rules and regulations made by the various regulatory bodies established under the FSA, replaced previous laws dealing with unit trusts (the UK equivalent of United States mutual funds) and revised the law on closed-end investment companies. In some aspects, as regards futures and options, the FSA is modelled on the United States regulatory system but in important respects it remains tied to the paternalistic approach inherited from the past.

Under the rules adopted by the Securities and Investments Board, the world of funds, like that of King Lear, is split into three parts: authorised unit trusts (domestic funds which can be marketed to the general public); unauthorised collective-investments schemes (which can be marketed to and through authorised institutions to certain categories of investor); and recognised schemes (foreign funds organised in countries with comparable regulations). Among the latter, special treatment is accorded to funds established in the EC and in the 'designated' English islands, including Guernsey, Jersey, the Isle of Man and Bermuda. The rules also distinguish between authorised unit trusts which are ungeared and those which are allowed gearing of up to 20 per cent of funds under management.

Authorised futures and options funds (AFOFs)

As mentioned briefly in Chapter 1, under the SIB regulations, AFOFs are permitted to buy and sell approved futures and traded options and certain OTC options and warrants as long as their obligations or rights arising under such contracts are fully (100 per cent) covered by holdings of cash, near cash (e.g. short-term gilts or short-term bank deposits) or 'transferable' (essentially listed) securities or an equivalent derivative contract with equal and opposite exposure. Subject to certain adjustments, up to 10 per cent of the value of an AFOF may be invested in buying traded options without cover. AFOFs may use combinations of securities and derivatives and may also construct synthetic portfolio funds. They can also use strategies such as 'buy/write' which combine securities and derivatives to increase potential returns or reduce risks of losses. AFOFs are not permitted to invest in base metals, oil and gas or other physical commodities. However, they may invest in covered futures or call options on physical commodities provided the transaction is closed-out before delivery. AFOFs may also enter into certain types of OTC futures or options with approved banks or other entities authorised to undertake OTC futures or option business, and they may hold up to 10 per cent of the fund value in gold. Unlike geared futures and options funds, which are not permitted to borrow, an AFOF may borrow up to 10 per cent of the fund value for investment purposes.

Geared futures and options funds (GFOFS)

GFOFs may commit up to 20 per cent of the value of the property of the fund to uncovered initial futures margin or option premiums (thus so-called 90:10 or 80:20 funds are permitted). GFOFs may also purchase additional options with up to 10 per cent of the value of the fund's property. The SIB has stated that it regards this level of gearing as being the maximum appropriate for a product to be marketed to the general public.

GFOFs are permitted to invest in derivatives of products and of instruments which they are not otherwise permitted to hold, provided the transactions are closed-out before delivery or, in the case of involuntary assignment, provided the underlying commodity is immediately sold.

GFOFs' holdings must be diversified among a variety of contract types and categories of investments. Rather than specify a maximum percentage of the value of the property of the fund which may be used as initial margin in respect of derivatives in any one of the permitted derivative product categories, the SIB has imposed a general obligation upon the fund to ensure that its investment in derivatives is prudently diversified. This requirement can be met by investment in derivatives which are diversified in nature such as broadly based market indices. Neither GFOFs nor AFOFs are yet permitted to change performance-related fees.

Marketing in the United Kingdom

Both AFOFs and GFOFs are designed to be marketed to the general public subject to a combination of the FSA, SIB regulations and rules issued by the SROs. The use of cold calling on non-private investors to sell both AFOFs and GFOFs is permitted, subject to 'cooling-off' periods and other restrictions. AFOFs may only be sold by cold calling to private investors who are 'established customers' of the calling entity. Private investors may only be sold GFOFs by cold calling by investment managers with whom they have contracted specifically for portfolio management or portfolio review services. Both AFOFs and GFOFs may be sold by off-the-page advertisements in which promotional material is coupled with an application form, subject to compliance with the risk-warning requirements. Standardised risk warnings with respect to fund products have been rejected by the UK regulators in favour of a requirement that fund promoters make 'absolutely clear' the degree of risk involved in investing in a futures fund. The 'Generic Risk Disclosure Statement' agreed between the CFTC and the SFA in relation to trading in futures and options does not apply to UK funds but provides useful guidelines.

GFOF promoters are further required to explain clearly that units in a GFOF may fluctuate widely in price and that all or a substantial proportion of the initial amount invested may be lost. AFOFs, but not GFOFs, are permitted to project future performance based on past performance. AFOFs' past-performance tables are required to set out performance for the shorter of the period from the launch date to the present, or for the past five years. GFOFs are required to show performance from the launch date to the present even if more than five years has elapsed. Comparison of past performance of AFOFs and GFOFs with indices and other investments is allowed provided the comparison is 'fair' and that, where appropriate, additional SRO rules are observed. It is anticipated that new rules now under consideration will specify the United States format for performance tables.

As with other unit trusts, private investors in AFOFs and GFOFs have the right during a short 'cooling-off' period to cancel their purchase of units and receive a refund. Although any decrease in the value of units between purchase and cancellation is the investor's risk, this fact must be made clear when his or her cancellation rights are explained. GFOF promoters must clearly indicate that the geared nature of a GFOF investment may lead to a considerable shortfall in the amount recovered upon exercise of cancellation rights.

Non-public funds

Unauthorised schemes, including offshore funds, may not be promoted to the general public in the United Kingdom. They may, however, be promoted by an authorised person to the following categories of customer:

1. Other authorised persons.
2. Persons 'whose ordinary business involves the acquisition and disposal of property of the same kind as the property . . . to which the scheme relates'.
3. Non-private customers, essentially 'business', or 'professional' 'investors' as defined in the SIB's rules.
4. Existing participants in the scheme or in schemes with substantially similar underlying property and risk profile.

5. Existing customers, including newly accepted customers provided they have not been solicited as customers for the purpose of participating in unregulated schemes.
6. Exempted persons as defined in the FSA. These include listed money-market institutions, members of Lloyd's and certain public officials.
7. Permitted persons as defined in the FSA, primarily companies whose investment business is incidental to their main business.
8. Tax exempt pension schemes and charities not falling within the non-private customer category, subject to complying with SRO suitability requirements.
9. Persons who have notified an unauthorised person not associated with the authorised person that they wish to receive details of particular types of unauthorised schemes.

The practical effect of all this is to allow unregulated funds to be sold on a *de facto* 'private placement' basis in the United Kingdom. Why the regulators failed to create an express private placement exemption is hard to explain.

The principal results of the paternalistic approach to defining the permitted range of investors, investments, methods of marketing, and imposing a particular and anachronistic legal structure (the unit trust) on futures funds established in the United Kingdom has presented significant obstacles to the development of the industry. There is little attraction to advisors and promoters in establishing funds under UK regulation when the distribution costs are high, the investment returns are limited by rule and the fees to be earned are low by international standards. The result has been the rapid growth of offshore funds which do not suffer from these restrictions, and their marketing by various routes to UK investors. These include funds established in other jurisdictions 'recognised' by the United Kingdom.

Unless and until a 'disclosure', as opposed to 'paternal', philosophy is adopted, modified perhaps, as is already the case in the United States, by relief from certain disclosures for private placements to sophisticated investors, this situation is likely to continue. The rapid development of a number of jurisdictions including Ireland and Luxemburg within the EC, as well as elsewhere, is likely to further erode the desirability of establishing funds in the United Kingdom, unless these issues are successfully addressed in the current regulatory review. Reform of the legislation on closed-end investment companies, while also now being considered, is long overdue. If and when the EC UCITS directive is amended to provide for the cross-border distribution of futures funds, it is likely that the United Kingdom's hitherto assumed competitive advantage will further erode.

Recognised low-tax jurisdictions

From a UK regulatory perspective, 'recognised' and usually low-tax, jurisdictions now fall into essentially two categories: UK designed territories and the remainder. Funds set up in any of these jurisdictions generally may not be offered or sold to residents of that jurisdiction.

UK designated territories

Bermuda, Jersey, Guernsey and the Isle of Man are UK designated territories. Each has a regulatory system which the SIB has recognised as affording investors protection equivalent to that provided under the FSA. These include the obligation to make available collective investment scheme particulars; controls over funds' investment and borrowing powers and over the manner in which fund units are priced. At present there is little UK regulatory benefit attached to incorporation of a futures fund in a designated territory. Although futures funds have been permitted to become UK authorised unit trust since 1991, none of the four designated territories has yet applied to include futures funds within their designated classes of schemes. It is, however, expected that one or more of these jurisdictions will make such an application in the near term. If such an application were to be approved by the SIB, this would enable futures funds established in that jurisdiction to be marketed to the UK general public (subject to the FSA investment advertising regulations) while retaining the tax benefits of an offshore location.

Bermuda

Bermuda funds are either mutual funds governed principally by the Companies Act 1981, which also controls the marketing of shares through its prospectus requirements, or unit trusts governed by contractual agreement between the parties.

The Bermuda Monetary Authority publishes guidelines relating to the formation and marketing of funds. The guidelines cover the prospectus contents requirements and also require Bermuda funds to appoint Bermuda entities as management company, custodian, trustee of unit trusts, registrar, transfer agent and auditor. The delegation of these responsibilities to sub-custodians and sub-registrars by the Bermuda entities is permitted, provided that notice is given to the Bermuda Monetary Authority. There is no specific Bermuda futures-fund legislation.

The Bermuda regulatory framework is the least restrictive of the four UK designated territories. There are no regulatory controls on the operation of funds in Bermuda. The principle on which Bermuda relies is essentially that of self-regulation achieved by requiring the use of Bermuda entities to protect Bermuda's and its investors' interests.

Jersey

Jersey funds are constituted as either unit trusts or companies. In either case, funds established in Jersey are regulated under the Collective Investment Funds (Jersey) law. Funds cannot be established without the consent of the Finance and Economics Committee of the States of Jersey granted under the aegis of the Financial Services Department. Approval is governed by published policy guidelines. Particular caution is shown in approving futures funds. There are in essence two classes of collective investment funds – the recognised-fund class and the unclassified-fund class. A recognised fund must offer the investor the same protection afforded investors under the FSA.

Any futures fund launched in Jersey currently falls into the category of unclassified funds. The Financial Services Department has what it calls a 'flexible' approach to unclassified funds. First, the department looks at the track record and reputation of the promoter. Second, the department assesses the fund from the investors' perspective looking particularly at a number of issues including investor protection, ease of redemption, target audience and investment focus. Third, the department seeks to minimise structural risk by insisting on the removal of elements which it considers unacceptable, such as the absence of a custodian for an open-ended company or the lack of any mechanism which adequately diversifies counterparty risk where significant investments in OTC derivatives are proposed. Risk to investors which is inherent in the nature of a fund's proposed investments will not be a bar to approval if clear risk warnings are given.

There are not hard and fast rules about what the department will or will not accept. The department relies on fund promoters to ask for what they want; the department will then either accept the fund as it stands, accept the fund but with certain amendments, or reject the fund outright. A highly geared fund with a minimum investment of US$1 million aimed at the professional investor is much more likely to be given a green light than a highly geared fund with a minimum investment of US$5,000 aimed at retail investors. However, if a highly geared fund aimed at retail investors also offered a return of capital guarantee, its chances of approval will improve.

Guernsey

Investment funds in Guernsey may be either open- or closed-ended. Open-ended funds must be authorised by the Guernsey Financial Services Commission under the Protection of Investors (Bailiwick of Guernsey) law.

Closed-end funds require the approval of the Commission under the Control of Borrowing (Bailiwick of Guernsey) Ordinaries. An entity must first be licensed by the Commission before carrying out any of the following activities in Guernsey: promotion, subscription, registration, dealing, management, administration, advising or custody in relation to an open-ended fund. Before granting any licence, the Commission must be satisfied that all individuals to be involved in the activity in question are fit and proper. A licence is not required to carry out these activities in relation to closed-end funds but the Commission will refuse to approve any closed-end fund unless it is satisfied that those involved in the operation of it are fit and proper.

The Commission has been cautious about approving futures funds and is unlikely to agree to be the first jurisdiction of incorporation used by a futures-fund promoter. A small number of futures funds have so far been authorised by the Commission. In considering whether to not to authorise a futures-fund the Commission insists on a proven track record of futures-fund performance and normally only authorises futures funds on condition that they are marketed only to business, professional and experienced investors and subject to a substantial minimum investment, usually at least US$50,000.

Isle of Man

Funds established in the Isle of Man are regulated by the Isle of Man Financial Supervision Commission under the Isle of Man Financial Supervision Act. There are in essence two classes of collective investment funds – authorised funds and restricted funds. An authorised fund must offer the investor the same protection afforded investors under the FSA. Futures funds constituted under Isle of Man law or operated from the Isle of Man currently fall into the restricted-funds category.

A restricted fund requires authorisation from the Commission and must have a manager and trustee each of whom must be a body corporate independent of the other with a place of business in the Isle of Man. Both the manager and trustee must hold investment business licences granted under the Isle of Man Investment Business Act. Restricted funds are also required to file their constitutional documents which must provide for a number of prescribed matters in accordance with the Commission's published guidelines. These include: investment objectives; borrowing, hedging and investment powers; adequate descriptions of charges; and powers of manager and trustee and means for their removal.

There are not regulations governing the types of restricted fund which may be established in the Isle of Man. The Commission has expressed the wish to keep this aspect of its regulatory regime as flexible as possible. A number of funds investing in futures and options have been launched in the Isle of Man. Futures funds which are restricted to investors who are sufficiently expert to understand the risks involved can be geared provided appropriate risk warnings are given to investors.

Closed-end investment companies are not within the Financial Supervision Act. Such companies are treated in the same way as ordinary companies wishing to raise capital by way of public offer shares. They must comply with the prospectus requirements of the Isle of Man Companies Acts.

Other low-tax jurisdictions

Other low-tax jurisdictions include the Bahamas, British Virgin Islands, Cayman Islands, Dublin's International Financial Services Centre, Luxemburg and Netherlands Antilles. These jurisdictions are not 'recognised' for UK regulatory purposes. Reciprocal recognition arrangements under EC directives have limited impact in relation to futures funds.

Bahamas

There is no specific regulatory or legislative framework in the Bahamas governing futures funds or other pooled-investment vehicles. Collective-investment vehicles in the Bahamas may be international business companies (IBCs) or unit trusts. The former are more flexible and are therefore the more common choice except where the jurisdiction in which the fund is to be marketed has regulations which militate in favour of the use of a unit trust.

British Virgin Islands

There is no specific regulatory or legislative framework in the British Virgin Islands (BVI) concerning investment funds in general or futures funds in particular. The most common vehicle used for the operation of a BVI investment fund is an IBC. The BVI Companies Ordinance is a flexible piece of legislation which allows for the speedy incorporation and efficient operation of funds with the minimum of procedural formalities. IBCs are not required to have any directors or officer resident in the BVI. Management and control can be exercised anywhere in the world.

IBCs also have no minimum or maximum number of shareholders. Investment in an IBC is made by the purchase of shares in the company and withdrawal from a fund is usually by way of redeeming or re-purchasing shares. The directors of an IBC are permitted to redeem shares without formality where the IBC's Articles of Association provide that shareholders have the right to redeem their shares. There is not legal obligation to file any form of accounts, particulars or directors or shareholders, prospectuses, or any information concerning its activities. Amendments to constitutional documents must be filed.

Cayman Islands

The Cayman Islands Mutual Funds law has just been adopted. It sets out a framework which regulates an area which was previously not subject to any specific Cayman statutory regulation. The Mutual Funds law regulates collective-investment vehicles which are established or incorporated in, or managed from the Cayman Islands and which issue equity interest. Equity interests are defined to exclude debt issues. The Mutual Funds law divides regulated Cayman funds into three categories: (1) 'section 4(2)' funds; (2) 'private sector' mutual funds; and (3) licensed mutual funds. Differing regimes are imposed on each category. The Mutual Funds law does not cover closed-end investment vehicles and exempts from its provisions funds with less than fifteen investors – provided the investors can remove the fund operators by majority vote.

A section 4(2) fund is one which is listed on a designated stock exchange or which requires a minimum investment of an amount which has not yet been fixed but which is expected to be at least US$50,000. A section 4(2) fund is simply required to file certain information from its offering document and annual audited accounts with the Inspector of Mutual Funds and to pay an initial filing fee and an annual fee of an amount which has not yet been fixed but which is expected to be approximately US$600. A fund which qualifies as a section 4(2) fund may opt to be regulated in one of the other two categories.

A private sector mutual fund is one which designates a Cayman licensed mutual-fund administrator as its principal office. Before accepting such designation, the mutual-fund administrator is charged with ensuring that: (1) the fund promoter is of sound reputation; (2) the fund administrators are of sound reputation and have sufficient expertise; and (3) the offer of interest and business of the fund will be carried out in a proper manner. A private sector mutual fund is also required to file a copy of its offering document and annual audited accounts with the Inspector of Mutual Funds. The payment of the initial filing fee and annual fees is the responsibility of the licensed mutual-fund administrators. There is no regulation of investment objectives or other commercial matters.

A fund which does not meet the criteria for a section 4(2) fund and which does not wish to use Cayman-based administrators may apply to the Inspector of Mutual Funds to become a licensed mutual fund. The application procedure includes the filing of a copy of the offering document together with a prescribed form containing details of the fund promoter, investment advisors, custodian and other service provider and payment of an application fee expected to be about US$600. The licence will be granted if the inspector is satisfied that the three-point test set out above in relation to private sector mutual funds is met by the administrators and service providers. A licensed fund is required to file annual audited accounts with the inspector and to pay an annual fee expected to be about US$600. There is no regulation of the investment objectives of a licensed fund or of other commercial matters.

Dublin International Financial Services Centre

Funds carrying on business from the Dublin International Financial Services Centre (IFSC) established for the sole benefit of non-Irish investors are exempt from Irish taxation on income and on gains arising from their investment activities. In addition, no Irish withholding tax applies to any distributions of income or gains on any undistributed income of such funds. A reduced Irish corporate income tax rate of 10 per cent applies to the profits of fund management companies established in the IFSC which obtain the requisite certification from the Irish Ministry for Finance. To qualify for tax exempt status, IFSC funds must be constituted either as unit trust authorised under the Irish Unit Trusts Act or as collective investment companies established under Part XII of the Irish Companies Act and designated by the Irish Central Bank.

Two categories of futures and options funds may be established within this regime – Capital Protected Futures and Options Funds and Leveraged Futures and Options Funds.

The Irish Central Bank must approve the capital protection measures used by Capital Protected Funds – particular attention is paid to the segregation of assets held for capital protection. A maximum of 5 per cent of a Capital Protected Fund's net assets may be held in any single futures or options contract and a maximum of 10 per cent of the fund's net assets may be held in contracts on a single commodity or financial instrument. Borrowing is not permitted. The fund prospectus must disclose the contracts and instruments in which the fund will invest – and these must be approved by the Central Bank. The prospectus must also fully describe the risks of investment in futures and options and the methods used by the fund to ensure that its liabilities do not exceed its net assets. Before it will grant authorisation, the Central Bank must be satisfied that the fund manager and investment advisors have adequate experience in the area of futures and options investment.

Leveraged Funds, which do not provide a return of capital guarantee, are subject to the same general rules as Capital Protected Funds with certain additional requirements. Fund property must include liquid assets with a total minimum value which at all times equals or exceeds the sum of margins posted and premiums paid on open transactions. There must be a minimum subscription per investor of IR£10,000 (or its foreign currency equivalent). The fund prospectus must contain a full description of the risks involved in leveraged futures investments, a prominent recommendation that not more than 5 per cent of an investor's portfolio be invested in the fund, and a prominent risk warning drawing attention to the above average risk involved in the investment and its suitability only for investors in a position to accept such risk.

Luxemburg

The Luxemburg law of 30 March 1988 distinguishes two basic classes of investment funds. Futures funds are 'Part II funds' which may be organised as contractual funds (*fonds commun de placement*) or as corporate entities. Minimum capital for such funds is Lux Fr50,000,000 (currently approximately US$1.4 million). This must be in place within six months after the establishment of the fund. The minimum initial investment per investor for futures funds is Lux Fr500,000 (currently just over US$14,000). A Luxemburg fund must have a depository bank which is either a bank organised under Luxemburg law or a Luxemburg subsidiary of a foreign bank. The depository bank monitors the assets of the fund and assumes custodial duties. Under Luxemburg law, the central administration of the fund's assets is also required to be in Luxemburg.

Prior to organising a Luxemburg fund, the sponsors must apply to the Institut Monetaire de Luxemburg (IML) for approval of the fund. The IML monitors the activity of all Luxemburg funds, reviews investment policy and comments on all documentation involved in the organisation of the fund. The approval process can take several months depending on the complexity of the fund's investment policy. However, funds which do not employ novel structures or investment policies can generally secure approval in a matter of weeks.

Netherlands Antilles
These is no specific regulatory or legislative framework in the Netherlands Antilles concerning investment funds in general or futures funds in particular.

The corporate vehicle used for the operation of a Netherlands Antilles offshore fund is the *naamloze vennootschap* (NV) company. An NV company must have its corporate seat in the Netherlands Antilles but individual managing directors need not reside there. It has become standard practice for the Netherlands Antilles Central Bank to require a company to have a local representative in order to obtain 'offshore' status.

An NV company is therefore typically managed by one or more managing directors including a local trust company which handles the day-to-day operation of the fund. The trust company often provides various administrative and other, including custodial, services. The trust company, in cooperation with the civil-law notary who executes the deed of incorporation, will obtain the various licences and will make the necessary filing with the Commercial Register.

A general meeting for shareholders of the fund must be held once a year in the Netherlands Antilles. Shareholders may be represented by written proxy. The general meeting has the power and authority to dismiss the managing directors and appoint new directors. One of the items on the agenda of the general meeting must be the adoption of the annual accounts of the NV company.

European Community

The EC directors which have potential impact on futures funds are currently more remarkable for what they exclude than for what they include.

UCITS Directive

The Undertakings for Collective Investments in Transferable Securities (UCITS) Directive is designed to set up a common framework for mutual recognition of investment funds by EC member states. Its scope is currently restricted to funds which invest in transferable securities. Although UCITS funds may use derivatives for 'efficient portfolio management' (i.e. hedging) the directive is not designed to accommodate futures funds. The European Commission has been receptive to industry representations that the UCITS framework be extended to cover funds whose primary purpose is investments in derivatives. However, its preoccupation with the need to implement the

Investment Services and Banking directives and other matters, is likely to keep the issue marginalised for some time. For the present those marketing futures funds in Europe will not be able to benefit from a single country approval providing a 'passport' to the other EC member states. There is, as yet, not 'single market' in futures funds.

Investment Services Directive (ISD)

The aim of the Investment Services Directive (ISD) is to provide a means for those carrying on investment business in the European Community to be authorised in one member state and for that authorisation to provide a 'single licence' or 'passport' to do investment business in other member states. The ISD regime is divided into 'instruments' and 'investment services'. An entity authorised in one member state to engage in services within the ISD will be permitted to carry on these activities in the other member states in relation to instruments within the scope of the ISD without additional authorisation.

The current version excludes the management of collective-investment schemes from the list of services. Units in UCITS schemes are included among listed instruments but the current version only permits these to be managed as part of a client's portfolio of investments. Financial futures and options are included among 'Passportable' instruments; however, the scope of what is included in the definition of these terms is not yet clear. Although various interests lobbied for the inclusion of commodity futures and options, the lack of such products on continental exchanges limited the support for these initiatives. It is very unlikely that as the ISD is brought into force in each country, management of financial futures funds will be within its scope and almost certain that commodity futures and options will remain excluded.

Japan

The Japanese Commodity Fund law was enacted in 1991 and regulations under the Commodity Fund law have been in force since 1992. Japanese fund regulation is controlled by three ministries with overlapping jurisdiction: the ministries of Finance (MOF), International Trade and Industry (MITI), and Agriculture, Forestry and Fisheries (MAFF).

MOF regulates financial companies, banks and securities dealers, and supervises the Japanese financial markets. In addition to the funds permitted under the Commodity Fund law, MOF allows investment in derivatives by securities funds provided at least 50 per cent of the fund is invested in securities or securities derivatives. MITI regulates trading companies and leasing companies, and supervises the Japanese metals, energy and rubber markets. MAFF has jurisdiction over the grain markets and has been keen to encourage active domestic commodity futures markets for hedging purposes.

The regulations issued by the three ministries follow broadly similar guidelines and were hammered out as a compromise during a year of negotiation between the passage of the law in April 1991 and the coming into force of the regulations in April 1992. Fifty per cent of a commodity fund's assets must be invested in grains, energy and other commodity derivatives. A maximum of 30 per cent of a commodity fund's value may be committed as margin or option premium in relation to overseas financial derivatives contracts or other permitted financial derivatives. Investment in Japanese financial futures other than stock-index futures is not permitted. Investment in domestic stock-index futures is restricted to 1 per cent of the fund's value. In addition, guidelines restrict investment in overseas stock-index futures to 10 per cent of the fund's assets.

For the present, the minimum investment in Japanese commodity funds is Y100 million (currently approximately US$935,000). However, fund operators with a proven track record in the promotion of foreign derivatives funds may sell Y50 million investments. Although fund operators are permitted to repurchase fund shares, no secondary market is permitted.

Both Japanese companies and foreign companies with an office in Japan are eligible to register as fund operators. Each commodity fund is required to have a general operator and may also have a co-general operator. A co-general operator may only act as fund operator in conjunction with a general operator. Selling agents, a third category of registered fund-related entity, may only market fund interests. General operators must maintain minimum capital of Y1 billion, co-general operators must maintain at least Y500 million and selling agents Y20 million. As of July 1993, 29 entities have been authorised as general operators, 25 as co-general operators and 14 as selling agents. In October 1994, Japan's first six domestic CTAs were authorised and under MITI and MAFF guidelines set up the Japan CTA Association as a self-regulatory organisation.

There are regulations which require strict separation between brokers and operators. Fund operators which are 50 per cent or more owned by a futures broker may not use that broker. The legislation and regulations also establish detailed reporting and disclosure requirements for fund operators.

Unless an offshore fund is registered with the MOF or listed on an approved stock exchange, it may only be sold in Japan by private placement. Offers must be restricted to a maximum of 49 'designated financial institutions'. Designated financial institutions include banks, life and non-life insurance companies, credit associations, credit cooperatives, mutual federations, pension funds and certain government-affiliated organisations.

Conclusion

Outside the United States, futures funds are only gradually gaining acceptance. Although frustrating from a commercial point of view, this may be inevitable, even desirable from a policy point of view. The development of non-United States futures markets has been uneven. Some exchanges have surged forward; others seem to show organic growth; still others, particularly in continental Europe and Asia, are still struggling to establish themselves. All this implies an uneven commercial and regulatory infrastructure. There seems to be some movement toward regulatory convergence between the United States and the United Kingdom, but that will not soon guarantee a 'level playing field'. Futures-fund promoters will, for the foreseeable future, be obliged to tailor their products and distribution to disparate markets with inconsistent and overlapping regulation. Professional advice will remain essential if legal and regulatory problems are to be reduced if not avoided.

3
Taxation issues and derivatives

Introduction

This chapter considers the international taxation issues which are relevant to portfolio investors. It does not attempt to address indirect taxes such as value added tax or stamp duty or overseas tax consequences. It is based on law and practice as at October 1993.

First, it briefly reviews the taxation regimes for different funds in the United Kingdom, that is investment trusts, unit trusts, pension funds, insurance companies, with particular reference to the taxation of borrowings and the use of derivatives.

On 20 August 1993, the Inland Revenue in the United Kingdom issued draft legislation on the taxation of financial instruments to complement the proposals on the taxation treatment of foreign-exchange gains and losses included in the Finance Act 1993. As the new legislation will not affect calendar year end companies before 1 January 1996, this chapter considers the current tax treatment as well as the new proposals.

The chapter then addresses some investment and regulatory restrictions (principally for investment trusts and unit trusts) which may explain why the use of derivatives in particular is not as extensive as one might otherwise expect. Finally, we consider certain taxation issues in the United States.

Taxation consequences for different players

In addition to considering the general rules, it is necessary to consider in turn the tax regimes applicable to the main portfolio-investment vehicles, particularly the treatment of currency risk-management techniques. The vehicles which will be covered are:

1. investment trusts;
2. unit trusts;

3. pension funds and unauthorised unit trusts;
4. insurance companies.

It is important to appreciate that sterling is the only currency recognised by the UK tax system and this will continue to be the case under the new proposals for taxing currencies for non-trading activities. (It is in practice possible to negotiate with the Inspector of Taxes to translate some foreign currency items in to sterling *en bloc*.) Under the foreign exchange regulations, it will also be possible to elect to use a functional currency other than sterling in certain circumstances.

General rules

Before talking about the general rules it is helpful to explain the differences between the four main types of transaction that will normally be used for currency risk management:

1. an on-balance-sheet position;
2. a forward currency contract;
3. a futures contract;
4. an option.

Comparison of transactions

An on-balance-sheet position is any asset or liability that is denominated in a currency other than sterling. It may be holdings of shares or debt securities, currency, (i.e. cash), currency deposits or currency borrowings. For tax purposes foreign currency denominated share equity and reserves can effectively be disregarded.

A forward currency contract is an unconditional agreement to buy one currency in exchange for another currency.

A futures contract, as has already been explained, is an agreement to buy or sell a standard quantity of a specific financial instrument or commodity at a predetermined future date and at a price agreed between the parties. The exact technical distinction between a futures contract and a forward contract is not entirely clear but it follows normal usage. The essential difference appears to be that a forward contract will proceed to completion in the absence of default whilst a futures contract typically can be closed out without proceeding to delivery and/or may be settled for a net consideration. A currency swap is a future.

An option contract gives the holder the right, but not the obligation, to buy or sell the relevant underlying financial instrument, commodity, future or currency at a predetermined exercise or strike price, at one or more future dates. In return for this right the holder or purchaser of the option pays a premium to the seller or writer of the option. A warrant is an option.

The essential difference between a future and an option is that whereas a future carries a commitment to assume a long or short position, an option merely conveys the right but not the obligation to assume such a position. The practical effect of this is that an option purchaser has losses limited to the value of the premium but has unlimited scope for profits. The converse is, of course, true of the option writer: profits are limited to the amount of the premium but he or she has unlimited scope for losses.

Tax treatment for a normal taxpayer

Trading

In any case where any of the above items are entered into as trading transactions, any gain or loss will be taxed based on the relevant trading accounts. However, there can be significant timing differences since, for instance, under current rules a provision for an unrealised loss on a contract may well not be tax deductible. In this particular instance, on the accounting date it is not possible to say what the exchange rate will be when the contract matures, only what it is currently, and thus the loss is not certain ever to occur.

Capital

Capital transactions, which would include long-term investments and borrowings, are taxed under the capital gains regime. Assets are taxed by comparing the proceeds (converted to sterling at the sale date) when they are eventually sold with the cost (in sterling determined at the purchase date) as adjusted for UK inflation. Currency and currency deposits are separate chargeable assets in their own right. For example, each payment out of a foreign currency bank account strictly requires a separate calculation to be made. Either by concession or practice these rules are not generally strictly applied. Sterling, sterling debt securities and ordinary sterling debts (unless previously assigned) are generally not chargeable assets.

The relevant date is when a contract becomes unconditional. It is not relevant when delivery of the asset takes place. Thus a forward exchange contract involves the immediate purchase of one currency and the immediate sale of another. Since the currency sold will often not yet have been purchased, in practice it is not possible to calculate the gain or loss and the Inland Revenue may be persuaded to agree to include the item in a later year's tax computation.

Unfortunately where an asset has a life of less than fifty years, it is treated as wasting and this will result in the cost, less any value receivable on maturity, being amortised over the predicted life. This used to apply invariably to a futures contract; however, the rule is specifically disapplied for most option contracts and following the Budget on 30 November 1993, it will no longer be applied to futures contracts. (It is not applied to debt securities because on redemption full value is received and curiously it has never been suggested that debt purchased at a premium is caught.)

Options entered into on capital account also involve a further complication. When an option is created, the writer sells an asset, the option, and has an immediate capital gain, while the purchaser acquires an asset. If, however, the option is exercised these transactions when the option was granted are ignored and rolled into the purchase or sale of the underlying asset. Again this creates practical problems since at the end of a tax year it may not be known if exercise will take place. It can also create planning opportunities if the asset transferred on exercise is not itself subject to the capital gains rules for example, sterling. Gains or losses on capital liabilities, for example, a foreign currency loan, are not taxable at all.

Where a capital contract also generates periodic cash flows (e.g. interest on a deposit, recurring swap payments) these generally retain an income characteristic. It should be noted that such swap payments only obtain tax relief by concession – under strict law no relief is possible and such transactions are not therefore suitable for aggressive tax planning.

Miscellaneous income

It is also conceptually possible for taxpayers to be assessed under a miscellaneous income account where non-trading items are not held for the long term and are thus not capital. For an investor this is only likely to apply where there is considerable activity in derivatives and fortunately there is specific legislation which prevents this treatment for 'commodity or financial futures' or 'qualifying options'. These terms should cover any exchange-based contract or a contract entered into with a bank or counter-party regulated under the FSA.

Tax-exempt bodies

It follows from the above that a capital gains tax-exempt body, for example, a unit trust or investment trust, will only be taxable on gains in so far as the gains arise from trading or the use of specific futures and options.

Investment trusts

Taxation of income

Investment trusts are companies, listed on the Stock Exchange. They pay tax on their income less allowable management expenses at the standard rate of corporation tax, currently 33 per cent.

Taxation of capital gains

Provided the investment trust complies with the requirements set out in S842 TA 1988 it is exempt from tax on its capital gains. These requirements must be met for each accounting period.

Currency risk

Borrowings

Borrowing in foreign currencies is a form of currency risk management used widely by investment trusts for hedging. Gains/losses from such transactions are treated as a 'tax nothing' and are hence not taxable/allowable.

Investment trusts are excluded from the new legislation on the taxation of exchange gains and losses and, therefore, the tax treatment is not likely to change in the near future.

Derivative instruments

The tax treatment of futures and options for investment trusts is currently explained in the Inland Revenue's Statement of Practice (SP 14/91). The Statement of Practice covers financial futures and options. This would include forward contracts, exchange traded and OTC contracts and options and warrants.

A future or option which is clearly ancillary to a trading transaction on current or income account will give rise to trading profits or losses, as, for example, when a company has borrowed money at a floating rate of interest for trade purposes and enters into an interest-rate future or option with a view to protecting itself against rises in interest rates.

A future or option which is clearly ancillary to a transaction which is not a trading item on current account will be capital and hence not taxable, for example:

1. A company has existing loans denominated in US dollar and uses a futures or options contract to protect itself against the rise in the US dollar.
2. A company whose base currency is the US dollar holds yen-denominated securities and in order to eliminate the perceived risk of a fall in their value, enters into a forward contract to sell for US dollars an amount of yen equivalent to the yen value of the securities.

There are also transactions which are not clearly ancillary to another transaction. It is necessary to look at these in their own right to see whether they are capital or trading. This may cause uncertainties – if transactions are regarded as capital by the investment managers but income by the Revenue, for example in the following situations:

1. Futures and options are used in conjunction with a holding of cash bonds etc. so as to create synthetic assets.
2. Futures and options are used to take a position in a foreign currency in which the company does not have a portfolio, and has no intention of acquiring a portfolio, creating an exposure to fluctuations in that currency.

This uncertain treatment not only creates a potential tax expense on the transaction itself but also has implications for the investment trust status.

The Inland Revenue Consultative Document on Financial Instruments is discussed later on. It should be noted that the proposals only cover interest and currency contracts; contracts based on securities are still covered by SP 14/91.

Authorised Unit Trusts (AUTs)

Taxation of income

AUTs are treated as companies. They pay tax on their income less allowable management expenses currently at a rate of 22.5 per cent. Following the Budget on 30 November 1993, the rate applicable to unit trusts increased to 25 per cent from 1 April 1994.

Taxation of capital gains

AUTs are exempt from tax on their capital gains.

Currency risk

Borrowings

Borrowing is generally restricted to 10 per cent of the value of the fund's assets. Gains/losses from such borrowings would be a 'tax nothing' item and hence not taxable. Unit trusts are excluded from the new legislation on the taxation of exchange gains and losses.

Derivative instruments

Authorised unit trusts are specifically exempt from tax on income from transactions in futures and options. The SIB regulations restrict the use of derivatives for most AUTs and therefore this exemption is not as generous as it seems.

Forward contracts are not specifically exempt and AUTs are not covered by SP14/91. The SIB regulations would restrict the use of such contracts, and should in effect result in all such transactions being treated as capital (and hence exempt).

Authorised unit trusts are excluded from the new legislation on the taxation of foreign-exchange gains and losses and the proposals in the Consultative Document on the taxation of Financial Instruments.

Pension funds

Taxation of income

Income derived from investments or deposits and underwriting commission is exempt from income tax provided the scheme is approved and the income is held for the purposes of the scheme. (A non-approved pension fund would be taxed in the same way as any other trust.)

Taxation of capital gains

Provided the scheme is approved, capital gains are exempt from tax.

Currency risk

Borrowings

Pension funds may, if permitted by their trust deed, borrow in foreign currencies to hedge against the movement of non-sterling assets. Gains/losses from such transactions are treated as a 'tax nothing'.

Derivatives

As stated above, income from investments is exempt from income tax. The Taxes Act specifically states that income from futures and options contracts received by approved pension schemes shall be deemed to be income from investments, that is, income from such contracts is exempt. Forward contracts are not specifically exempt, and approved pension funds are not covered by SP14/91. Again the trust deed creating the fund may contain restrictions on the use of such contracts.

Unauthorised exempt unit trusts

A common investment vehicle for pension funds is an unauthorised unit trust. The most frequent form of such trusts is the unauthorised exempt unit trust, where investors are restricted to bodies which are exempt from tax, other than by reason of residence. Their investors normally comprise pension funds and charities.

Taxation of income

The trustees of an unauthorised unit trust are subject to income tax at the basic rate of income tax. No relief is given for management expenses.

Taxation of capital gains

Unauthorised unit trusts are exempt from tax on their capital gains provided the unit holders are all exempt bodies.

Currency risk

Borrowings

Gains/losses from borrowings would be a 'tax nothing' item and hence not taxable/allowable. Unauthorised unit trusts are excluded from the new legislation on the taxation of exchange gains and losses since they are not treated as corporates.

Derivative instruments

Like investment trusts, the tax treatment of financial futures and options is explained in the Inland Revenue's Statement of Practice (SP 4/91).

Unauthorised unit trusts are not treated as companies for taxation purposes and are therefore not covered by the proposals for Financial Instruments.

Insurance companies

Taxation of income

Insurance-company business is divided up into several components for tax purposes and these are subject to different rules.

Tax is charged at the normal corporation tax rate to the extent that the total amount assessed represents the shareholders' (or company's own) profits, and at the basic income rate to the extent that it represents the investment return on the life policy holders' funds. Profits attributable to pension policy holders will normally benefit from the same tax reliefs as an approved pension fund.

Taxation of capital gains

Insurance companies are subject to tax on their capital gains, essentially on their British life-assurance business, calculated by reference to normal capital gains tax principles. The computations tend to be complicated as insurance companies often have a far larger number of disposals than other companies which are subject to tax on their gains.

The Revenue considered that insurance companies were inappropriately avoiding tax on their capital via unit trusts and offshore funds. This effectively enabled companies to sell securities and re-invest the proceeds within the unit trust or fund without realising a taxable gain. Legislation was introduced in 1990 to counteract this by deeming unit-trust and offshore-fund holdings to have been sold and immediately re-acquired at market value at the end of each accounting period. This legislation has effect for all accounting periods beginning on or after 1 January 1993.

Currency risk

Borrowings

Gains/losses on long-term borrowings are 'tax nothings' and would not be taxable/allowable.

Insurance companies are included in the legislation on exchange gains in accordance with special rules for insurance companies set out in the regulations.

Derivative instruments

Income and gains from derivative instruments are taxable as income or capital gains in accordance with the general rules for companies.

Insurance companies are included in the proposals for financial instruments, with certain modifications to accommodate the special circumstances of insurance companies.

Application of proposed tax regimes

New regime for financial instruments

A Consultative Document was published on 20 August 1993 and the Revenue asked for representations on these proposals by 31 October 1993. Legislation has subsequently been included in the Finance Act 1994.

Qualifying companies

The proposed legislation will cover all companies within the charge to corporation tax. Authorised unit trusts are excluded.

Special provisions are required to adapt the rules for investment trusts and insurance and mutual trading companies.

Qualifying contracts

Interest rate contracts and options and currency contracts and options are included. Commodity or equity based contracts are excluded.

Treatment of profits and losses

The profit or loss on a qualifying contract will be computed on the basis shown in the company's statutory accounts if the basis used is:

a marked-to-market basis or;
an accruals basis; which
satisfies the conditions laid out in the proposals.

If some other method of accounting is used the profits or losses for tax purposes will be computed 'using an appropriate basis to be agreed between the taxpayer and the Inspector of Taxes but with the Inspector having the final decision'.

Profits or losses on qualifying contracts held for trading purposes will be included in the computation of trading profits/losses.

Non-trading profits or losses will be aggregated with non-trading exchange gains and losses. Any surplus of non-trading profits and gains over non-trading losses will be taxable as miscellaneous income.

Non-trading losses can be:

1. set against other profits in the same accounting period;

2. surrendered as group relief;
3. carried back against non-trading profits on qualifying contracts and non-trading exchange gains for the three preceding years; or
4. carried forward against future non-trading profits on qualifying contracts and non-trading exchange gains.

Implications for investment trusts

Proposed treatment

Instead of the distinction between revenue and capital, a distinction is now drawn between trading and non-trading. An investment trust would not be normally be trading.

As a result of the changes, gains which were previously capital (and therefore not taxed) are taxable. Conversely, losses are tax deductible, fortunately in the case of investment trusts, currency based derivatives are excluded from the new rules.

The legislation includes a provision to treat non-trading profits (but *not* losses) as income from shares and securities for the purposes of S842 TA 1988.

Insurance companies

Modification to the general rules are proposed for the computation of insurance companies' income and gains.

Foreign-exchange legislation

The provisions came into force on 23 March 1995 simultaneously with the financial instruments proposals. They will affect individual companies from the start of their next accounting period after the appointed date.

Qualifying companies

The foreign-exchange legislation applies to corporates. Unlike the financial instrument proposals, it excludes investment trusts as well as authorised unit trusts.

Treatment of profits and losses

Profits and losses are calculated by revaluing currency, currency debts (receivable and payable) and currency contracts into the local currency. In addition, if equities are held on trading account these are also revalued (insurance companies are subject to special rules). The revaluations take place whenever an item is acquired or disposed of and on each balance-sheet date. The gain or loss represents the movement since the valuation. (For a non-trader the local currency will always be sterling.) There will no longer be tax nothings in the form of currency borrowings or simple debts.

Trading gains and losses are included within the Schedule D Case I computation. Non-trading gains are assessable as miscellaneous income.

There are various complex rules to defer the taxation of gains on commencement or where they are unrealised or where transactions comply with restricted hedging rules.

Special requirements for retail funds

Investment trusts

S842 TA 1988 requirements

The tax requirements for investment trusts are set out in S842 TA 1988. Approval is given by the Inland Revenue after the end of the accounting period; approval will not be given unless the following conditions are satisfied throughout the accounting period:

1. The company is not a close company and is resident in the UK.
2. The company's income is derived wholly or mainly from shares and securities. The Revenue generally accept 70 per cent as being 'wholly or mainly'.
3. No holding in a company, other than an investment trust, represents more than 15 per cent by value of the investing company's investments. For this test all holdings in companies which are members of a group are aggregated. The test applies at the latest time when an addition to the investment is made, that is, the trust is not forced to sell investments if the value happens to rise to greater than 15 per cent of the company's assets at a later date.
4. The company's shares are quoted on the Stock Exchange.
5. The Memorandum and Articles of Association prohibit the distribution of gains from the realisation of investments.
6. The company does not retain more than 15 per cent of its income from shares and securities.

Accounts/taxation basis

The Revenue have stated that the tests should be based on income shown in the tax computation, although this has not been tested in the courts and it is possible that they should be based on income shown in the accounts. In practice the tests are not always straightforward, particularly where there is doubt whether income from certain transactions is income from shares and securities, for example, futures and options.

Futures and options

In the case of futures and options, SP 14/91 provides guidance about how they should currently be taxed. There are certain transactions, however, which although accounted for as capital could be seen to be income by the Revenue and taxed as such. For the purposes of S842 TA 1988, this income would not be income from shares and securities and such a treatment could cause the company to fail the income test. Income from trading in derivatives would not be income from shares and securities.

The *Consultative Document on Financial Instruments* issued in 1991 proposed that investment trusts should be excluded from the new regime but, following representations, the revised *Inland Revenue Consultative* issued on 20 August 1993 proposed that investment trusts are included. Following further representations, the 1993 Budget press release stated that qualifying instruments used by investment trusts to manage currency risk would be excluded, but that non-trading gains from interest-rate contracts (which would have previously been treated as capital and hence exempt) would be taxable as miscellaneous income but treated as income from shares and securities for the purpose of S842 TA 1988.

This treatment could also impact on the retention test, increasing the amount capable of being retained.

Unit trusts

SIB regulations – types of funds

The following types of funds are covered by the *Financial Services (Regulated Schemes) Regulations 1991* published by the SIB:

securities funds;
futures and options funds (FOFs);
geared futures and options funds (GFOFs);
warrant funds;
property funds;
fund of funds;
money market funds;
feeder funds;
umbrella funds.

Of the above, FOFs, GFOFs, property funds and warrant funds were first permitted when the regulations were revised in 1991.

Investment constraints

The following concentrates on securities funds – by far the most common type of unit trust. Certain investment constraints are included in the regulations to ensure that such schemes have a sufficiently diversified spread of risk. A number of constraints exist for such funds.

1. The funds can invest in approved securities quoted on recognised stock exchanges. The maximum amount which can be invested in non-approved securities including unquoted investments is 10 per cent.
2. The investment in any one investment should be limited to 5 per cent of the value of the fund. However, holdings of up to 10 per cent of the fund are permitted provided that the sum total of such holdings is less than 40 per cent of the value of the fund.
3. A securities fund may invest up to 35 per cent in Government Securities issued by any issuer with no restriction. However, if this limit is exceeded then a maximum of 30 per cent may consist of one issue and there must be at least six issues in the fund.
4. A fund may invest up to 5 per cent of its property in other collective-investment schemes providing that these schemes meet certain requirements regarding the nature and spread of the investments.
5. Up to 5 per cent of the fund may consist of warrants. However, a warrant or partly paid security is not permitted if its exercise would cause the scheme to exceed its investment and borrowing powers.

Currency risk

Borrowing

The traditional means of currency hedging has been the cumbersome back-to-back loan procedure, that is, a foreign currency loan matched by a sterling deposit. The lack of flexibility of back-to-back loans has discouraged managers from hedging in the past. The SIB Regulations now permit borrowings which are repayable out of the property of the trust, but are limited to 10 per cent of the value of the property. This limit does not apply to foreign currency loans which are the subject of back-to-back arrangements.

Derivative instruments

Since April 1988, managers have been permitted to use a number of sophisticated financial instruments – options, futures and forward currency contracts – to reduce currency and investment risk by way of efficient portfolio management (EPM). The SIB's Regulations allow EPM transactions provided the exposure is fully covered by cash or other property sufficient to meet any obligation to pay or deliver. EPM transactions are only to be entered into to reduce or eliminate risk and not for speculation.

Derivative funds

Specialised funds investing in derivatives were allowed in the 1991 regulations

– FOFs and GFOFs. These funds are allowed greater flexibility with the use of futures and options.

FOFs

The difference between an FOF and a securities fund is that an FOF can invest in derivatives, not simply by way of EPM but as the general investment management policy.

It is permitted to invest in futures, options, etc., as long as the exposure is suitably covered from within the property of the scheme. Some limited investment without cover is permitted in the form purchased options.

GFOFs

GFOFs differ from securities funds in that a GFOF can invest and retain 20 per cent of the property of the scheme in initial outlay and this can lead to volatile markets and greater exposure to profit and loss than in the case of a FOF.

A GFOF cannot borrow. This excludes back to back arrangements in the context of EPM.

Since they were first permitted by the 1991 regulations there have not been a large number of these funds set up in the United Kingdom. This may be because investors are likely to be more sophisticated corporates and fund managers have preferred to set up such funds offshore.

Personal equity plans

Investment limits

Either £6,000 (for 1994/95) can be invested in any combination of:

UK ordinary shares;
qualifying EC shares;
units in qualifying authorised unit trusts;
shares in qualifying investment trusts;

or £1,500 can be invested in any combination of non-qualifying investments, that is:

units in non-qualifying unit trusts;
shares in non-qualifying investments.

Qualifying unit and investment trusts

Qualifying unit trusts and investment trusts are those which have over 50 per cent of its investment in UK/qualifying EC shares.

Non-qualifying unit and investment trusts

Non-qualifying unit trusts and investment trusts are those which have over 50 per cent of its investments in shares, but they are not UK/qualifying EC shares.

Units and shares in unit trusts and investment trusts which do not meet this requirement cannot be held within a Personal Equity Plan (PEP). (Prior to 5 April 1993 £1,500 could be invested in these.)

Futures and options and other investments

Futures and options cannot be held directly within a PEP, although they can be held indirectly by unit trusts and investment trusts, provided the other conditions for these funds are satisfied. Note that currently the following are not allowed to be held within a PEP:

unauthorised unit trusts;
futures and options funds;
geared futures and options funds;
fund of funds which invest in any of the above;
others not allowed include money market funds, property funds, warrant funds, etc.

United States – regulations on the tax treatment of hedging transactions

The United States Treasury Department recently issued regulations reversing the United States government's litigating position over the United States tax treatment of hedging transactions. That position – that gains and losses on hedging transactions were capital and not ordinary items – was accepted by United States courts in the *Arkansas Best* case. The regulations provide that hedges generally will generate ordinary gains and losses if acquired as a hedge of an ordinary asset or liability.

The regulations respond to a congressional request in the 1993 Tax Act conference report asking Treasury to study the tax treatment of hedging transactions.

Overview

The regulations provide for ordinary tax treatment of gains and losses from interest rate, inventory and other common business hedges. These regulations apply immediately and for all open tax years, thus allowing for settlement of hundreds of pending tax cases and audits.

Hedging-transaction definition

The regulations generally define a hedging transaction as a transaction that a taxpayer entered into in the normal course of business primarily:

1. to reduce the risk of price changes or currency fluctuations for 'ordinary property' held or to be held by the taxpayer; or
2. to reduce the risk of interest rate, price changes or currency fluctuations on borrowings made or to be made or on 'ordinary obligations' incurred or to be incurred.

The regulations thus cover anticipatory hedges as well as other hedging transactions involving ordinary property and obligations.

Transactions excluded from the definition of hedging transactions under the regulations include:

1. a hedge of a depreciable asset used in the conduct of a trade or business.
2. a hedge of the ordinary income (e.g. a dividend stream) produced by a capital asset.
3. a hedge of non-inventory supplies.

Gains and losses on these hedges will be capital.

Transactions that hedge aggregate risk qualify for ordinary treatment only if all (or all but a *de minimus* amount) of the risk being held is related to ordinary property and liabilities.

The regulations do not apply where a taxpayer hedges the risk of a related party.

The regulations do not provide for the integration of the hedge and the asset or liability being hedged. Instead, the regulations respect the 'separate existence' of these transactions.

Identification requirement

Taxpayers generally must identify a hedging transaction in order to receive ordinary tax treatment. The regulations state that an identification for financial accounting purposes generally is insufficient, unless the taxpayer's books and records indicate that such an identification is being made for tax purposes as well.

There are specific identification requirements for inventory hedges, debt hedges for a limited period, anticipatory debt hedges, and hedges of aggregate risk.

Identification can be on a transaction by transaction basis. Alternatively, the regulations permit taxpayers to establish a system under which identification is effected by the type of transaction or by the manner in which the transaction is consumated or recorded.

For hedges entered into on or after 1 January 1994, identification of each hedge on the day entered into is required in order to receive ordinary treatment. Hedges entered into before 1994, and still open on 31 March 1994, must have been identified before the close of business on 31 March 1994.

Timing rules

The Internal Revenue Service (IRS) also issued regulations governing the timing of income or loss recognition on hedging transactions.

The timing rules (applicable only to hedging transactions that are eligible for ordinary gain or loss treatment under the regulations described above) generally require that a gain or loss from a hedge be taken into account in the same period as the income, gain or loss on the item being hedged.

Under the timing rules, taxpayers are generally permitted to choose a method of accounting for hedging gains and losses. The regulations recognise that more than one method of accounting may be permissible, and taxpayers have some leeway in choosing their method. Once a taxpayer chooses a method, that method must be applied consistently unless the IRS grants permission to change.

The IRS anticipate that hedge accounting methods used for financial accounting would satisfy the regulations. However, the IRS also recognises that the financial accounting rules in this area are not yet fully developed and may change in the future. Consequently, the financial-accounting treatment for hedges is not automatically a valid method under the regulations.

The proposed regulations provide specific limitations for the timing of gains and losses on hedges of aggregate risk, hedges of items marked-to-market, hedges of inventory, hedges of debt instruments, anticipatory hedges, notional principal contracts and dispositions of hedged assets or liabilities. Hedges of debt instruments, for example, generally have to be accounted for according to the terms of the debt instrument and the people to which the hedge relates.

Current United States tax treatment of certain hedging transactions

The Tax Court has allowed the Federal National Mortgage Association ('Fannie Mae') to treat losses on its liability hedges as ordinary rather than capital losses. *Federal National Mortgage Association v Commissioner*, 100 TC 541 (1993) adds new confusion to the uncertainty created by the Supreme Court decision in *Arkansas Best Corp v Commissioner*, 485 US$212 (1988) which overturned taxpayers' settled expectation about the United States tax treatment of hedging transactions.

Prior to *Arkansas Best*, for 30 years *Corn Products Refining Co v Commissioners*, 350 US46 (1955) was applied quite liberally by the IRS and taxpayers to a variety of hedges, both financial and foreign currency. Under the *Corn Products* doctrine, any asset, including hedges, acquired and held in the ordinary course of a taxpayer's business, if held for a 'business purpose', fell outside the definition of a 'capital' (i.e. investment) asset and, therefore, gain or loss on its disposition was ordinary. *Corn Products* appeared to create an extra-statutory exception to the Section 1221 definition of capital asset.

Arkansas Best

Arkansas Best dramatically limited the *Corn Products* doctrine. *Arkansas Best* rendered a taxpayer's 'intention' in holding an asset (i.e. investment vs. trade or business) irrelevant and held that all assets other than those specific assets enumerated in Section 1221 (1)–(5) as exceptions (inventory, accounts receivable, copyrights in the hands of the creator and depreciable business property) are capital assets. The court in *Arkansas Best* held that *Corn Products*, properly read, did not sanction an extra-statutory exception to the Section 1221 rule that an asset is capital unless a specific exemption applies, but rather recognised that in some cases, future contracts which hedged the price of goods incorporated into goods held as inventory and sold in the ordinary course could be 'essentially equivalent' to the inventory itself and, therefore, could fall within the Section 1221 inventory exception.

Enactment of Section 1256

In 1986, two years before the *Arkansas Best* decision, Congress had enacted Section 1256 which requires taxpayers to mark-to-market certain futures and foreign-currency contracts ('Section 1256 contracts'). Section 1256 also generally provides that gain or loss on such marked-to-market contracts is 40 per cent short term and 60 per cent long term. Section 1256(e) provides that Section 1256 contracts which a taxpayer elects to identify as hedges are not subject to the marked-to-market or 40/60 rules.

The legislative history to Section 1256(e) makes clear that Congress assumed that financial instruments acquired in ordinary course to reduce risk of price changes on goods or currency fluctuation or interest-rate fluctuations on indebtedness would not be treated as capital assets. *Arkansas Best* levelled the assumptions on which 1256(e) was based and taxpayers who identified Section 1256 contracts as hedges were in the unfortunate position of having elected ordinary treatment for gains in those contracts but being subject to the IRS imposing capital treatment for any losses.

Enactment of Section 988

Section 988 of the United States Code (which makes all foreign currency gains and losses ordinary) effectively eliminated this problem for certain hedges and interest-rate hedges denominated in a non-functional (non-dollar) currency entered into after 21 October 1988. However, the post-*Arkansas Best* problem described above has continued for hedges involving dollar-denominated instruments.

Fannie Mae decision

The holding in *Fannie Mae* is narrow and arguably consistent with *Arkansas Best*. The Tax Court confirmed that the only exceptions to capital-asset treatment were those enumerated in Section 1221(1)–(5), but held that these exceptions to capital-asset treatment could be given the same expansive reading that the Supreme Court gave the inventory exception in *Corn Products*. Fannie Mae, the court stated, was entitled to rely on the rationale of *Arkansas Best* only to the extent that its portfolio of mortgages qualified for one of the statutory exceptions to capital-asset treatment.

Both the taxpayer and the IRS conceded that the inventory exception did not apply. The court's great leap was fitting Fannie Mae's mortgage portfolio under the Section 1221(4) exception for 'accounts or notes receivable acquired in the ordinary course of trade or business for services rendered'. Because Fannie Mae's purpose is to make life comfortable for mortgage lenders, the court reasoned, it must therefore be providing a 'service' to them by making a secondary market.

Because acquiring mortgages is all that Fannie Mae does, it was relatively easy for the court to relate any debt issuance to the acquisition of Section 1221(4) assets. The *Fannie Mae* decision does not sanction ordinary treatment for issuers of debt who enter into interest-rate hedges but who cannot specifically relate their debt for the purchase of an asset specifically enumerated in the 1221 exceptions. Nor would it appear to apply for corporations in other businesses that routinely hedge their liabilities, unless they are financial intermediaries who profit from interest-rate spreads, like Fannie Mae, its sister organisations, and banks.

The Tax Court seems to have invited the next case with its statement that 'we do not need to face the question whether there still exists a nonstatutory exception to Section 1221 . . . but we leave it to another case on another day, where it may be squarely presented'.

The United States taxation of capital gains

With the exception of securities and commodities dealers and purchasers holding as part of a 'straddle' or hedging transaction, purchasers will normally hold options and futures as capital assets and accordingly be subject to capital-gains rules. The United States tax code provides different rules for short-term and long-term gains (under 1 year and over 1 year respectively). Since 1987, however, the distinctions between ordinary income and capital gains have not been as important as they once were because the tax rate on capital gains for corporations and ordinary income is the same for corporations. The gain differential for individuals has varied since 1987 but capital gains are presently taxed at a maximum individual tax rate of 28 per cent, almost 12 percentage points less than the maximum individual tax rate (39.6 per cent) on ordinary income. Long and short gains have to be accounted for separately and the rules for dealing with ordinary and capital losses are different.

Corporations

- Corporations are liable to tax on long-term gains at the same federal rates as apply to ordinary income, that is, 35 per cent where income exceeds US$18.33m. Annual income below this level is taxed at federal rates between 15 per cent and 35 per cent (surtax of 3 per cent applicable in certain cases may increase the marginal rate to 38 per cent).
- Net capital losses may be carried back three years or forward five years and offset against capital gains in chronological order.

Individuals

- Individuals and other non-corporate taxpayers are liable to federal tax on their ordinary income, and short-term capital gains at graduated rates between 15 per cent and 39.6 per cent. Income is subject to a deduction for itemised deductions and personal allowances. The add-back of personal allowances and deductions for high-income individual taxpayers may in some cases increase the marginal federal tax rate of 28 per cent on capital gains to 31 per cent.
- These taxpayers are liable to tax at rates up to a maximum of 28 per cent on their *net* capital gains, i.e. net long-term capital gains less net short-term capital losses (subject to the personal allowances add-back noted above).
- Net capital losses can be set against US$3,000 of ordinary income in the current year. Excess losses can be carried forward and set against future year capital gains and US$3,000 of ordinary income for an unlimited number of years.

Securities and commodities dealers

- Security dealers are taxed on their gains and losses under the normal rules for 'ordinary income'. In addition, certain methods for valuing year-end inventory must be used. Dealers will not, however, be liable to United States tax unless they are United States persons or they have a branch or permanent establishment in the United States.
- Activities of a dealer are distinguishable from those of a trader, broker, investor or speculator. A dealer's profits must be derived from a mark-up of the products it sells to its customers in the ordinary course of its business.

Thus, a specialist or a stock-exchange dealer who accepts orders in selected stocks from other members of the exchange will be treated as a dealer, but a specialist who merely matches buy or sell orders received from other brokers will not.
- It should be noted that a diversified investment house may be a dealer in some products and trade for its own account in some other products and trade for its own account in some of the same or other products.

United States marked-to-market rules for securities dealers

The 1993 Revenue Reconciliation Act, signed by President Bill Clinton on 10 August 1993, requires certain 'dealers' in securities to mark-to-market those securities on the last day of a taxable year, thereby recognising taxable gain or loss. At the time the legislation was enacted, banks, insurance companies, mutual funds and even some manufacturing companies publicly urged the United States authorities to give early evidence on what a 'dealer' is for the purpose of these rules.

In early October 1993 a government official stated publicly that efforts would be made to issue guidance on who is a dealer under the marked-to-market rules before the 31 October deadline for identifying securities in inventory on that date. The guidance, Revenue Ruling 93–76, was issued on 25 October but has so far proved to be a disappointment to many financial services companies.

General rules

Under the new law, a 'dealer' must mark-to-market two types of securities: (a) securities held in inventory; and (b) any security held at year end not in inventory. Several exceptions, listed below, to the marked-to-market rules apply, even to securities in the hands of a 'dealer':

1. securities held for investment;
2. debt acquired by a dealer in the ordinary course of business but not held for sale;
3. a security which is a hedge of another security not subject to the marked-to-market rules; and
4. a security which hedges a position which is not a security.

The law requires clear identification of a security falling within an exception before the close of the day on which the security was acquired.

Definition of dealer

Revenue ruling 93–76 states that taxpayers that regularly originate and sell loans are dealers. However, the ruling does not affirmatively state that those who make but do not sell loans are not dealers.

The ruling clarified that the classification of a security under financial accounting principles – including Federal Accounting Standards Board Statement No 115 – is not dispositive of the treatment of the security for federal-tax purposes and, in particular, the eligibility for one of the four exemptions described above.

The IRS ruled that a taxpayer that is not a dealer as defined in the statute will not be deemed a dealer because it makes protective identification of all its securities for purposes of the exemptions described above. In addition, a taxpayer whose sole business consists of trading in securities will not be deemed a dealer.

Identification procedures

A dealer's records must clearly indicate the specific security or hedge being identified for an exemption from the marked-to-market rules, and the identification must clearly indicate that it is being made for purposes of these rules.

According to the ruling, taxpayers are not required at this time to use any special procedures to comply with the identification requirements of the statute. The IRS stated that until further guidance is published, any reasonable method could be used, as long as the identification was made on, and retained as part of, the dealer's books and records.

On the other hand, the ruling said that the dealer may identify specific accounts as containing only hedges that are covered by a particular exception, so that placing a security or hedge in the account identifies that security or hedge as being covered by that exception.

Straddles and hedging transactions

- The marked-to-market rules are not applicable to 'straddles', defined for United States tax purposes to include most offsetting positions in the same, or substantially identical, property. Code Section 1092 contains special rules for hedging transactions. The United States rules governing straddles and certain other types of hedging transactions are set forth in Sections 1092 and 1256 of the Code and are quite complex.

Pension funds

- Some major institutional investors (e.g. pension funds) are exempt from tax on ordinary income and capital gains.

United States taxation of gains arising from derivative instruments

Different rules apply to regulated derivative contracts (mainly but not exclusively futures) and other derivative instruments (mainly but not exclusively options).

Regulated contracts

The United States tax code draws a distinction between 'regulated contracts' (Code Section 1256 contracts) and non-regulated contracts. The rules apply equally to corporations or individuals. More specifically, Code Section 1256 applies to:

1. any regulated futures contract;
2. any foreign currency contract;
3. any nonequity option; and
4. any dealer equity option.

These terms and their significance are explained below.

Regulated futures contracts

Regulated futures contracts are governed by Code Section 1256. A regulated futures contract is defined as a contract which is:

1. traded on, or subject to, a qualified board or exchange; and
2. which the amounts required to be deposited or withdrawn depend on a system of marking to market (a system of variation margins).

A qualified board or exchange is a national securities exchange registered with the SEC, a domestic board of trade designated as a contract market by the Commodities Futures Trading Commission or any other exchange or board of trade having rules that the IRS determines are adequate to carry out the purposes of Code Section 1256.

Non-equity options

A non-equity option is any listed option which is not an equity option.

Equity options

Broadly, as would be expected, an equity option is any option:

1. to buy and sell stock, e.g. a New York Stock Exchange (NYSE) traded option; or
2. the value of which is determined directly or indirectly by reference to any stock (or group of stocks) or stock index.

There is, however, an important exception. The expression 'equity option' does not include any option with respect to any group of stocks or stock index if the option is regulated by the CFTC and the CFTC has designated the contract or, in the case of other contracts (notably non-United States contracts), the United States Treasury has determined that the contracts meet the requirements for designation. Therefore, CFTC-regulated or Treasury-designated index options are non-equity options governed by Section 1256.

Dealer equity options

These are any equity options purchased or granted by an options dealer in the ordinary course of his business and listed on an exchange on which the options dealer is registered. The definition does not appear to be relevant to London International Financial Futures Exchange (LIFFE) contracts.

Rules that apply to Code Section 1256 contracts

Under Section 1256 each regulated contract held at the close of the taxable year is marked-to-market and any resulting gain or loss is taken into account for that tax year.

The termination of a regulated contract, either by delivery of the underlying asset, assignment of the contract, lapse of the contract or in any other manner, is treated as a sale of the contract at its market value on the date of termination or transfer. This is the actual price paid or received in most cases.

The aggregate gain or loss which arises from the termination of futures contracts during the year, or from marking to market of futures contracts held at the year end, is treated for tax purposes as follows:

40 per cent of the gain or loss is treated as if it were a *short*-term capital gain or loss;
60 per cent of the gain or loss is treated as if it were a *long*-term gain or loss.

The capital gain or loss would then be treated according to the basic rules for corporations or individuals as above.

Exceptions to the normal rules

- As stated above, Code Section 1256 and the 40/60 split do not apply to regulated futures contracts held by a corporation or individual as part of a hedging transaction entered into in the normal course of their business. Any gain/loss arising from a regulated futures contract held as part of a hedging transaction will be wholly treated as ordinary income or loss.
- The automatic 40/60 split also applies to regulated futures contracts relating to foreign (non-United States) currency contracts unless an election is made to treat any gains or losses as ordinary income.
- The rules contained in Code Section 1256 do not apply to non-United States persons unless such persons are engaged in a United States trade or business. Therefore no United States tax is imposed on any gain realised by a person who is not resident in the United States for tax purposes.

- Where a straddle exists, all contracts are deemed to be terminated on the date of delivery under any one of the contracts where the taxpayer takes delivery or exercises part of the straddle. A straddle is an offsetting position in actively traded personal property which involves two or more contracts governed by Code Section 1256.
- As stated above, securities and commodities dealers recognise ordinary income or loss on sales of contracts.

Non-regulated contracts

- Taxpayers are liable to tax on long-/short-term capital gains at the time of disposition under the general charging provisions for capital gains.
- Non-regulated contracts are not marked-to-market at the year end nor are gains/losses subject to the 40/60 per cent short-term/long-term split contained in Section 1256.
- Gains and losses must be reported separately to gains/losses arising from regulated contracts.
- Straddles involving non-regulated futures contracts are subject to special loss-limitation rules contained in Code Section 1092. This prevents the conversion of ordinary income and short-term capital gains into long-term capital gains on straddle transactions.

Option contracts: corporations and individuals

As indicated above, different rules apply to equity and non-equity options. Non-equity options are governed by Code Section 1256; certain contracts within the definition of an equity contract are defined as non-equity.

Conclusion

Tax issues clearly influence the use of derivatives by portfolio investors and fund managers. There are significant differences in the taxation rules between different territories and even within a single country, the consequences of entering into a derivative may depend on the tax status of a particular investor. Furthermore, many tax systems are in a state of flux as legislators update old laws to reflect the rapid development of the derivatives markets in the last decade. Up-to-date advice related to the precise circumstances of the investor will normally be necessary to ascertain the current tax treatment of a particular derivative transaction.

4
Performance indices and benchmarks

In the context of fund management, the word 'benchmark' is often interchanged with the word 'index'. To go back to basics for a moment, 'benchmark' is defined in the *OED* as 'standard or point of reference; surveyors mark at point in line of levels'. 'Index', on the other hand, is defined as: '1, number expressing prices etc. in terms of a standard value; 2, list of subjects usually alphabetical, of the contents of a book'. In fund management, a benchmark and an index are generally understood to be reference points for performance comparison. However, to the purist, an index is rather more than this; it must be an investable commodity or instrument comprising either an equally weighted or equity-weighted basket of clearly defined items.

The value of using a benchmark depends upon whether you believe in assessing performance in absolute or relative terms. As a fund manager you are more likely to subscribe to relative assessment. As an investor you are more likely to subscribe to the absolute camp. Performance benchmarks, and indices, can be constructed in many different ways and will be affected by a range of variables. A benchmark is usually an index, such as the S&P 500 or the FTSE 100, but this is not always the case. To most users, a good benchmark is one that is representative of its market, clean and accurate. To the cynics, benchmarks are used primarily for marketing purposes and a good benchmark can be defined as one that can be beaten.

So, what are all the different options available to the investor? How are they constructed, how can they be used and what value do they add to overall portfolio construction and evaluation?

Stock indices

The last decade has witnessed a proliferation of new stock indices and benchmarks for the equities investor. Users are increasingly adopting the rifle as opposed to the shotgun approach. What is the point of comparing your investment in UK small companies with the performance of the FTSE 100? The FT–Actuaries World Indices Consortium has compiled well in excess of 400 indices and sub-indices. These are compiled jointly by The Financial Times Limited, Goldman, Sachs and Co., and County NatWest/ Wood Mackenzie in conjunction with The Institute of Actuaries and the Faculty of Actuaries, and represent approximately 75 per cent of the capitalisation of the world stock markets.

Before going on to consider the issue of indices or benchmarks and their use in assessing the performance of managed derivatives investments, it is worth first taking a look at the strict rules to which the above consortium adheres in its construction and maintenance of different indices.

The aim of the consortium has been to create and maintain a series of high quality equity market indices for use by the global investment community. To achieve this aim, the consortium has sought to establish that the indices are recognised as being:

- comprehensive;
- consistent;
- flexible;
- accurate;
- investible;
- representative;
- user-driven.

The consortium has created a World Index Policy Committee which is referred to as 'The Panel'. All policy decisions made concerning the indices are the responsibility of the Panel which (as outlined in the FT-Actuaries World Indices rule book) consists of:

1. One representative of each consortium member.
2. One member nominated by each of the parties as representing an actual or prospective main user of The World Indices.
3. A chairman who is a member of the Institute of Actuaries and/or the Faculty of Actuaries.
4. A second representative of the Institute of Actuaries and/or the Faculty of Actuaries.

All decisions of the Panel are by majority vote with the chairman having a second or casting vote.

The Panel's role is to do the following:

- Determine and review the overall policy and objectives of the Indices.
- Establish the country and stock-selection criteria.
- Ensure that the indices are theoretically and operationally correct and accurate.

- Monitor and assess submissions made by end-users.
- Consider and agree additions, deletions and sector classification changes for implementation at each quarter end and at other times when extraordinary conditions dictate.

The development of indices in the derivatives industry has taken place on two fronts: first, the commodity indices, which are similar to most stock indices in that they reflect the price changes of a basket (either weighted or unweighted) of commodities traded on recognised futures exchanges; second, the skill-based indices which seek to show how the managers investing in the commodity and financial futures and options and other derivative markets have performed as a group over a given period of time. We shall call the latter 'skill-based market performance indices'.

Commodity indices

The first of the commodity indices was the index developed by the Commodity Research Bureau (CRB).

The Commodity Research Bureau's Futures Price Index was developed in 1957. It was designed to monitor broad changes in the commodity markets and is treated as an inflation indicator. The index averages the prices of the following 21 futures markets within 6 groups:

Meats:	Cattle Hogs Bellies	**Industrials:**	Crude oil Cotton Copper Unleaded gas Heating oil Lumber
Metals:	Gold Silver Platinum		
Softs:	Coffee Cocoa Sugar	**Grains:**	Corn Wheat Soybeans Soybean oil Soybean meal
		Miscellaneous:	Orange juice

The weightings can be seen in the pie chart in Figure 4.1.

The index is calculated in three stages. First, each of the index's 21 component commodities is arithmetically averaged using prices for all of the futures months which expire on or before the end of the ninth calendar month from the current date, excluding non-cycle months. This means that

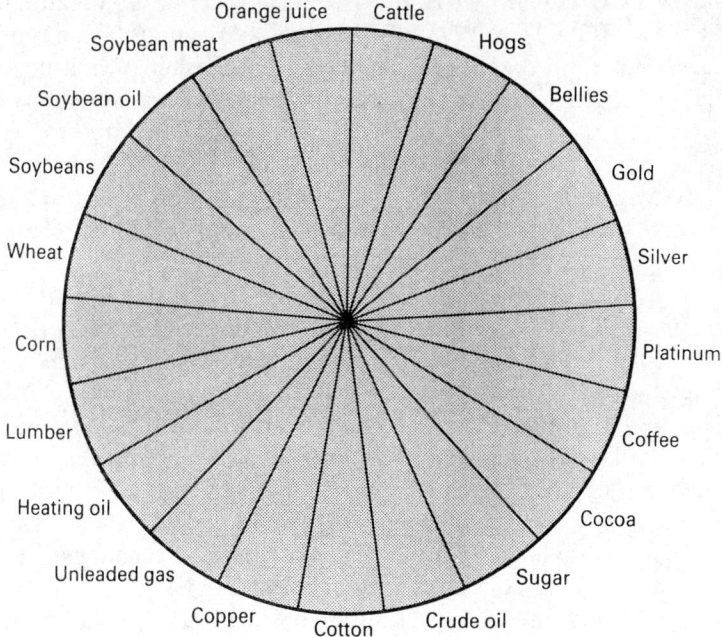

Figure 4.1 Pie chart of CRB index.

the index extends between 9 and 10 months into the future depending on where one is in the current month.

The next step is to geometrically average the 21 component averages by multiplying all of the numbers together and taking the twenty-first root. Then the resulting value is taken and divided by 50.7161, the 1967 base-year average for these commodities, and then multiplied by an adjustment factor of 0.94128. This adjustment factor is necessary because of certain changes that have been made to the index since 1987. In July 1987 the index changed from including 26 commodities averaged over 12 months to 21 commodities averaged 9 months. The second change happened in July 1989 when the non-cycle component months were eliminated; and the third change took place in July 1992 when oat futures (traded on the Chicago Board of Trade) were substituted with unleaded gasoline – which is traded on the New York Mercantile Exchange (NYMEX).

To complete the index calculation, the above result is multiplied by 100 in order to convert the index into percentage terms.

Goldman Sachs Commodity Index (GSCI)

In the 1970s Goldman Sachs and Co. launched the Goldman Sachs Commodity Index (GSCI). In 1992, GSCI futures and options began trading on the Chicago Mercantile Exchange. The GSCI is a basket of non-financial commodities with active futures markets. Each commodity is weighted by quantity of world production in order to effectively measure the impact of commodity performance on the world economy.

The GSCI, unlike the CRB, incorporates yield as well price movement in its total return. The price movement reflects spot price changes in the underlying constituent commodities. The 'yield' indicates all returns that are not related to simple price movements. It includes the interest earned on the money used as margin to buy and sell futures contracts, as well as the returns which result from rolling forward positions in commodity-futures contracts.

Like the FT-Actuaries World Index Consortium, the GSCI has strict requirements that a commodity must meet before being either considered or included in the index.

- The commodity must be a physical commodity. No financial commodities or instruments are considered for inclusion.
- The commodity must have a futures contract traded on an exchange in an OECD country.
- The futures contract must be denominated in US dollars.
- If the exchange operates on the basis of perpetual forward prices (e.g. the London Metals Exchange (LME) 3-month, 15-month prices) a fixed date price at least one month forward must also be available (e.g. LME Final Intermediate Closing Prices).
- Contract prices in US dollars must be published daily by the exchange and be available to Goldman Sachs & Co. from the exchange or via a third party data vendor.
- In order to ensure that the GSCI is an investible index, several liquidity requirements are imposed. Changing liquidity over time may result in commodities being added to and/or deleted from the GSCI.

To be added to the GSCI in a given year, a commodity must have had a total futures-contract volume on its most active exchange of at least 750,000 contracts in the previous year. If in the course of the year the contract specifications change slightly, or a contract is replaced with a new, essentially similar contract, the volumes of the new and old contracts in that year may be aggregated.

If a previously included commodity's contract volume in its most active year falls below 375,000 in a given year, it will be removed from GSCI in the following year.

- In order to be added to the GSCI in a given year, a commodity must have an equivalent physical traded ratio (EPTR) greater than 33 per cent in the previous year. EPTR is defined as the product of the annual US-dollar denominated contract volume on the exchange with the largest annual US-dollar denominated volume and the contract size on that exchange, divided by the world production quantity average (defined below).
- Since the GSCI is production weighted, an included commodity must not be a direct derivative of another included commodity. If derivative commodities were included in the GSCI, the effect would amount to 'double-counting' the production of these commodities. An exception is made in the case of a single commodity which comprises more than 33 per cent of the dollar weight of the index. In this case, derivative commodities can be considered for inclusion, but the weight of the primary commodity is adjusted to reflect its inclusion.

So which commodities are (or have been) included in the GSCI?

Table 4.1 Summary of history to date

Included contracts Commodity	Exchange	First year	Last year
Copper	COMEX	1977	1989
Copper high grade	COMEX	1989	current
Aluminium	LME	1991	current
Zinc	LME	1991	current
Nickel	LME	1993	current
Gold	COMEX	1978	current
Silver	COMEX	1973	current
Platinum	NYMEX	1984	current
Live hogs	CME	1976	current
Pork bellies	CME	1970	1975
Live cattle	CME	1970	current
Wheat	CBOT	1970	current
Corn	CBOT	1970	current
Soy beans	CBOT	1970	current
Sugar	CSCE	1973	current
Coffee	CSCE	1981	current
Cocoa	CSCE	1984	current
Cotton	NYCE	1977	current
Heating oil	NYMEX	1983	current
Gasoline (unleaded)	NYMEX	1988	current
Crude oil	NYMEX	1987	current

As of 23 June 1994, the weightings were as follows:

Commodity	Percentage
Crude oil	16.99%
Gasoline	12.44%
Heating oil	13.42%
Natural gas	12.61%
Live cattle	10.89%
Live hogs	8.43%
Wheat	5.57%
Corn	3.97%
Sugar	2.53%
Soy beans	2.15%
Cotton	2.54%
Coffee	1.52%
Cocoa	0.27%
Aluminium	3.03%
Copper	2.33%
Zinc	0.61%
Nickel	0.46%
Gold	2.05%
Platinum	0.33%
Silver	0.31%

The above list is shown in the following pie chart. The GSCI is compared to the production-cost benchmark as part of the research and to identify the cost structure of an industry.

Table 4.2 Contracts excluded from the GSCI

Commodity	Exchange	Reason for exclusion
Oats	CBOT	Volume <750,000
Eggs	CME	Volume <750,000
Orange juice	NYCE	Volume <750,000
Iced broilers	CBOT	Volume <750,000
Plywood	CBOT	Volume <750,000
Gasoline (leaded)	NYMEX	EPTR <33%
Potatoes	NYMEX	EPTR <33%
Lumber	CME	EPTR <33%
Feeder cattle	CME	Derivative of live cattle
Soy-bean meal	CBOT	Derivative of soy beans
Soy-bean oil	CBOT	Derivative of soy beans
Copper	LME	No US-dollar price published until July 1993

Performance indices and benchmarks 71

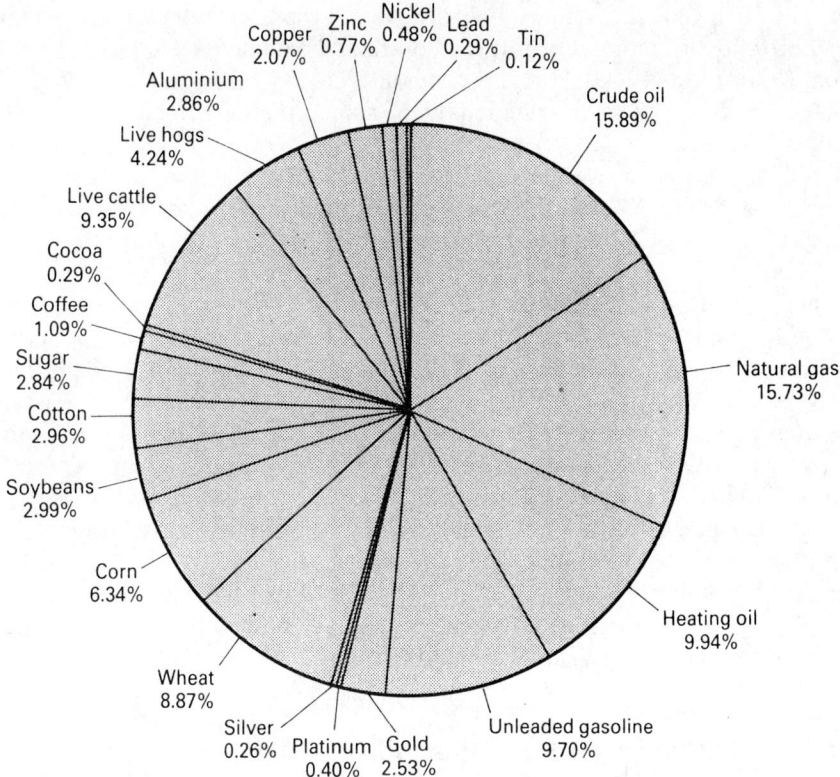

Figure 4.2 Goldman Sachs Commodity Index.

Table 6.2 is a list of other reasonably active contracts which historically have not been included in the GSCI and the reason for their exclusion.

GSCI weighting

The weight of each commodity is the quantity of that commodity produced world-wide. The actual number used for world production is a five-year moving average (lagged three years) of the world production quantity. The majority of the production statistics used are from the *United Nations Statistical Yearbook* and *Industrial Statistics Yearbook* which have been published annually since 1961 and 1969 respectively. In addition to the data from these publications, several other sources of data have been used from time to time.

So how is the GSCI calculated?

The GSCI actually consists of two separate indices, the Spot Index (GSCI) and the Total Return Index (GSCI). The Spot Index represents the sum of the US-dollar value of the world production average (WPA) for each commodity normalised to 100 on 2 January 1970. The GSCI represents the total return on the portfolio of commodity futures contracts contained in the GSCI. The Total Return Index (GSCI) is also normalised to 100 on 2 January 1970.

The Spot Index (GSCI) is defined by the sum of the settlement prices of the futures contracts held (CP) multiplied by the World Production Weight (WPC) divided by a normalising constant (NCH). The World Production Weight values are equal to the world production average values divided by a price-scaling factor (generally 1 or 100) so that exchange quoted prices may be used.

The Total Return Index (GSCI) represents the cumulative total return realised by an investor holding the portfolio of futures contracts in GSCI. It is normalised to 100 on 2 January 1970. GSCI is calculated by taking the product of the daily returns of the portfolio. Investors are constantly looking for assets which are negatively correlated with standard portfolios of stocks and bonds and which provide acceptable returns. Commodity indices, which generally show a negative correlation to stocks and bonds (see the study commissioned by the Chicago Mercantile Exchange (CME) from Ibbotson Associates Inc.) can be used for outright alternative investment, tactical asset allocation and hedging. For further information and insight into the application and use of commodity indices we suggest that you contact both the Commodity Research Bureau and Goldman Sachs and Co.

Skill-based Market Performance Indices (MPIs)

Most investment managers in the managed derivatives industry (some would say in fund management in general) have clearly identifiable investment styles. Such differences in style mean that managers investing in the same markets and instruments can generate very different performance results. It is, therefore, extremely difficult to measure performance and to select an appropriate benchmark for so doing. Investment managers in this field tend to report their results on a monthly basis. Most of the skill-based benchmarks that currently exist are equity weighted and include the results of different numbers of traders depending on each benchmark's selection criteria. There are two particular problems facing end-users of these MPIs; first, how can you be sure that the benchmark being used is a relevant yardstick against which to compare your investment? Second, how 'good' is the data from which the benchmark has been compiled?

Towards the end of 1992, TASS Management was commissioned by two leading industry associations – the Futures Industry Institute and the Managed Futures Association – to research and create a new performance benchmark. By the time this book is printed, the index is likely to have been launched, and the construction and maintenance parameters published. However, at the time of submitting this manuscript to the publishers, answers were still pending on a few issues. Nevertheless, at the risk of boring you with further detail on index construction, we thought it might be helpful to take a look at the issues that had to be considered and the problems that had to be overcome in the research of this new benchmark. They offer some enlightening insights into the whole issue of performance presentation in the managed derivatives industry.

At the outset it was decided that the development of the performance benchmark should be divided into two distinct parts:

1. the computation of an adjusted monthly rate of return (ROR) for each investment programme;
2. the computation of a monthly 'market performance index' (MPI).

These two issues had to be regarded as separate because they do not lead to the same definition of 'performance'. It can be argued that the percentage rate of return should be regarded by the investor as a return on investment and should be in net terms in order for the managers to be comparable. The MPI is an indicator of how the universe of managers performed during the considered period. This should be presented in gross and net terms to identify any bias due to the different fees charged by different managers.

When the research started, it was decided to include only the results of managers investing in exchange-traded instruments and/or foreign exchange on a leveraged basis. The universe comprised, initially, the active commodity trading advisors and derivative fund managers as well as those who were active for a period since 1980 (and for whom public records exist) but who have since ceased trading. The project was divided into two parts. First, the performance data validation; second, the construction of the actual benchmark (the MPI).

Data validation

To understand the minefield that had to be negotiated when validating the data, it is useful to have some idea of the current performance-reporting requirements in the industry. In the United States, both the Commodity Futures Trading Commission and the Securities Exchange Commission have laid down specific guidelines. Outside the United States such guidelines do not exist. Many of the managers based outside the United States adhere to these guidelines when preparing their performance results for distribution, but there are a number who do not. Furthermore, despite the seeming strictness of these guidelines, there is room for varying degrees of flexible interpretation.

Performance in this industry is generally presented in a composite, spreadsheet format, as shown in Table 4.3.

Composite track records are not necessarily representative of the returns that each client achieved. Furthermore, they do not show the different levels of risk that might have been taken by the manager on behalf of some clients. The reasons for this are numerous, but the most important sources of bias are:

- the timing of capital additions and withdrawals during the time period (usually a month);
- non-actual equity;
- fees.

The question that had to be asked concerning every composite performance record included in the universe was 'does this record provide a fair representation of what a new investor might have achieved if he or she had invested at some date in the past?' Depending on the treatment of the above-mentioned sources of bias the answers varied considerably.

Phase 1: computing an adjusted monthly percentage rate of return (ROR)

Introduction

In general terms, the ROR for a given investor at a given period in time is the ratio between the net trading profits/losses (achieved under the advice of the trader) and the actual equity the investor deposited in his or her account.

Ideally we should deal with each investor's account separately in order to build the ROR for each trader. Unfortunately, this is not practical. We therefore have to work from composite performance results assuming that each trader only has 'one' investor. However, in order for this simplification (and regulatory requirement) to be valuable, the ROR of each investor must be

Table 4.3 Sample SEC/CFTC track record

Date	Beginning net asset balance actual $	Beginning net asset balance actual $	Adj. bnav fully fnd accounts actual $	Cash added nominl $	Cash withdrw nominl $	Notional added nominl $	Notional withdrw nominl $	Notional funds nominl $	Realized profit nominl $	Comms. paid nominl $	Gross realized profit nominl $	Other interest nominl $
Jan 93	0	0	0	0	0	0	0	0	0	0	0	0
Feb 93	0	0	0	0	0	0	0	0	0	0	0	0
Mar 93	0	0	0	0	0	0	0	0	0	0	0	0
Apr 93	0	0	0	0	0	0	0	0	0	0	0	0
May 93	0	0	0	0	0	0	0	0	0	0	0	0
Jun 93	0	0	0	0	0	0	0	0	0	0	0	0
Jul 93	0	0	0	0	0	0	0	0	0	0	0	0
Aug 93	0	0	0	0	0	0	0	0	0	0	0	0
Sep 93	0	0	0	0	0	0	0	0	0	0	0	0
Oct 93	0	0	0	0	0	0	0	0	0	0	0	0
Nov 93	0	0	0	0	0	0	0	0	0	0	0	0
Dec 93	0	0	0	0	0	0	0	0	0	0	0	0
Jan 94	0	0	0	0	0	0	0	0	0	0	0	0

comparable. In essence, the investor accounts should be treated in the same way. This means that at the end of the month, each client has the same ROR associated with a similar risk. If this is not the case, then the monthly ROR is said to be biased, and thus cannot be compared to the ROR of other traders.

As stated above, the different sources of bias are:

- additions and withdrawals (DE) of equity (both actual and non-actual) during the month;
- non-actual equity (NE) i.e. notional equity, committed funds (CF) and any other form of equity which is not actually deposited in the account;
- fees (FE);
- interest income (II).

Additions and withdrawals of equity

There are two methods for dealing with DE. The first one is very accurate but requires a substantial amount of information and computation. The second is very simple, does not require a lot of information but is based on a restrictive assumption.

With the first method, we need to know the precise days and amounts of additions and withdrawals. The starting equity (SAE) is then adjusted by adding to it or removing from it the addition (withdrawal) according to the day on which the transaction has taken place. There is one major drawback to adjusting the SAE for DE in this manner. Even if it is possible to obtain the necessary information from the traders (which is most unlikely), it assumes that a trader makes a daily adjustment to all positions based on new levels of equity. Research to date indicates that this is not the case.

Table 4.3 (continued)

Net accrued interest nominl $	Change open tr. equity nominl $	Change accrued comms. nominl $	Change other income nominl $	Change mgmt. fees nominl $	inc. fees nominl $	net perfrm nominl $	Gross ending balance nominl $	Ending nav nominl $	vami index fully fnded	month retrn fully fnded	qtr. retrn fully fnded	year retrn fully fnded
0	0	0	0	0	0	0	0	0	0	0		
0	0	0	0	0	0	0	0	0	0	0		
0	0	0	0	0	0	0	0	0	0	0	0	
0	0	0	0	0	0	0	0	0	0	0		
0	0	0	0	0	0	0	0	0	0	0		
0	0	0	0	0	0	0	0	0	0	0	0	
0	0	0	0	0	0	0	0	0	0	0		
0	0	0	0	0	0	0	0	0	0	0		
0	0	0	0	0	0	0	0	0	0	0	0	
0	0	0	0	0	0	0	0	0	0	0		
0	0	0	0	0	0	0	0	0	0	0		
0	0	0	0	0	0	0	0	0	0	0	0	0
0	0	0	0	0	0	0	0	0	0	0		

This approach can be demonstrated as follows. Let us suppose that a trader receives US$1,000 from an investor on the seventh trading day of the month and let us suppose that there are 22 trading days. The trader then has an increase in the portfolio for a fraction of the month. This fraction is equal to

$$\frac{22-7}{22} + 1 = \frac{16}{22}$$

that is, the trader has been in possession of US$1,000 for 16 out of the 22 days. Therefore, the starting equity should be increased by

$$1000 \, \frac{22-7+1}{22}$$

The withdrawals of capital are treated in the same way.

This supposes that the days of the additions and withdrawals are known. The trader knows this, but as we have stated above, neither TASS nor any other third party is likely to be provided with such detailed information.

The second method consists of treating additions and withdrawals (DE) in an 'informal' way. We want to be sure that DE do not distort what the ROR would have been in the absence of any DE. However the calculation is done, it is important that all traders 'appear' to treat DE, even if in reality they do not do so, in the same way for the purpose of being included in the benchmark universe.

We could assume that the additions and withdrawals are spread evenly over the 22 trading days during the period. The accuracy of this approximation depends on how well the hypothesis are fulfilled. It can be argued that when additions and withdrawals represent a small proportion of the trading equity, and if the rate of return is considered on an annual basis, then the approximation can be regarded as accurate. There will, of course, be monthly distortions, but at the end of the year they should cancel out each other. When the additions and withdrawals represent a large proportion of the trading equity, it might be more appropriate to use an *ad hoc* approach.

Non-actual equity
Non-actual equity is money that is available for investment/trading but which has not actually been deposited in the derivative fund manager's account at the broker or bank. As mentioned earlier, it includes equity referred to as 'notional equity' and 'committed funds'. Foreign-exchange traders using credit lines are considered to be trading non-actual equity. The inclusion of non-actual equity in the computation of the rate of return is essential. If NE is not included in the performance then the rate of return is overestimated (either positively or negatively).

Non-actual equity can be seen as a leverage factor influencing not only the rate of return but also the associated risk. Therefore, different investors in the same trading programme with different amounts of NE will not achieve the same rate of return with the same associated risk if the rate of return and associated risk is computed solely on the basis of actual equity.

When all the client accounts are compounded, if some of them have NE which is not identified, then the starting equity represents equity which is not equal to the nominal equity (i.e. total equity including both the actual and non-actual). Of course, for a fully funded account, actual equity is equal to nominal equity.

Brokerage commission and fees

The subject of fees draws many different opinions. Clients investing with the same trader can be charged different fees and commissions depending upon what has been negotiated. Furthermore, the increasing application of 'wrap' fees in the market makes the task of breaking out the different charges extremely difficult. In order to compute the rate of return for each trader, it is important to include all the possible commissions and fees charged to an investor's account.

To be able to combine all the investors that a trader might have to compute one rate of return for the trader, the investors should be treated alike and be charged the same. As stated above, this is not always the case. Therefore, the monthly rate of return should reflect the variability of these fees among clients; that is, the rate of return should actually be an (estimated) interval between the lowest rate of return and the highest rate of return a client might expect to receive (assuming that the appropriate adjustments have been made for additions and withdrawals, non-actual equity and interest income). Such information is extremely difficult to obtain but is most necessary.

Interest income (II)

Interest income can be the most biased value in the computation of the rate of return. Its effect on trader performance can be distorted for a number of reasons. Some traders do not include interest income in their results. Of those who do include interest income in their results, some charge fees on it and others do not. Finally, some traders who manage non-actual equity charge a 'notional interest income' on the non-actual equity, whereas others do not.

Non-actual equity influences the interest income because it is equity which is not actually in the client's account and therefore receives no interest income. If this client had a fully funded account he or she would have received interest income corresponding to the full equity level. Therefore, it can be argued that the necessary performance tables need to be adjusted to include a 'notional interest income' on the non-actual equity. This can be done simply enough by multiplying the non-actual equity by the interest rate, and adding the result to the actual interest income to compute the adjusted interest income (II*).

It is in the trader's interest to identify exactly how much non-actual equity is being managed because the rate of return is always corrected positively when adjusted interest income is added to the performance.

The interest rate can be determined from the trader's monthly figures. It is the ratio between the published amount of interest income and the starting actual equity. It is not necessarily equal to the 'market' interest rate, such as the Treasury Bill rate, for two reasons. First, some fees can be hidden in interest income; and second, not all equity is necessarily in the form of Treasury Bills. We therefore reckon that it makes more sense to estimate the interest rate from the trader's monthly figures.

The monthly effect of interest income and adjusted interest income is not expected to be very great. However, over an annual period the effect could be quite substantial.

II and fees

If the rate of return is to be computed in net terms, then interest income should be included for all traders because so many of the traders charge fees on the interest earned.

Computation of the rate of return (ROR)

The rate of return for a given trader is the ratio between the net performance (NP) and the total equity (TE) he or she was supposed to be managing.

By TE we mean the sum of the starting actual equity (SAE) (which does not include non-actual equity) adjusted by additions and withdrawals (DE) incurred during the period, notional equity (NE) adjusted by the difference between additions and withdrawals of NE (DNE), and 'committed funds' (CF) adjusted by additions and withdrawals of CF (DCF). We therefore end up with:

$$TE = SAE + 0.4777 \times DE + NE + 0.477 \times DNE + CF + 0.477 \times DCF$$

The NP includes the gross profits/losses, the adjusted interest income (II*), the different fees (management fees, incentive fees, realised brokerage commission). The gross profits/losses are the sum of the realised (RPL) and the unrealised (UPL) profits and losses. If we denote by MF the management fees, IF the incentive fees, BC the realised brokerage commission, the NP can then be written as:

$$NP = RPL + UPL + II^* - MF - IF - BC$$

The adjusted II (II*) is given by:

$$II^* = \frac{II}{SAE} \cdot (NE + CF) + II$$

Research to date shows that the minimum information needed to compute the rate of return for each trader consists of the following variables:

- starting actual equity (SAE);
- notional equity (NE) (part of non-actual equity);

- committed funds (CF) (part of non-actual equity);
- additions and withdrawals of actual equity (DE);
- additions and withdrawals of notional equity (DNE);
- additions and withdrawals of committed funds (DCF);
- realised gross profits/losses (RPL);
- unrealised gross profits/losses (UPL);
- brokerage commission for realised profits/losses (BC);
- interest income (II);
- management fees (MF);
- incentive fees (IF).

The adjusted rate of return for each trading programme is then given by:

$$ROR = \frac{RPL + UPL + II^* - BC - MF - IF}{SAE + 0.477 \times DE + NE + 0.477 \times DNE + CF + 0.477 \times DCF}$$

where II* is given by the equation above.

If a trader manages only actual equity, the rate of return simplifies to:

$$ROR = \frac{RPL + UPL + II - BC - MF - IF}{SAE + 0.477.DE}$$

Market performance index (MPI)

Once the data validation has been finalised and the adjusted rate of return for each derivative fund manager's programme calculated, we can then get to the contentious issue of how the benchmark (or index) should be constructed and, furthermore, whether one benchmark is sufficient for relevant and effective performance comparisons.

The purpose of the skill-based benchmark (MPI) that TASS has been commissioned to research is to provide investors with a benchmark of how the managed futures industry has performed over a given period of time. In essence, the MPI should reflect the performance of the 'average manager' within the universe. Due to the considerable variation in fee structures offered by the derivative fund managers it is important to show the MPI in both gross and net terms.

If the MPI is to represent the performance of the 'average derivative fund manager' within the universe, it should, therefore, be a weighted average of the performance of all the DFMs. The big question is, how should these weights be defined and what should they reflect.

There are three main characteristics which prevent the computation of a simple, naive performance average – the risk associated with the performance, the length of the DFM's track record and the amount under management with each DFM. Furthermore, if a DFM offers a number of investment programmes to investors should each of these be treated separately?

The risk taken by a manager plays an important role in the evaluation of performance. Higher risk should be associated with higher expected returns. These two values, expected rate of return and associated risk are not known and must be estimated. The expected rate of return is estimated by the mean rate of return (over a given period) and the risk is the standard deviation. A mean performance among different DFMs, therefore, is meaningless if the DFMs do not use similar risk. One way of dealing with this is to create three different MPIs – low, medium and high risk – each with a separate universe of managers using similar leverage.

Should the MPI be in the form of a number or a percentage?

We are of the opinion that if a trader offers three different trading programmes then each of these should be treated separately. There are two reasons for this; first, the different programmes do not usually have the same ROR, and rarely have the same amount of money under management.

Length of track record. Money under management. Leverage. Fees.

The length of the DFM's track record plays a more technical role. As stated above, the important factors in the evaluation of the performance are the expected rate of return and the risk level, both of which have to be estimated. The accuracy of the estimation depends on the amount of data available. It is difficult to give an exact number of the minimum number of observations that one needs to compute accurate estimates and, furthermore, it is not possible to state statistically whether it is better to include one length of track record than another. However, research to date shows a general decreasing variability of the rates of return after one or two years of performance history.

The amount that a DFM has under management should be a principal factor determining the weighting of the MPI. The influence of a DFM's rate of return in the computation of the MPI must be proportional to its total equity when compared to the sum of all equity represented by the DFMs selected for inclusion in the MPI.

The 'average trader' performance, referred to above, results from a combination of all the DFMs. The performance of different DFMs can be compounded only if the managers are comparable. This, as we have already learned, is not always the case because of various sources of bias.

Let us suppose that two traders have achieved the same performance, but their published monthly rate of return is different. What might be the causes of this difference?

- The inclusion or not of interest income (II).
- The treatment of additions and withdrawals (DE).
- The inclusion or not of notional equity (NE).
- The inclusion or not of committed funds (CF).

As discussed earlier, some traders may keep a proportion of the interest income as a fee, or charge a fee on the interest income, whereas others do not. For this reason II should not be included in the gross version of the MPI.

How important is non-actual equity in the computation of the MPI? In calculating each DFM's monthly rate of return we have seen that it is important to include NE to ensure that different client records are comparable. It is important to include NE in the computation of the MPI as well, but for a different reason. In the MPI's case, it is not a question of comparability in terms of risk, but a question of 'What is the real performance one can expect when investing in managed futures?' To leave out the non-actual equity would introduce a serious bias to the results.

Whether or not it is better to evaluate returns in relative rather than in absolute terms is a decision for the investor. The issues concerned with developing a respected, accurate benchmark are extensive and, at times, emotive. We recognise that it is impossible for anybody to develop a perfect index which will satisfy all investors and participants in the marketplace; we aim, however, to create an index which can stand up to the scrutiny of serious data validation and which satisfies a broad base of intelligent market opinion.

5
The traders and investment managers

Introduction

The absolute return industry would not exist without the traders and fund managers. Their skill supports an array of businesses and individuals including bankers, brokers, accountants, lawyers, fund administrators, data providers, consultants, managers of managers and many more. The traders and investment managers are as different in style and substance as the multifarious businesses and investors that yearn for and feed off their success. They may be referred to as derivatives fund managers, commodity trading advisors, leveraged fund managers, hedge fund managers or absolute return investment managers. At the end of the day, however, they all have one objective: to deliver absolute (positive) performance results on a consistent basis to their investors. For doing this they are generally compensated by taking a percentage of the profits.

If you ask a traditional fund manager about how his fund has performed over a given time period, he or she will usually tell you that the fund has either out- or under-performed the benchmark to the tune of x per cent. The benchmark could be down 10 per cent and the fund down 8 per cent and you will be told that the fund has beaten the index by 2 per cent. Some consolation. Most absolute return investment managers will tell you that they are either up or down x per cent on the year so you can work out immediately how much money you have made or lost over the period. The news might not be great, but it is not disguised.

The issue of benchmarked versus absolute investment management is worthy of at least a chapter in its own right. You will find that most participants in the absolute return end of the market are of the view that benchmarking, or indexing, are simply ways that allow mediocrity in fund management to be tolerated. Tolerance of mediocre performance is reducing. Investors are becoming more knowledgeable about the markets and are expecting more from their fund managers. You only have to look at the billions of dollars invested with the so-called hedge fund managers over the past five years to get an indication of this.

In order to play the absolute return game the manager or trader must be able to short the market so that whether it goes up or down, the manager has an opportunity to make a profit. And this is where derivatives (both listed and over the counter) can come in. Of course the manager may short sell a stock, but it may be much simpler and nimbler to sell a stock future, a stock index future or buy a put option, depending on the overall strategy.

Hedge fund managers – derivatives fund managers – commodity trading advisors – leveraged fund managers. Are they so different and why are there so many labels?

'Commodity trading advisor' was a term which the US regulators introduced in the 1970s to define an individual or a company managing client money in the listed commodity and financial-futures and options markets. At that time there were so few financial-futures contracts that most of the trading activity was done in the commodity markets and hence the label. Although the term has not changed (despite the fact that more than two-thirds of trading activity now takes place in the financial rather than traditional commodity markets), its meaning has evolved to encompass most independent specialists managing client funds in these markets.

In 1993, the regulators in the United Kingdom addressed this issue of anachronistic labelling by classifying UK-based and registered commodity trading advisors as derivatives fund managers. The rest of the world, however, still seems to use the CTA label, so take your pick.

Leveraged fund managers include commodity trading advisors, derivatives fund managers and, as you will see below, certain so-called hedge fund managers.

A hedge fund was originally a long equity or bond fund which could go short. The first of these funds was launched in the United States in the 1940s. As recently as 1988 in the introduction to George Soros' book, *The Alchemy of Finance* (updated in 1994), a hedge fund is described as a mutual fund that can go short. However, the perception in the market today is that hedge funds are anything but hedged; and in fact, the substitution of the word 'leverage' for 'hedge' paints a more accurate picture. So we now have a situation in which traditional hedge funds, which have a strong equities bias, are lumped in the same category as the more aggressive, opportunistic, trade-anything funds and performance comparisons are made which pay little or no attention to this distinction between hedged and leveraged funds.

If we take the original definition of a hedge fund then any manager who goes short – and naturally this includes the CTAs and DFMs – is a hedge fund manager. How investors who neither work directly in this industry nor who have a degree in 'relational labelling' are supposed to sort their way through this maze is anyone's guess. Some simplified and more relevant labels have become essential if the 'absolute return fund-management industry' is to develop beyond its current narrow, albeit sophisticated, investor base.

In 1993 seven fund managers who describe their funds as 'hedge funds' made the top ten largest earners on Wall Street. Indeed the names George Soros, Michael Steinhardt, Julian Robertson and Mark Strome have become so well known that they are almost household names. Their funds gave their typically wealthy and sophisticated investors substantial returns, although the picture by the end of 1994 was not so rosy.

The majority of funds that refer to themselves as hedge funds are stock funds. TASS Management estimate that over 75 per cent of all hedge fund strategies involve buying and selling equities and bonds on companies. Out of that number, less than 10 per cent are flatly devoted to the derivatives market. However, a reasonably large number of equity biased hedge funds currently do use derivatives.

It is difficult to obtain a clear picture of the hedge fund community. The single largest problem in investigating the world of hedge funds is that secrecy is the code of conduct. This code is reinforced by the economics of the marketplace and the United States security laws.

United States investment laws also hamper ready information about hedge funds. United States based managers, which account for at least 80 per cent of such managers, usually use private placements called limited partnerships as their fund vehicle. These limited partnerships are not allowed to have more than 99 investors; each of their investors must be an 'accredited investor' (very wealthy, very professional and very knowledgeable); they may not solicit business by advertising in the press or any other public medium.

Because of these conditions, and many others, it is extremely difficult for any potential investor or other third party to find out exactly what they do without actually investing in or working with such a fund.

Investment approaches

The investment approaches offered by absolute return managers vary extensively. The asset focus is generally equities, fixed income, commodities, currencies and property. Fine wines, art and other more exotic assets occasionally make an appearance, but can hardly be regarded as mainstream at this point. Some managers concentrate on the cash markets, using derivatives either to gear or to hedge. Others take all their positions in the derivative markets – both listed and unlisted – while the non margined equity generally sits in United States Treasury Bills or other so-called 'risk-free' instruments.

The derivatives players, whether they are dealing in commodity, financial or equity futures and options tend to fall into three categories. Their approach may be driven by fundamental considerations, technical considerations or a bit of both. The majority of technical traders have developed a fully computerised, systematic approach to trading and act on each and every signal generated by the system (black box); the only discretion likely to be incorporated is the timing of position implementation and the size of the position. Some systematic traders incorporate a degree (the amount varies) of discretionary judgement based on certain fundamental analysis and override the system's signals from time to time. The fundamental traders within the CTA community tend to be global macro-economic players. They may use technical analysis to help them decide when to get into or get out of a market, but their decisions are generally based on whatever market, economic and political information they have been able to glean. Some managers in this category prefer to be called discretionary traders – *chacun à son goût*!

What is interesting about the equities players is that they are almost all discretionary managers whose decisions are based on company and market fundamentals. Although many equity traders have quantitative models to analyse relevant data and to identify key stocks, as well as the more esoteric over-the-counter instruments in which they may be dealing, most of these managers are stock pickers with backgrounds in securities analysis.

As mentioned earlier, the majority of managers, some 75 to 80 per cent are currently based in the United States. Some focus on a single geographic market, such as the United States, Europe, Asia, South America, or on emerging economies such as India or Thailand. The majority are dealing in mature equity, although the focus on small cap growth stocks and emerging markets has grown over the past couple of years. Value stocks, growth stocks, new issues, distressed securities, special situations and bankruptcies are among the categories of equities that the funds invest in. Short sellers are fewer than several years ago, although after the success of the short sellers in 1994 we have noticed several key stock groups hiring short specialists.

While the global, macro, 'trade anything', leveraged players represent less than 10 per cent of the universe, they account for approximately 30 per cent of the assets under management in the absolute return arena. As mentioned above, the number of hedge funds that use derivatives is small; however, the hedge funds who do use derivatives are usually very large, with assets over US$500 million. These larger hedge funds may use derivatives extensively in their investment strategies. The array of derivatives range from stock options, convertibles, warrants and swaps to many more complicated instruments. Although futures are often disclosed in fund documents, their use is still relatively small.

The futures markets are used more commonly by the CTA and DFM community, as well as the large banks and investment houses. The latter two, in their capacity as counterparties, create 'baskets' of investments for their hedge fund clients. These baskets may include metals, emerging market debt instruments, speciality stock baskets – such as small cap and high technology stocks – and collateralised mortgage obligations. After the bank creates the product and sells it to the hedge fund, the fanks often go to the futures markets to hedge their risk.

Following on from the above description, the equities players are almost all discretionary managers. We have yet to come across more than a few equities-biased absolute return manager with a totally computerised approach to investing. Although some of them use quantitative models to identify market sectors and specific stocks to pick in addition to valuing the more esoteric OTC instruments that they are dealing in, most of these managers are stock-pickers with backgrounds in securities analysis. Furthermore, the majority are currently based in the United States. Some focus on one geographic market such as the United States, Asia or Europe, others take a more global approach. The majority are dealing in mature equities markets, although despite the lack of derivative instruments in many of the emerging markets, the growth in activity in this sector has increased over the past couple of years and continues to do so. Value stocks, growth stocks, new issues, distressed securities and bankruptcies are among the categories of equities that the funds invest in. Most take a directional approach but there are a growing number of so-called market-neutral strategists on the scene. Short sellers have been thin on the ground over the past few years, but the first half of 1994 has seen an increase in the number.

In Europe, if we separate the derivatives and currency players from the equities/fixed-income players we find that the absolute return managers in the equities markets are the newer kids on the block; the majority have track records no longer than three years. Some of the more established managed derivatives players, however, have been around for ten years or more. At the time of writing it is estimated that there are approximately 110 independent derivatives fund managers in Europe and approximately 40 equities-fixed-income-biased managers in the 'absolute' group. However, as more and more of the talented (and, unfortunately, the not-so-talented) traders and managers decide to leave the relative security of a job within a bank, traditional fund-management house or other institution in search of independence and a fat share of the profits (assuming any are made) then these paltry numbers may grow substantially.

The market is always seeking the next Tudor Jones, Louis Bacon, Bruce Kovner, George Soros, Julian Robertson, Michael Steinhardt and Leon Cooperman to name but a few of the leading absolute return managers from the United States. Until 1994 a number of these managers had achieved an almost surreal status as wonder investors who rarely got it wrong. How things can change for some. Many investors who thought that they had found the holy grail to consistent and continual profit (with a few minor hiccups along the way) were brought down to earth with a bump in the early part of 1994. The greatest enemy to most managers is size. As the asset base grows will the manager be able to continue to produce the results without having to migrate to another market in which he or she has little experience?

Much has been written about some of the leading managers in the United States. Little about the managers on the other side of the Atlantic. At the risk

Traders and investment managers 87

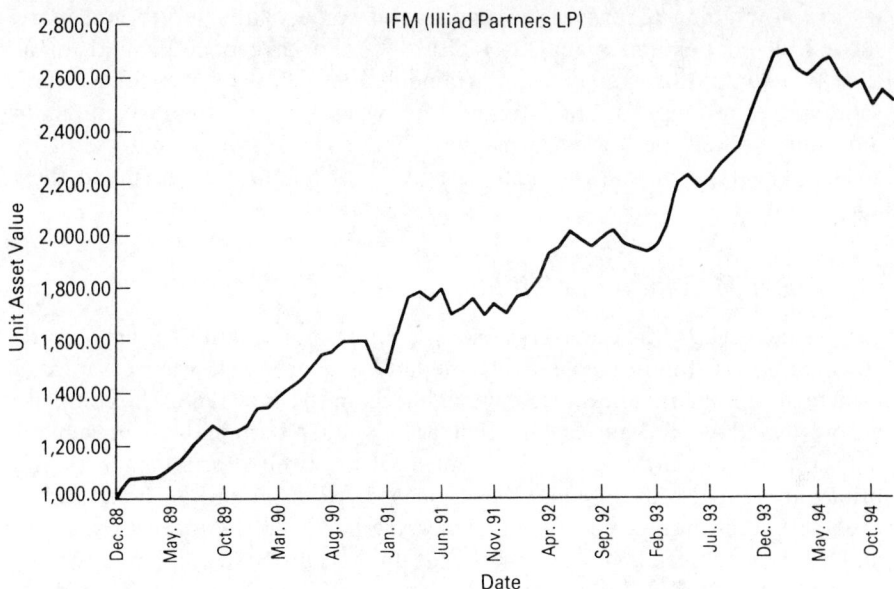

Figure 5.1 IFM (Illiad Partners) 1 LP.

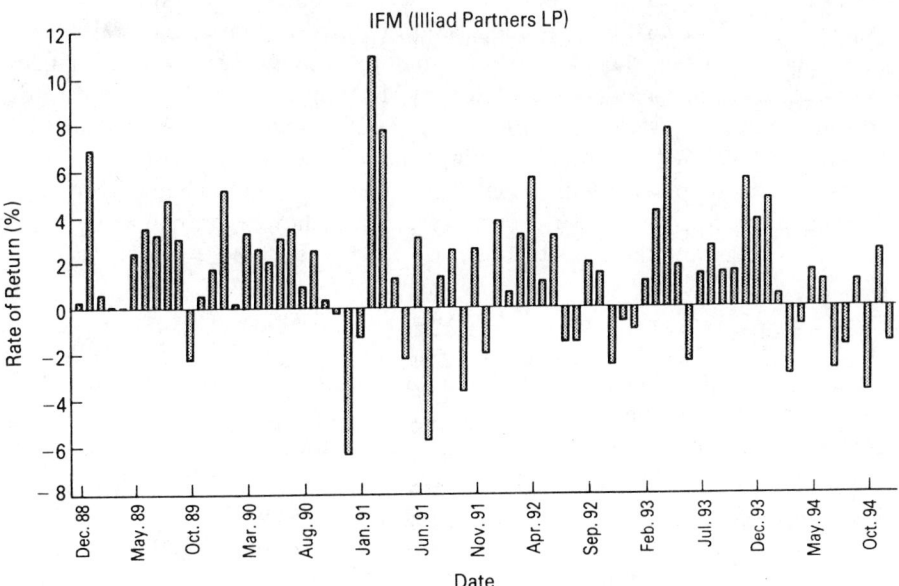

Figure 5.2 IFM (Illiad Partners) 1 LP.

of putting our heads on the block and being guillotined in a few years' time, we are now going to provide a snapshot of some of the larger and more successful independent managers in Europe who have been around for at least two years (not exactly a time frame over which we can produce some valid statistical analysis, but a time frame which includes two exceptionally different market conditions), who may, if they have not done so already, achieve the type of status which has investors queuing up to make their allocations.

IFM Asset Management Limited

Established in 1984, is one of the oldest (in terms of length of track record) absolute return fund-management company in Europe. It was set up as a principal trading firm and started managing client funds in 1988. The company is now owned by AIG and St James's Place Capital although the management team retains a healthy economic interest. Of the twelve fund managers, the principal managers are David Craig, Richard Atkinson and Nicholas Rallis, each with a different area of expertise. Craig heads up the foreign exchange and fixed-income trading. Atkinson heads up the European and United States equity trading; and Rallis heads up the Japan and Asia Pacific equity trading.

Like most of the absolute return managers, IFM measures itself against cash, not against an index. They have a bias towards arbitrage and hedged investments, although this does not preclude incorporating a directional approach. Until it became unfashionable to use the phrase in the spring of 1994, some of IFM's investment strategies were defined as market neutral. Whatever one's views on the overlap or mutual exclusivity of arbitrage, relative-value and market-neutral strategies, IFM's approach encompasses three distinct investment styles: a mathematically derived quantitative approach; an analytically derived quantitative approach; and a qualitative approach. Performance in comparison with some of their competitors has been perceived as boring: an average of 19 per cent per year since they began managing client money with an annual range of 14 per cent to 28 per cent.

Buchanan

Like IFM, Buchanan is one of the more quantitative and computerised alternative investment managers on the equities side of the industry. Set up in 1992 the company applies a disciplined and systematic approach to investment using an extensive array of quantitative techniques. The objective is to exploit inefficiencies and anomalies in the international equity and derivative markets placing an equal emphasis on forecasting both return and risk.

The three principals – Peregrine Montcrieffe, Kevin Rowe and Sharanbir Brijnath – used to work together at Credit Suisse First Boston. Montcrieffe was an executive director and both Rowe and Brijnath were founder

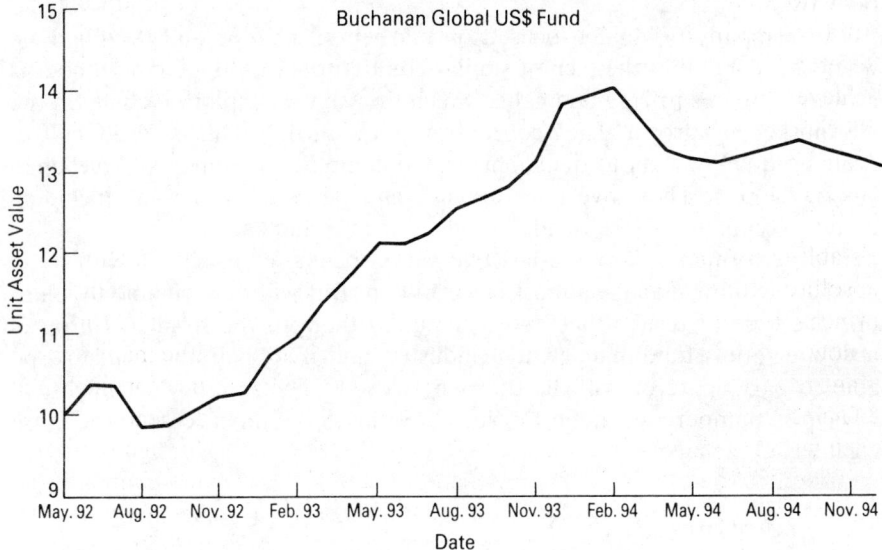

Figure 5.3 Buchanan Global USD Fund.

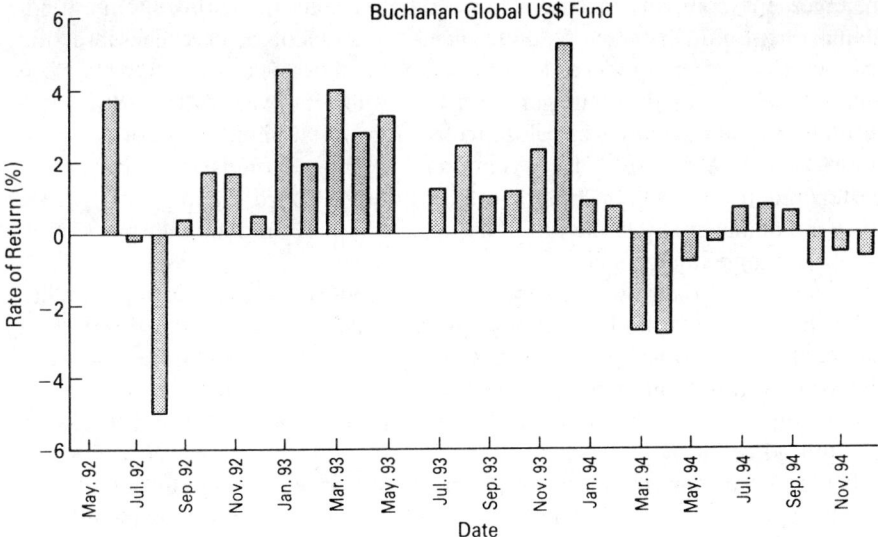

Figure 5.4 Buchanan Global USD Fund.

members of the proprietary trading department. Despite emerging out the same box, three more different individuals you cannot imagine – a case of blending complementary skills to achieve their business and investment objectives.

The company originally focused on markets in Europe and the Far East where they feel that the lack of similar competitors (although the number is growing) creates pricing anomalies which they aim to exploit. Activity in the US market has grown. They concentrate on securities which are difficult to evaluate quickly without the sophisticated computer systems that Buchanan has developed. They invest in the cash and derivatives markets including holding companies, closed-ended funds, warrants and convertibles.

The performance over the last two years speaks for itself and with these results they now manage almost US$1 billion. But will they be able to maintain the type of results that have catapulted them to the front of Europe's absolute return fund-management industry, and if so, will new investors be able to participate or will the doors be closed? The industry's growth will always be hampered if the institutions have limited if any access to the more established managers.

Barran & Partners

Established in the spring of 1993. When you talk to Diana Barran of Barran & Partners you are talking to an individual who is passionate about the merits of 'the absolute performance' concept and the weaknesses of 'the relative performance' concept. The partners' decision to establish their own fund-management company resulted from a belief that the conventional fund-management industry often failed to meet its clients' objectives. The obsession with measuring performance relative to a particular stock or bond index often led, on the part of the manager, to a preoccupation with delivering relative returns. As long as they were close to the appropriate index, all was in order. The fact that a number of conventionally managed funds regularly underperform their relevant benchmark, often without the slightest apparent concern from the managers, was one of the key reasons for Barran and her partners to take the plunge and go solo.

As masters of their own destiny and investment principles, Barran's aim has been to construct a fund which not only is designed to meet the objectives of its clients, but also has been structured to avoid conflicts of interest between the client and the fund manager. Furthermore, they aim to avoid many of the restrictions which can hamper most conventional fund managers (at least in the United Kingdom).

Barran's investment philosophy provides an interesting snapshot of conventional fund management and the ridiculous situations in which many funds are placed from historic habits and current regulations. Barran particularly highlights the asset-class restrictions and the lack of risk management.

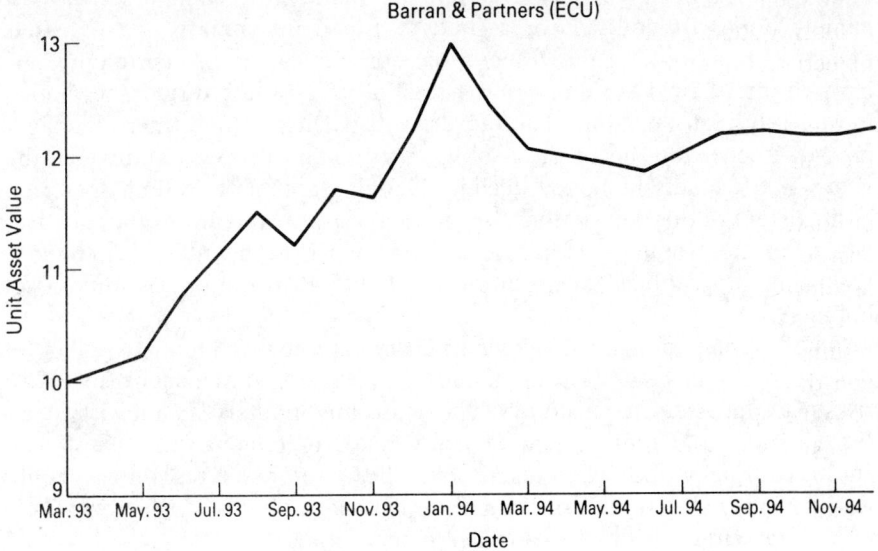

Figure 5.5 Barran & Partners (ECU).

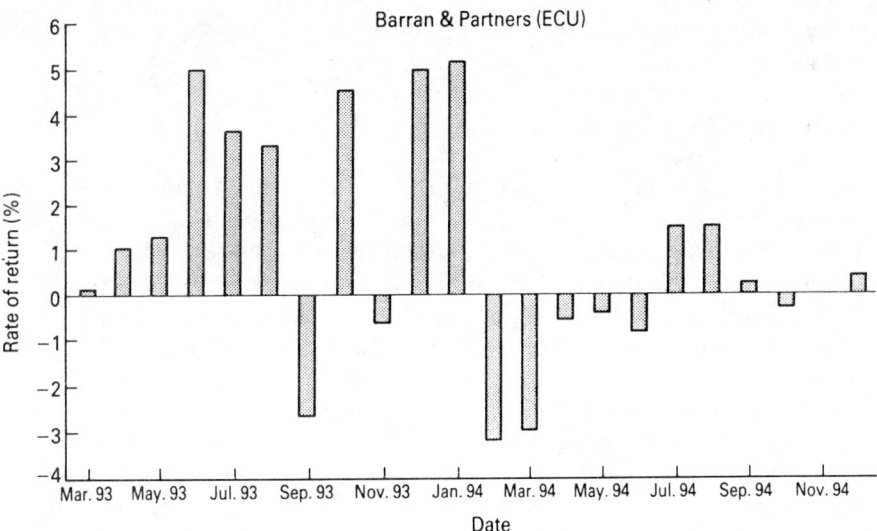

Figure 5.6 Barran & Partners (ECU).

The majority of investment funds are constrained by guidelines which dictate that their investments should be made in certain asset classes, namely bonds or equities, or a predetermined benchmark mix of assets or subject to a predetermined sector or geographical mix. Accordingly, during periods when these individual assets fall in absolute terms, the fund is most likely to follow suit. Therefore, even when the investment manager predicts such a fall, he or she is obliged to remain invested and watch the value of the assets managed decline. Hedging and short selling are often non-existent or difficult options. In contrast, Barran, and most other alternative investment managers, are not constrained by conventional guidelines regarding geographical distribution, asset-class distribution or liquid-asset holdings.

On the subject of risk management, Barran is convinced that a corollary of the conventional asset-class restrictions is that the fund manager often takes risks with the assets managed which he or she might otherwise not wish to do. For example, the requirement of many funds to remain fully invested in equities during periods when short-term deposits offer high real returns, could lead the manager to take risks with his or her client's funds which are unlikely to product better results than a risk-free alternative.

Barran's Magus Fund has a single-investment approach, although it offers individual sub-funds which have different currency exposures to meet the requirements of the underlying investors. Much to the irritation of some of their peers, the principals of Barrans have incorporated a 'hurdle rate' before their performance fee kicks in. Furthermore, the principals have to invest in their fund. They are not allowed to invest elsewhere. Encouraging for the investors; but how long will the principals want to have all their eggs in one basket?

Gottex Fund Management

The spring of 1993 also saw the launch by Gottex Fund Management of their Global Swap Fund, one of the first funds primarily dealing in European interest-rate swaps. Gottex Fund Management is a subsidiary of Gottex S.A. which is a broker and market maker in interest rate and currency swaps. The principal traders are Joachim Gottschalk, who has been a swap dealer for many years, and Clayton Freind, who brings the quantitative skills to the table.

For those of you who are familiar with interest rate swaps and understand very clearly how a fund dealing in these instruments will manage its assets, you might like to skip the next few paragraphs. However, for those of you unfamiliar with such strategies, we should like to explain how an interest-rate swap works and have borrowed one of the clearest descriptions of a single currency interest rate swap example from Ermitage (who in the spring of 1994 launched a fund to which Gottex is the sole advisor).

There are four main elements to the decision-making process:

1. Money market deposit rates vary according to the length of time for which the money is to be placed. The first stage is to determined what is on offer. For Deutschmark deposits as at 1 March 1994 rates were as follows:
   3-month deposit   5.92%
   6-month deposit   5.72%
   1-year deposit   5.42%
2. The next stage is to determine why these differences occur. They are the result of the market's expectations of what will happen to interest rates in the future. These expectations are known as implied forward rates and can be calculated from the above table.
   (a) DM1,000,000 can be placed for 1 year at 5.42%. The guaranteed return at the outset is DM54,200.
   (b) DM1,000,000 can be placed for 6 months at 5.72%. The guaranteed return for this period is DM28,600. The market expectation is that DM25,600 can be earned over the next six months so that the return under (a) above can be matched. The implied forward rate is therefore 5.12% (ignoring the effect of compound interest).
3. The next stage is that Gottex will formulate its views on future interest-rate movements in order to determine whether the market's expectations are reasonable. If, for example, they believe that the DM deposit rate in six months' time will be higher or lower than 5.21%, then a potential profit can be made from an interest rate swap transaction.
4. An interest-rate swap is an agreement between two parties to exchange two streams of interest income. One party will pay the other interest computed at a fixed rate and will receive interest computed at a variable rate in return.
   (a) If Gottex in the example believe that the DM deposit rate in six months' time will actually be 4% (lower than the implied forward rate), then they may elect to pay interest on a nominal borrowing of DM1,000,000. These interest payments are made in two six-monthly instalments, with the second payment being made at the prevailing floating rate. In exchange, Gottex can elect to receive interest on a nominal load of DM1,000,000 for one year at the fixed market rate of 5.42%.

   If their view is correct, their outgoings (ignoring compounding) will be six months' interest at 5.72% and a further six months' interest at 4%, that is, DM28,600 + DM20,000 = DM48,600. However, the guaranteed income is 5.42% over 1 year = DM54,200.
   (b) Alternatively, if Gottex believe that the DM deposit rate is six months' time will actually be 7% (higher than the implied forward rate), then they can elect to pay interest on DM1,000,000 for one year at the fixed rate of 5.42 per cent, in exchange for the right to receive interest on DM 1,000,000 in two six monthly instalments. The second interest receipt will be at the floating rate in six months' time.

If their view is correct, the income (ignoring compounding) will be six months' interest at 5.72% and an additional six months' interest at 7%, that is, DM28,600 + DM35,000 = DM63,600. The outgoings will have been fixed at DM54,200 and a nice profit will have been made.

Gottex do not limit themselves to trading single-currency interest-rate swaps; they also trade cross-currency swaps for example, by undertaking to pay a fixed-rate interest stream in Deutschmarks in exchange for receiving a floating-rate interest stream in pesetas. Such a swap can take advantage both of interest-rate differentials between two countries and of anticipated future movements in exchange rates. The potential gain or loss arising from exchange-rate movements, may be left open or may be hedged. Either way it is limited to the interest-rate flows and cannot affect the nominal sum.

Interest-rate swaps do not involve the actual lending or borrowing of the principal sum (in the above example DM1,000,000). The effect of this is can be a high level of gearing on the assets under management which will magnify the potential gains or losses.

Simon Gillis

Also in the spring of 1993 *Simon Gillis* started managing his first fund which was launched by Global Asset Management. Gillis started off as an Foreign Exchange (FX) trader at Cargill and went on to work at Goldman Sachs for seven years until the end of 1992. At Goldman he became co-head of proprietary trading and head of FX trading. Although Gillis can trade any financial or commodity contracts, he specialises in the currency and fixed-income markets from a macro standpoint. The investment approach is discretionary and is driven by fundamental analysis.

Gillis' case is slightly different from the others profiled in this chapter. At the end of 1992 he decided to leave Goldman Sachs and set up independently. Having spent some time researching where to have the office, how to get registered with the regulators, how to identify the clients and raise the money to manage, how (if at all) to staff the new operation, how to organise the back office and so forth, Gillis decided not to go totally independent. After a few months (and, one presumes, some persuasive talk from Global Asset Management), Gillis decided to join their team as a specialist in house fund manager. He can focus almost exclusively on the trading while Global Asset Management (GAM) takes care of everything else. Chapter 9 considers these issues in more detail and predicts that in the future we shall see fewer fund managers setting up their own independent boutiques; there are a number of reasons for this and we shall not bore you by repeating them here.

Traders and investment managers 95

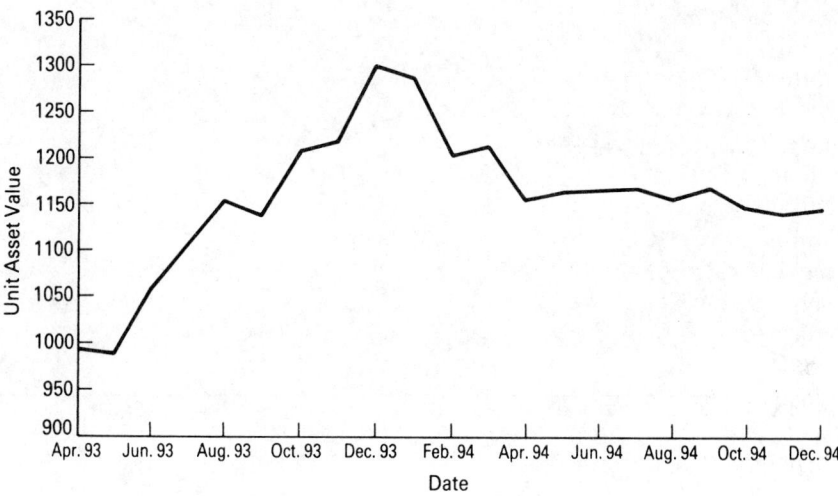

Figure 5.7 Gottex Fund Mgt. (BDA).

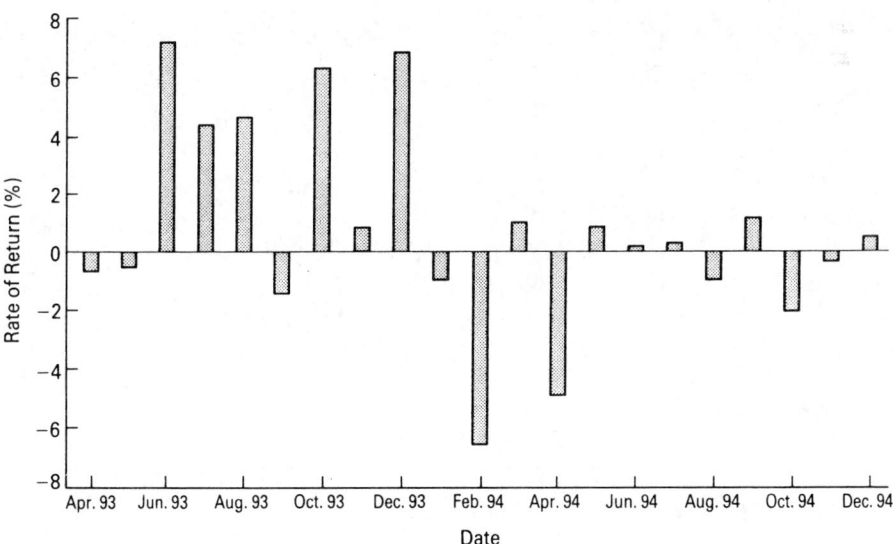

Figure 5.8 Gottex Fund Mgt. (BDA).

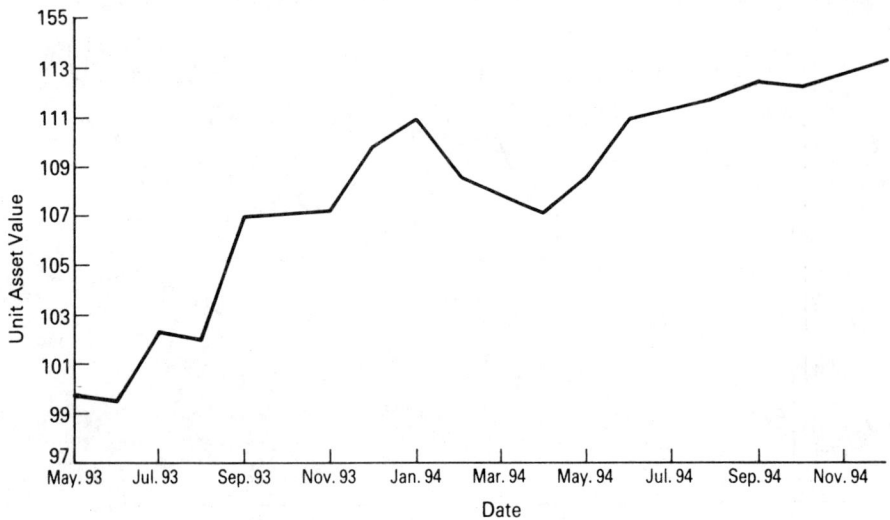

Figure 5.9 Simon Gillis.

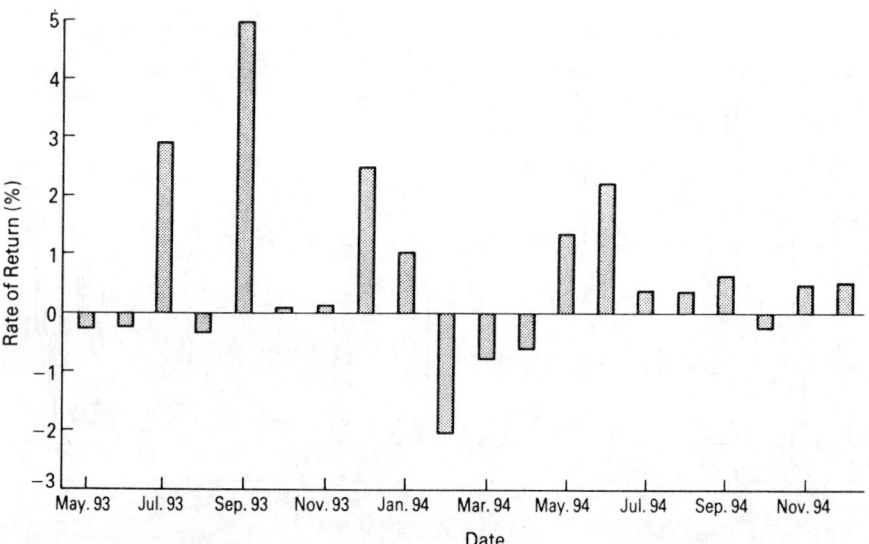

Figure 5.10 Simon Gillis.

Traders and investment managers 97

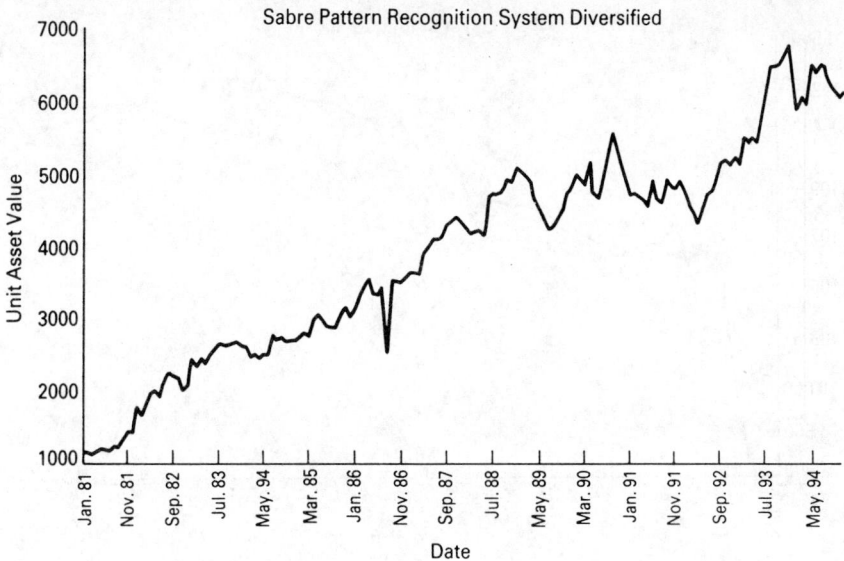

Figure 5.11 Sabre Pattern Recognition System Diversified.

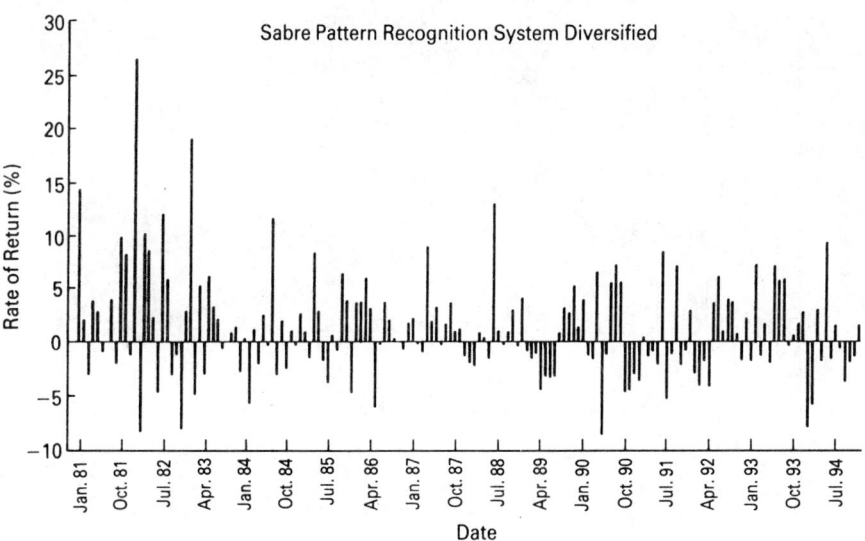

Figure 5.12 Sabre Pattern Recognition System Diversified.

Figure 5.13 Silver Knight Composite.

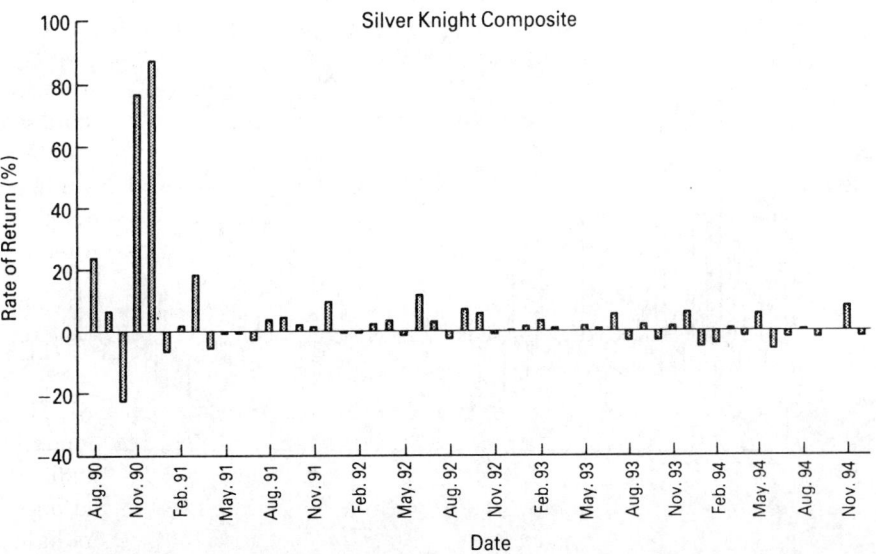

Figure 5.14 Silver Knight Composite.

Value Management and Research (VMR)

At the end of 1993 the first independent-German based absolute return fund-management boutique was set up by Florian Homm. Value Management and Research (VMR) seeks to capitalise on valuation discrepancies in European equities. The company's principal shareholder and investment manager is Florian Homm who honed his fund-management expertise at Tweedy Browne Europe where he was a partner and managing director; Bank Julius Baer (Deutschland AG) where he established and managed an Emerging Europe Fund; Fidelity Investments in Boston where he managed the Broadcast and Media fund, was also Fidelity's chief analyst for German equities and, according to Peter Lynch, a fund manager with Farstmann Lets in New York, contributed significantly to the Magellan fund performance record from 1987 until the middle of 1990; and Merrill Lynch.

Homm's investment philosophy is driven by the fact he believes that substantial valuation anomalies exist in European equities because of very different accounting standards and practices across different countries. Although the trend towards homogenisation of financial and accounting standards, as outlined in the EC Accounting Directives and International Accounting Standards (LAS), will continue to accelerate, eventually removing many of the investment opportunities that currently exist, few investment managers seem either eager or able to exploit many of the valuation discrepancies. Homm is convinced that until every buyside and sellside analyst works with roughly the same tools, the VMR portfolios have a strong chance of generating superior relative performance.

As the company name would suggest, Homm seeks to invest in value stocks. VMR's adopts a bottom-up stock-selection approach. Extensive research is conducted in-house and the overall approach has been strongly influenced by both Benjamin Graham and Peter Lynch. The track record as an independent is far too short, like most of the managers in this selection, to determine what might happen in the future. There are those who reckon that as the homogenisation of Europe's accounting and financial standards progresses, so Homm's investment opportunities will dwindle and performance will suffer accordingly.

Sabre Fund Management

Robin Edwards and Peter Swete set up Sabre Fund Management in 1981. The company has the distinction of being the longest established independent derivative fund manager in Europe. Both Edwards and Swete are qualified accountants; not such an unusual qualification for Peter who runs the business, but slightly more unusual for the head trader whose competitors have generally come off an institutional trading desk or the floor of a futures exchange.

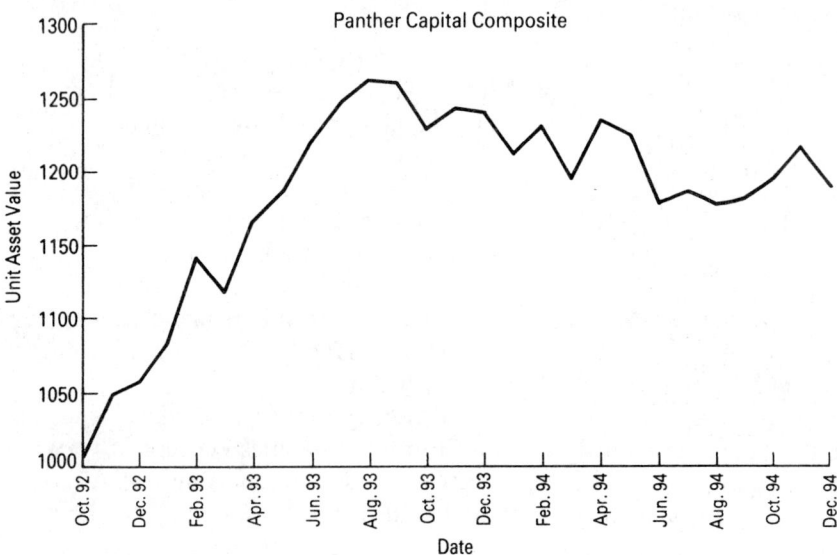

Figure 5.15 Panther Capital Composite.

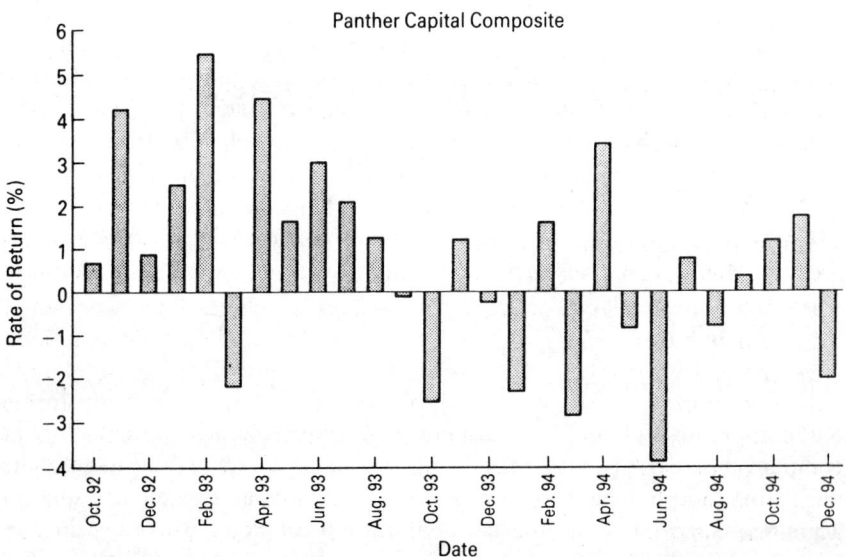

Figure 5.16 Panther Capital Composite.

Edwards started dabbling in the futures and currency markets when he was living in Australia in the mid-1970s. He then moved to Luxemburg and spent three years developing the fund-management approach used by Sabre – the Pattern Recognition System (PRS). This is a technical trend-following system which trades a wide range of derivative instruments including agricultural commodities, equity, bond, interest-rate and currency-related futures and options contracts on the United States, European and Japanese exchanges. Their Pattern Recognition System relies on the technical analysis and statistical evaluation of a proprietary price database. The technical analysis is based primarily on chart analysis and the PRS aims to take positions in markets in which a major change in prices seems imminent.

The PRS is not a totally mechanical, systematic approach. Sabre does not rely solely on its computer trading models; it also relies on the discretionary skills of the trading team to add value to what the system is advising them to do. Separate the system from the team leader and you may or may not get good results.

Like most technical trading approaches, Sabre analyses the price movements of an extensive array of futures and forward contracts – 60 in total to be precise – on an ongoing basis. It maintains a pattern library of both failed and successful trading patterns which are referred to when formulating trading strategies. Since 1981 Edwards and his team have achieved for the diversified investment programme an average annual return of 15.89 per cent. However, they did suffer three extremely weak years in 1989 (–5.39%), 1990 (+1.77%) and 1991 (+0.18%). These years resulted in a substantial review of the PRS, particularly the computerisation of certain research processes which had previously been done manually, and the changes implemented at the end of December 1991 took time to impact the results but to date seem to have paid off.

Silver Knight

Mark Shipman started Silver Knight in 1990. With a background in operations, money management and futures dealing he and his wife mortgaged their home to raise the necessary funds to establish their investment-management business. Like many of these boutique fund-management operations, the office started off in a room in the house, slowly spread to take over more and more space until the time finally came to move out into 'formal' business premises. None of which would have happened if the fluke had not become a coincidence which seems to have become a trend. Silver Knight's trading philosophy is implemented through a mechanical trading system into which the historical data (going back for 15 years) on over 30 futures and options markets is fed. Their system is designed to trade a diversified portfolio of futures contracts identifying trends in the early stages of their development and then exploiting the strong bias they give to a market.

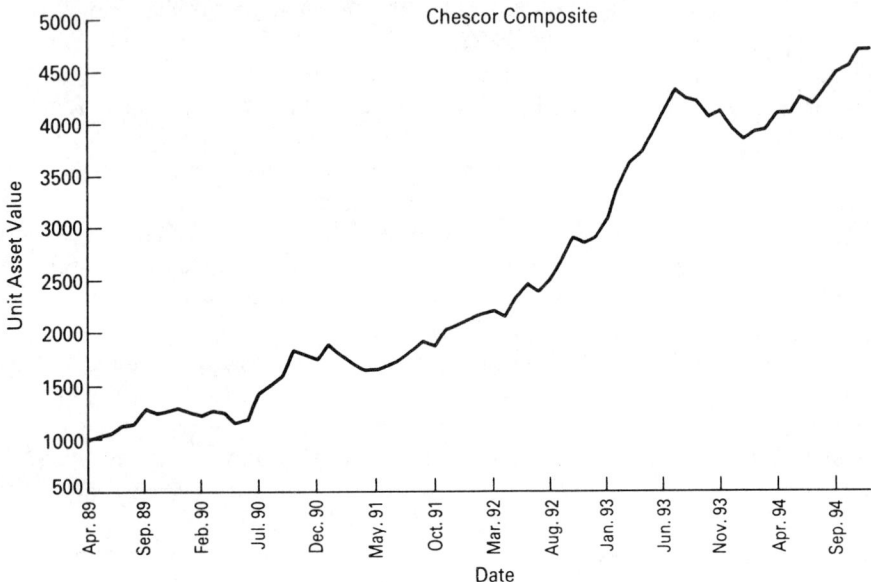

Figure 5.17 Chescor Composite.

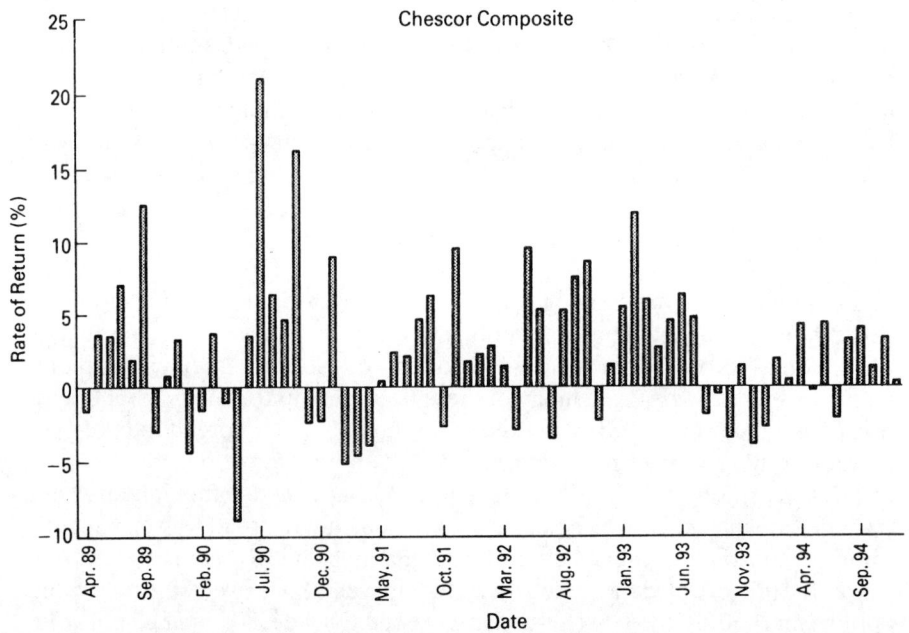

Figure 5.18 Chescor Composite.

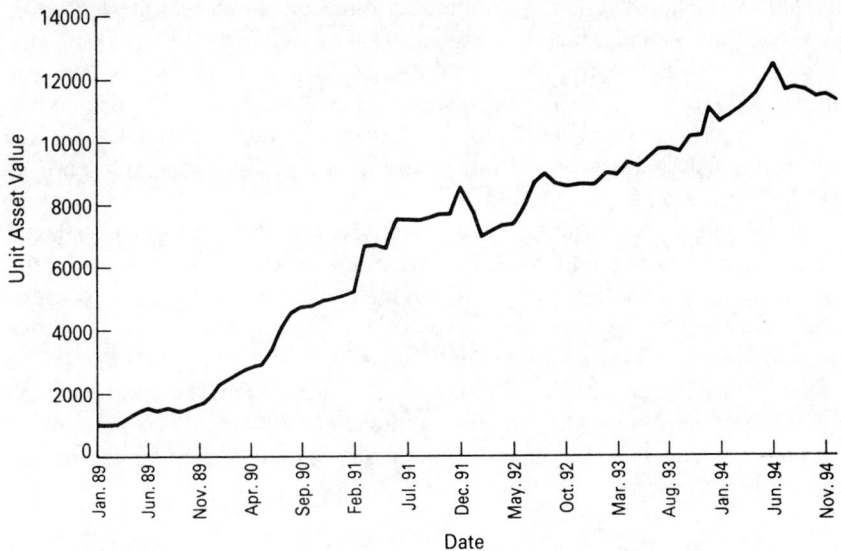

Figure 5.19 Capital Futures Management.

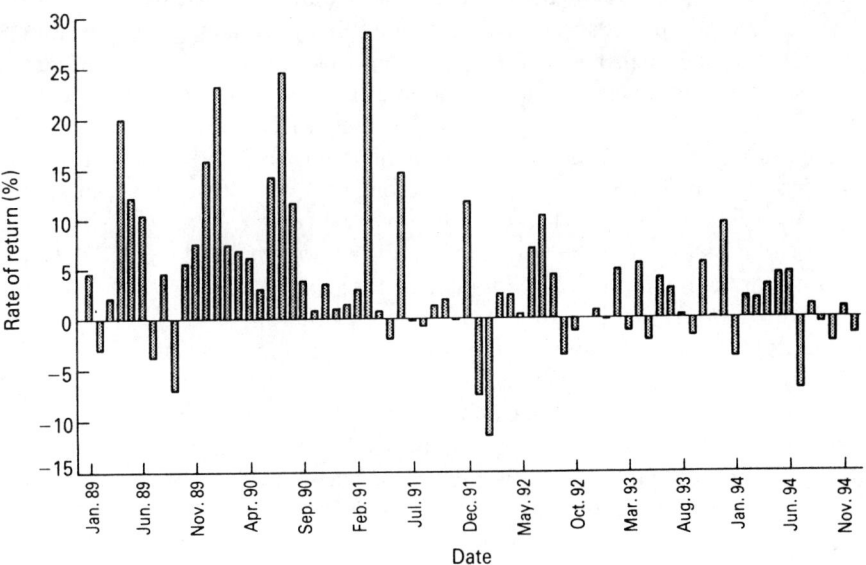

Figure 5.20 Capital Futures Management.

As with an increasing number of mechanical trading systems on the market today, Silver Knight's system is not limited to this one model. It also incorporates a volatility model which is designed to alert users when the risk-reward parameters become unprofitable. Unlike some derivatives managers, they use trailing stops to both limit the downside and protect profits. The problem is that if these stops are too close, choppy markets will ensure that any positions are continuously being stopped out resulting in a stream of small or not so small losses.

Silver Knight's growth in assets was relatively speedy. Performance started to disappear from the end of 1993. Many interested commentators in the market wondered whether they were having trouble digesting the new funds and whether or not the original, and successful, trading strategies would have to be amended to cope with the increased size. If US$100 million is the maximum that a manager like Shipman can manage, then there is not much hope for the institutions who may take years to come to the decision to invest with such a manager. By the time they are ready to make the commitment, the door has been closed.

Panther Capital Management

Set up in 1992. Unlike Mark Shipman's mechanical investment approach, Michael Cohn, as the principal trader for Panther Capital, relies heavily on the fundamental analysis of markets. This approach is also supplemented by the use of technical analysis to improve the timing of entry and exit points of trades which are part of predominantly relative-value and arbitrage-orientated strategies. Before joining Panther Cohn spent a number of years trading at Merrill Lunch International, Kleinwort Benson and Goldman Sachs with a general focus on United States, European and international arbitrage. Making the adjustment from being a trader amongst a large and diversified team with the continual flow of information and research (both good and bad) that such an environment provides, to sitting almost alone in a quiet office with your screens is not an easy transition to make. In the early days on one of the occasions that I met Cohn I was put in the unusual situation of not being able to get a word in for at least an hour. At the time I foolishly thought that Cohn was simply taking advantage of the fact that there was someone different to talk to. I have since learned that his passion for the international capital markets and what Panther can do will be expressed volubly to anyone who expresses interest!

Panther is not a believer in trend-following systems. Such systems generally assume that technical analysis is the most effective way to determine market movements in the future. Panther's approach acknowledges the value of technical analysis but treats it as one component of the matrix of variables that may help them make the right bet on the forthcoming direction of a market. Analysis of the economic and political landscape is more their scene. But as Cohn will tell you, although their interpretation of the economic and political environment is usually the starting point of a trade idea, it is only the beginning of a lengthy and rigorous process.

As with a number of managers driven by fundamentals, before getting into a position Panther consider the relative value of intra- and inter-markets and the components of fair pricing. These include the relationship between cash instruments, indices, futures, the costs of carry and options pricing. Using an integrated futures and options modelling system they attempt to structure a strategy which will exploit the underlying mathematical properties of the trade. Each trade is structured to reflect a predetermined maximum acceptable level of risk and exposure to the market. This is accomplished mainly through the use of a combination of futures and options strategies.

The portfolio's risk is broken down into two categories: market risk which measures directional market exposure by asset class (such as interest rate, currency or equity), and relative-value and arbitrage risk which measures spread, credit, basis and volatility risk. Until early 1994, Panther's strategies have paid off. However, the substantial reduction in liquidity in the European bond and other markets has made it extremely difficult not only to execute but also to justify executing trades that in 1993 worked well. Twelve months ago the spread on a particular options transaction was three pips. Now it is out to fifteen, and that is on a good day. Are we going to see the move from coincidence to trend? Watch this space for future developments.

Chescor

John Percival from Chescor arrived in currency management via journalism and newsletter publishing. Having been a Lex columnist for the *Financial Times*, he launched a currency newsletter – the *Currency Bulletin* – in the early 1980s. Providing useful and respected tips and comments on a fortnightly basis on the movement of the dollar, Percival gradually turned his skill to currency management on behalf of family and friends. The results were so successful that in 1992 he decided to expand the currency-management activity and work for clients outside this cosy and familiar environment.

Unlike many of his competitors who are continually researching new trading opportunities in the more esoteric and exotic cross-currency markets, Percival focuses on trading the dollar. In his book, *The Way of the Dollar* published in 1989, which describes his approach to the market, you are hit in the face by one word – *sentiment*. Sentiment is what drives the markets up and down; if you are in tune with market sentiment you will make money, if you are not you will lose. Sounds fairly straightforward. But how does one 'tune in'?

The results since 'going public' have put Chescor among the top performing currency managers around the world on both a return- and a risk-adjusted basis. Like most managers, one of their biggest concerns is being able to maintain strong results as the asset base grows. Will they be able to continue

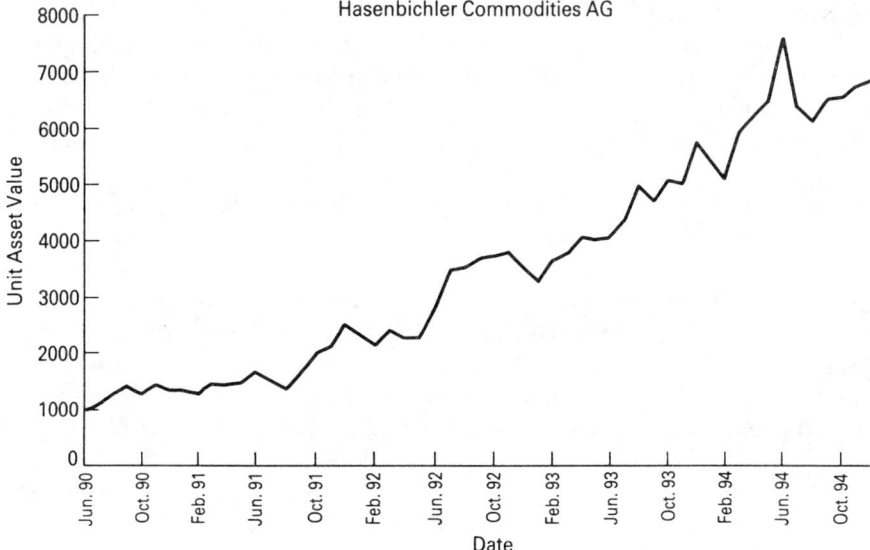

Figure 5.21 Hasenbichler Commodities AG.

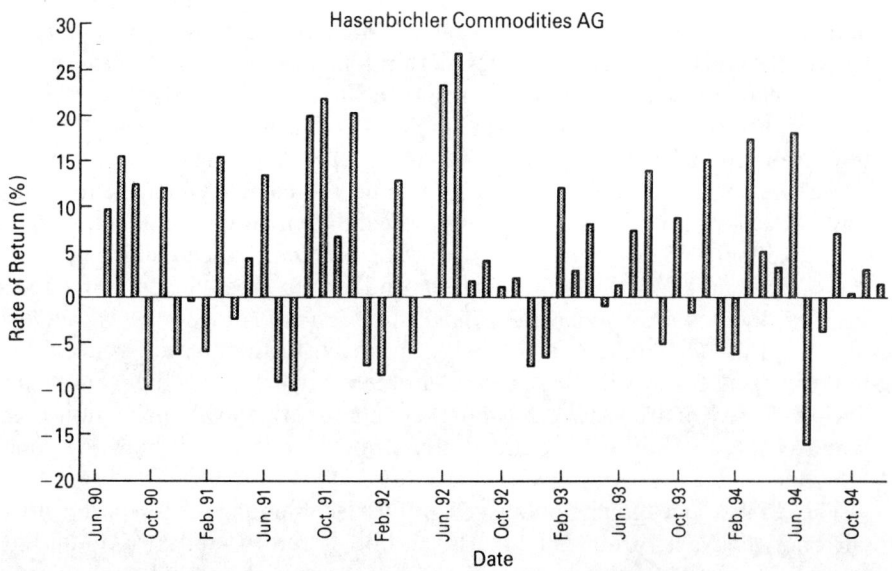

Figure 5.22 Hasenbichler Commodities AG.

to trade just the dollar or will Chescor have to migrate to other markets; and if they do, how successful will they be? Questions, questions.

If you take Le Shuttle to Paris you can find Capital Futures Management SNC, one of the more successful European based managers, and certainly the most successful French based manager to date. Capital Futures Management (CFM) was set up in 1991 by Jean-Pierre Aguilar. Aguilar started his career in 1986 when he joined LeGrand, LeGrand and Cie in Paris as a trader. In April 1988 he left and founded ATSM Finances S.A., a financial software company. When he established his CTA operation, Aguilar retained his involvement in the software company. Aguilar holds a degree in computer science from ENSIMAG and in finance from theEcole des Hautes Etudes Commerciales. Currently managing US $132 000 000, CFM has delivered average annual returns of 49.64 per cent over the past 4 years. So, how has this been done?

The CFM approach is highly systematic, although a discretionary overlay is used from time to time. The approach is also very diversified trading some 20 futures futures markets around the globe. CFM breaks these markets down into what they refer to as 5 asset classes. Long term interest rates, short term interest rates, stock indices, currencies (just the majors) and financial commodities (gold and crude oil). The trading system has three key features. First, it is a trend-following, volatility breakout, medium-term orientated system. There are many other similar systems on the market. CFM reckons that one of the key reasons why they have not suffered the same types of drawdowns (worst peak to trough losses relative to the peak) as many of their competitors over the past few years is because of the rigid stop-loss procedure employed by them. There are a number of successful discretionary traders who eschew the use of stops in the implementation of their trading strategies; perhaps we should get them together with Jean-Pierre for an interesting debate.

Like all successful managers, CFM places substantial importance on the risk management part of the trading system. Their risk management procedure is based on a portfolio insurance algorithm which aims at keeping the leverage of the portfolio constant. Typically after a loss making period the number of contracts per position will be smaller than when profits have been made.

If you travel south from Paris you come to one of the more unusual locations in which to find a futures fund manager. Hasenbichler Trading Services Ltd Malta (HTS–Malta) is run by Gerrit Rath and is an affiliate of Hasenbichler Trading Services Limited in the Bahamas. Gerrit Rath got into the futures fund management business via a somewhat unusual route. Having received a degree in communication engineering in 1979 he was involved in the ownership and management of a cultural management agency from then until 1991. This agency organised and ran a range of events from exhibitions to opera productions. During this time he also took a series of courses at the New York Institute of Finance (which, incidentally, has an affiliation with Simon & Schuster, the publishers whom you very kindly paid when you bought this book). From late 1989 to late 1991 Rath worked as a broker for Hasenbichler Warenhandel hedging base metals for clients.

The trading approach employed by Rath is totally systematic. It uses fully computerised trend following models operating over different time frames. Like most systematic traders, Rath trades a diversified range of commodity and financial futures markets. The same systems and parameters are used in each of the many markets traded. To try and control the risk in each market the signals generated are relative to price volatility. Hasenbichler, along with many other systematic managers, are extremely sensitive about providing any detailed information on how the trading system really works and why it seems to have an edge on the competition. A visit to Malta might shed some more light for the truly inquisitive.

Absolute return fund managers come in many shapes and sizes. They may use the cash, futures, options and other derivative markets in equities, fixed-income, currencies, commodities and other asset classes. The investment approach and geographic focus can vary enormously from manager to manager. What they all have in common is a belief in operating from the perspective of delivering absolute returns, a belief in the value of using the long and short side of the market and a desire to be compensated for their efforts by being paid a percentage (usually between 10 per cent and 35 per cent although the average is nearer 20 per cent) of the profits that they make.

6
Fund products

Keeping track of new products in this business is very much a moving feast – but our criteria has been successful money raising as much as anything else. We are going to outline and describe one major launch in each of the United States, the United Kingdom and Europe, and describe the general situation in the Far East. Additional material from some of these examples is in the appendices. The examples selected have been chosen for their relative simplicity and because they were reasonably retail oriented. Most OTC product is either tailor-made for clients or sold on a private-placement basis by the main investment banks. English documentation on Japanese funds is unavailable. This selection has been chosen to show a cross-section of what is available to reasonably sophisticated investors. The mix can vary considerably and we address general investor considerations in Chapter 8.

United States

Merrill Lynch has over US$1 billion under management in over 20 different possible derivative funds. Through Merrill Lynch Futures Investment Partners it selects and manages commodity trading advisors for its different multi-manager funds. One product was Merrill Lynch Global Horizons LP.

The marketing material in outline stated the following.

Today's investment challenge

Today, a global investment perspective seems essential for those seeking investment opportunity while attempting to control portfolio risk. The globalisation of the world's economy offers significant investment opportunities as well as risks. Major political and economic events have an influence – in some cases, a dramatic influence – on the world's markets, creating risk but also providing the potential for increased profitability.

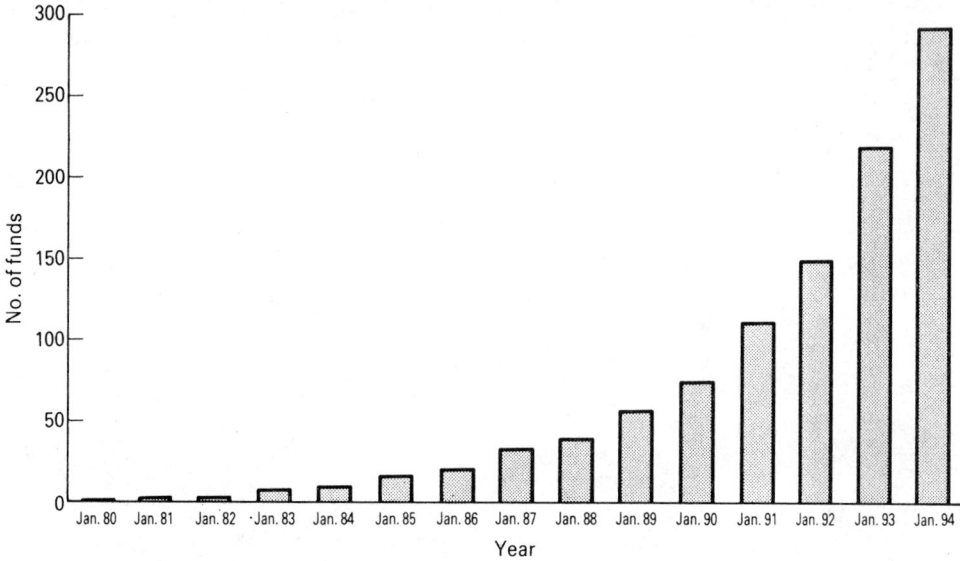

Figure 6.1 Bar chart showing growth in numbers of funds from 1980

Portfolios must have the ability to adapt to changing social, political and economic trends. A well diversified asset allocation strategy offers a desirable means of potentially building and protecting wealth in today's economic environment. As part of the asset allocation process, incorporating managed futures into portfolios can potentially increase profits while reducing portfolio risk.

Creating diversified portfolios

In the asset allocation process, portfolio holdings are invested among stocks, bonds, cash and non-traditional investments such as futures, to help achieve the dual investment objectives of long-term total return with reduced portfolio volatility. An investment's anticipated return, relative risk level and correlation to other investments, as well as the contribution of each investment to the overall portfolio are considered. Each investment responds differently to different economic cycles as well as shifts in the financial markets.

Managed futures are professionally managed investments in the global currency, financial, energy, metals and agricultural markets. These investments are made through futures contracts, options on futures contracts and forward contracts, and offer the ability to trade either side of the market. In addition, the profit and loss potential of futures trading is not dependent upon economic prosperity or interest rate or currency stability. As a result, positive, as well as negative, returns may be realised in both rising and declining markets.

Historically, the returns recognised on managed futures investments have exhibited a substantial degree of non-correlation with the performance of stock and bond investments, suggesting that a successful managed futures investment can be a valuable complement to a traditional portfolio. Allocating a portion of the risk segment of a portfolio to a managed futures investment can add a potentially valuable element of diversification to a traditionally structured portfolio of stocks and bonds.

The Fund

ML Global Horizons LP is a limited partnership organised with the objectives of achieving significant profits over time while controlling the risk of loss. The Fund will participate in major sectors of the international economy.

An 'aggressive' multi-advisor fund

Managed futures funds, like other investment products, are designed with a variety of anticipated risk/reward parameters in order to satisfy different investor objectives and risk tolerances. All such funds are speculative and involve a high degree of risk. However, certain types of funds are generally perceived as being more 'aggressive' than others. Although there can be no assurance that performance expectations will in fact be met, single advisor, single strategy funds are typically expected to have the greatest profit potential and greatest risk of loss, as well as being likely to experience the greatest volatility of performance. On the other hand, multi-advisor funds in which historically non-correlated strategies are combined are typically anticipated to exhibit less profit potential, risk of loss and volatility. The expected risk/reward parameters of futures funds may be varied by, among other things, adjusting the number of advisors, strategies and the markets traded. Generally, increased diversification among one or more of these categories is perceived to reduce anticipated performance volatility, profit potential and risk.

ML Futures Investment Partners Inc. (MLFIP) has sponsored numerous multi-advisor futures funds. In structuring the Fund, MLFIP has designed an investment with more 'aggressive' expected risk/reward characteristics than many of MLFIP's other multi-advisor investments. MLFIP anticipates that the performance of the Fund will exhibit considerable volatility (one widely accepted measure of risk). However, if major drawdowns can be avoided, the anticipated greater profit potential of a more limited number of advisors creates the opportunity to generate substantial gains over time, despite performance volatility.

Limited number of advisors

MLFIP intends to maintain a 'concentrated' multi-advisor approach for the Fund in an effort to reduce opportunity costs and increase profit potential. MLFIP believes that it may be possible to augment profit potential (although not to a level comparable to that of many single advisor funds) without materially increasing the risk of incurring a major drawdown by employing a more 'concentrated' advisor group, particularly as, even though limited in number, the initial Advisors collectively trade a wide variety of markets pursuant to diverse strategies. While MLFIP expects that the performance of the Fund will be more volatile than that of many other multi-advisors funds, MLFIP also believes that for investors willing to accept such volatility there is potential to increase their ultimate returns by limiting the number of advisors. (Initially there were three Advisors only.)

Fee structure

MLFIP has introduced a fee structure for the Fund which MLFIP believes to be innovative, and one which should lessen rather than increase risk during unprofitable trading periods. MLFIP has reduced the annual flat-rate brokerage commissions of 9% to 10% typically charged to its funds to 7.5% in return for MLFIP being entitled to a 10% annual Incentive Override payable only from Net New Gain (as defined in the Prospectus). From this brokerage fee, approximately 0.5 of 1% of the Fund's average month-end Net Assets per year must be paid out in ongoing administrative costs and either 2% or 4% for Advisors' consulting fees and ongoing compensation due on Units which remain outstanding for more than twelve months. In addition, all futures execution costs must be paid from this fee, and MLFIP will itself pay, without reimbursement from the Fund, the selling commissions due upon sale of the Units. As a result, a significant component of MLFIP's profit potential in sponsoring the Fund is dependent on MLFIP's receipt of Incentive Overrides, which, in turn, is contingent on the Fund generating Net New Gain (as defined in the Prospectus). In general, it is only if the Net Asset Value ('NAV') per Unit exceeds the highest NAV per Unit as of any previous calendar year-end (which may be significantly below the purchase price of a particular Unit), that MLFIP will receive additional Incentive Overrides. If the Fund generates Net New Gain in excess of 20% per year, MLFIP would recognise a higher overall net return from the Fund than MLFIP would under its more typical fee structure.

The general partner/trading manager

ML Futures Investment Partners Inc., a wholly-owned indirect subsidiary of Merrill Lynch & Co. Inc., is an integrated business, whose capabilities include research, trading, finance, systems, operation, sales and marketing. MLFIP is one of the largest managed futures sponsors in the United States (or elsewhere) in terms both of assets invested in futures funds for which it serves as trading manager or sponsor, and of financial and personnel resources. Since its inception, MLFIP has concentrated primarily on the structuring of multi-advisor products, and has devoted substantial resources to the development of the capacity to formulate advantageous trading advisor combinations, as well as to assess trading advisors on an individual basis. Advisor analysis includes the qualitative appraisal of an advisor's strategy and performance, combined with quantitative, statistical evaluation of the performance of individual advisors and of different possible advisor combinations.

MLFIP will monitor the performance of the Fund and its Advisors on a day-to-day basis, and will, from time to time, reallocate assets among, terminate and/or appoint new Advisors. At least quarterly, MLFIP will review the performance of the Fund and each Advisor in order to assess whether to change Advisor selections or allocations.

Investment managers

Fee structure
MLFIP has reduced the Fund's routine charges for the Incentive Override, payable only from Net New Gain (as defined in the Prospectus).

No initial sales charge
100% of investors' subscriptions will be available to the Fund. Redemption charges apply for the first 12 months after Units are sold.

100% interest credits
Merrill Lynch Futures will credit the Fund, as of each month-end, with interest as if 100% of the Fund's cash on deposit with Merrill Lynch futures during the preceding month were continually invested at the prevailing 91-day Treasury bill rates. The Fund's interest income as well as the assets on which such interest income is credited, is subject to the risk of trading loss.

Brokerage commissions; forward trading charges
The Fund will pay Merrill Lynch Futures a monthly flat-rate commission equal to 0.625 of 1% (a 7% annual rate) of the Fund's month-end available assets (including month-end interest credits and before deduction for brokerage commissions, Profit Shares or Incentive Overrides). From these commissions, all Advisor consulting fees, National Futures Association (NFA), clearing and exchange fees, ongoing compensation to Merrill Lynch Financial Consultants, as well as all brokerage expenses are paid. The Fund pays 'bid-ask' spreads and service fees on its forward trading.

Profit shares
Each of the Advisors will receive quarterly Profit Shares based on each Advisor's individual performance, not the overall performance of the Fund. Profit Shares may be payable by the Units even though the Units have declined in value.

Incentive override

MLFIP will be entitled to a 10% annual Incentive Override – payable only from Net New Gain (as defined in the Prospectus) after all charges. MLFIP believes the emphasis on compensation based on Net New Gain should lessen the risk of charges depleting the equity in the Fund, particularly during unprofitable periods. The Fund's fee structure will result in MLFIP recognising a higher net overall return from the Fund than MLFIP would receive under its typical compensation arrangements if Net New Gain exceeds 20 per cent of the Fund's average month-end assets in a given calendar year. There can be no assurance that the Fund will be profitable or avoid major losses. Incentive Overrides may be payable by certain Units even though such Units have declined in value.

Minimum investment

The minimum investment by a new subscriber is 50 Units ($5,000 during the Initial Offering Period; 50 Units multiplied by NAVE during the Ongoing Offering Period); 20 Units ($2,000 during the Initial Offering Period; 20 Units multiplied by Net Asset Value (NAV) during the Ongoing Offering Period) for both (i) trustees or custodians of eligible employee benefit plans and individual retirement accounts and (ii) existing Limited Partners subscribing for additional Units. Incremental investments, either at the time of initial investment or subsequently during the Initial or the Ongoing Offering Periods, are permitted in one-Unit increments.

Suggested term of investment

MLFIP believes that, in general, multi-advisor managed futures investments should be considered medium to long term investments. The Fund is intended as such an investment. While MLFIP has attempted to structure the Fund as a somewhat 'aggressive' form of multi-advisor investment, MLFIP does not believe that it is reasonable to expect that the Fund will achieve its rate of return objectives (if at all) in less than two to three years.

Monthly redemptions

Units may be redeemed, at the option of any Limited Partner, as of the close of business on the last day of any month on ten days' notice to MLFIP. Units are redeemed at NAVE, subject to early redemption charges of 3% of NAV on or prior to the end of the twelfth month after sale. Such charges will be paid to MLFIP.

Administrative convenience

The Fund is structured so as substantially to eliminate the administrative burden which would otherwise be involved in Limited Partners engaging directly in futures transactions. Limited Partners will, among other things, receive directly from MLFIP monthly unaudited and annual audited financial reports (setting forth, in addition to certain other information, the NAV per Unit, the Fund's trading profits or losses and the Fund's expenses for the period) as well as all tax information relating to the Fund necessary for Limited Partners to complete their federal income tax returns. The Global Horizons Fund raised about $70 million from its domestic and international efforts. Notable in its structure is the move to more incentive compensation on the part of Merrill Lynch. Global Horizons began with US$70 million in January 1994, issued at 100. At the end of January 1995 it had held its own at 100.74.

United Kingdom

An interesting product was Hypo Foreign and Colonial's Reserve Asset Fund approach – especially the Higher Income Plan. For a cautious and conservative market place with strict restrictions on futures and options funds as such, this unit trust had almost £450m under management by the end of 1994.

The Higher Income Plan was described and promoted – amongst professional advisors as a derivatives-based product designed to produce low-risk, higher income in an era of falling interest rates:

The higher-income plan

'The higher the income, the higher the risk?'

This is often true of individual shares, where a higher than average yield implies uncertainty over the sustainability of dividend payments. This is usually due to a company's operating or financial weaknesses which can result in dividend cuts. If dividends are cut, share price performance normally suffers. But the saying does not apply to the Higher Income Plan, because it employs modern investment techniques, using derivatives to enhance yield and reduce risk.

By converting future, potential capital gains into current income.

The fund does this by selling or 'writing' options against cash and shares held by the fund. This also reduces the fund's price volatility.

How selling 'calls' generates income

The fund holds shares. It writes call options on those shares. In return for giving the option holder the right to 'call' the shares at a set price for a set period, the fund receives a premium.

If the share price remains static or falls, the fund keeps the premium, the shares and any dividends on the shares.

If the share price rises, the call option is exercised and the fund does not participate in any potential further gains above the share price at which the options is exercised.

How is the fund structured?

The fund effects these transactions by purchasing debentures which have the relevant put and call options embedded in them to enable it to distribute premiums as income. The underlying fund is a unit trust using Efficient Portfolio Management in accordance with the SIB rules. In current market conditions, the investment strategy will produce an income of 10% p.a. which is not sensitive to changes in UK base rates.

What happens if interest rates rise or fall?

The fund's deposit income will be lower when interest rates are low. But Foreign & Colonial's calculations show that the projected 10% income return will be achievable with base rates in the range of 4% to 14%. The income generated by the fund will not be affected by base rate cuts within this range.

How selling 'puts' generates income

The fund holds cash. Against this, it writes put options. In return for giving the option holder the right to sell to the fund shares at a set price for a set period, the fund receives a premium.

If the share price remains static or rises, the fund keeps the deposit interest and the premium.

If the share price falls, the fund has to purchase shares from the option holder, but still keeps the deposit interest and the premium.

How will market movements affect the fund?

In the long term the trend of the UK stockmarket is upwards. The Higher Income Plan will benefit from long-term growth in equity values through its equity content, although some potential gains are converted into income. Short-term market movements should not affect the level of income. The fund will purchase 'out-of-money' put options as stop-loss insurance. This means that the maximum anticipated downside from a market fall in any option period is 6–7.5% regardless of the extent of the market fall. Options periods may be from one to twelve months but will typically be three months. This means that a sustained fall over a long period (e.g. two years) would result in capital erosion which would affect the fund's ability to generate the current level income. However, this stop-loss insurance may not protect the fund against a decline in one of the shares held by the fund greater than that of the FT/SE 100 Index.

This Plan versus other higher income investments

Equity income unit trusts

Traditional Equity Income Funds are completely different from the Higher Income Plan. An all-equity fund may generate a yield of up to 50% greater than that on the All Share Index. Such a fund might have a yield of 6.75% gross if the All Share yield is 4.5%.

But historic data suggests that investors wanting a good rate of growth in income and capital should avoid equity funds aiming for a much higher yield than that obtainable on the index. In this case, the risk is greater because of the inferior quality of share being purchased.

Investment trust income shares

There are two types of split-level investment trust income shares. One variety, normally called Income Shares, has many of the characteristics of annuities. Their redemption value is often fixed at a level below the current share price. In return for a high level of income, investors holding to redemption will suffer a capital loss. Preservation of capital will depend on selling the shares in advance of a price fall which is inevitable sooner or later. Ordinary Income Shares usually have rights to some element of capital growth. But usually these rights are secondary to the rights of capital shareholders, so a high rate of return on the trust's assets may be required for ordinary income shareholders to receive a satisfactory return.

Both varieties of share, because of their inherent gearing, are a far riskier type of investment than conventional equity funds, which in turn are riskier than the Higher Income Plan.

How can you be sure the Plan's concept will work?

Writing options against a share portfolio is a new concept in the UK market. But it is well established in the United States, where there are several mutual funds that do this. For example, the Analytic Options Equity Fund produced a compound average annual return of 11.4% from its inception in 1978. In the United States, over $800m is invested in funds of this type.

The market is huge

Retired people own the bulk of invested capital in the UK and look primarily for income . . . but have had interest rates halved over 24 months . . . making a high income, low risk investment an extremely attractive option . . .

Investors need to replace low-yielding deposits with long-term income investments that do not expose them to the high perceived risks of the equity market.

Summary

- 10 per cent tax-free income
- Income paid monthly
- Lower risk than normal equity fund
- A way of boosting income from existing PEPs through PEP

Transfer Plan

A way of getting a very high net yield of 8.0% after 20 per cent tax on dividends for those who have used up PEP entitlements.

Management of the Fund

This Fund is not 'mechanically' run and is very much a managed fund. The manager will always take a view on stock selection within the equity portfolio, and both the size and the extent of diversification of the portfolio. He will also take a view on the derivative strategy of the portfolio. This will embrace a wide variety of considerations including the level of options strike prices, both in terms of put and call options, the extent of any option sales, the maturity of the options which are to be sold and the diversification of those options maturities or expiry dates. In addition, the manager will consider the hedge or 'stop loss insurance' which protects the value of the portfolio in the event of market weakness. The characteristics and dynamics of the hedge will also form part of the overall portfolio strategy. Accordingly, the manager follows different options strategies to reflect his view of the market and the individual blue chip equities. If the view were bearish the manager would tend to write fewer put options and those that he did write would be as far out of the money as possible. This would mean that the premium derived from the put options would fall. On the other side of the equation, he could write more call options and write them very close to the money. This would produce more premium from the call option writing and would tend to offset the lower amount of premium generated from the sale of put options.

In its first ten months, the total return was 10.37%, very much in line with promotional expectations – and the investment manager's initial report stated:

> During the first eight months of the Fund's life the Managers have maintained a high level of monthly distributions to unitholders. This has been achieved despite the rapid growth in the fund size as a result of investor subscription. Unlike a conventional income fund, the Fund's income comes partially from dividends on the equities held but mainly from the high yield on the special debentures. The special debentures have been issued by borrowers of high credit standing. They have a high coupon which consists of a current market rate of interest plus the equivalent of premia on a number of notional options related to the shareholdings of the Fund to which the redemption price is formula-linked. The market interest and an amount equivalent to the premia on the notional options are paid as interest on the special debentures.
>
> As a result of the formula linking the redemption of the special debentures to the outcome of the notional options, special debentures generally

mature at a value below their issue price. This reduction in value may be compensated by increases in the value of the other investments of the Fund; indeed this has been the experience of the Fund during the period covered by this report.

Equity dividends have been better than expected, with increases in the dividend from many blue chip companies being greater than inflation. Interest rates have been stable, although they are expected to fall in the near future, while option premia have not changed significantly across the market.

The equity element of the portfolio, which accounts for almost 60% of the Fund's assets, is concentrated in some of the largest UK companies including British Telecom, BTR, Great Universal Stores, Marks and Spender, RTZ and Unilever. These have been chosen because of their financial strength, consistent performance and good prospects.

This Fund got some poor press when the yield was reduced to 9%. The monthly income feature caused some flexibility and performance problems, and generally its Capital performance has been weak. On balance however it has behaved much as expected.

Europe

1994 saw another successful derivatives fund placing by Citibank in the form of its Keynote Bonds in United States (fixed and floating) and Deutschmarks. A total of US$160 million was raised for the combined issue which took the form of Collateralised Enhanced Yield Notes of ten years' duration.

The investment manager and advisor selector was Kenmar – who have approximately US$450 million – under advice and management. There remains strong underlying interest in guaranteed- or bond-type structures amongst European investors and increasing acceptance of derivatives market usage as the means to improving returns in an era of lower interest rates.

The transaction outline was as follows for the United States fixed rate note tranche:

Transaction Outline
Issuer   Keynote US Fixed Limited
Rating   AAA (Principal and Minimum Coupon)
Amount   US$50–100 million
Maturity   10 years
Interest periods   Annual

Minimum Coupon*	First and Second Coupon Dates	6.00%
	Third Coupon Date	4.50%
	Fourth Coupon Date	3.00%
	Fifth Coupon Date	2.00%
	Sixth to Tenth Coupon Dates	1.00%
Coupon Enhancement	Depending on cumulative performance of the Investment Fund, with Minimum Coupon and Coupon Enhancement to be paid up to the Total Maximum Coupon according to an increasing payment schedule:	
	First Two Coupon Dates	6.00%
	increasing up to:	
	Tenth Coupon Date	8.00%
Premium on Redemption	Increasing value (depending on performance) of the Investment Fund**	
Put Option	Available on the second Coupon Date and on each anniversary thereof	
Form	Eurobond	
Denomination	US$10,000 and US$100,000	
Listing	Luxemburg	

* Subject to market prevailing conditions at launch
** Net Asset Value of Investment Fund will be available weekly

This was a professionally put together bond structure where 80 per cent of the funds raised were used to purchase an issue of medium-term notes issued by Deutsche Bank AG London, in the form of collateral notes. The balance was given to Kenmar Global Strategies Inc. Kenmar designs programs and manages investments in derivatives markets by retaining commodity trading advisors to trade in those markets. There is a section in Chapter 8 on multi-advisor funds and approaches. Kenmar were allowed to use a maximum leverage of 1.5 times on the trading account. Citibank basically performed all the other functions in the fund, particularly using its speciality service of portfolio monitor to monitor the trading account and the compliance with the terms of the funds trading policies.

The trading policies, in summary, were:

1. exchange-traded commodity futures contracts on approved exchanges in approved markets;
2. exchange-traded forward and option contracts as above;
3. off-exchange contracts in foreign exchange;
4. other instruments as agreed by the board;
5. no more than 45 per cent of the cash net asset value (CNAV) to be invested in initial margin and/or option premium;

6. no more than 40 per cent of the CNAV to be given to any one advisor;
7. no more than 35 per cent of the CNAV to be invested in any single market sector;
8. no more than 10 per cent of the CNAV in any single contract type.

Although the timing of the launch in March 1994 meant that the yield was locked in to some extent at low interest-rate levels, the derivatives trading started after the worst of the losses sustained by most CTAs in the early part of the year, and to the end of June the performance was encouraging. With all bond-related or guaranteed funds early profitability gives greater prospect of maximum use of the trading account to achieve the investment aims of the fund.

The trading account of about US$31 million began at the end of March 1994. After a good start performance suffered in line with the market.

Japan

After the excitement and anticipation for the growth of commodity funds in Japan after the changes in regulations, the reality has been more sombre. The recession in the Japanese market generally reduced demand and interest. By the end of 1994 the number of funds in issue was 70, of which 18 were opened in 1993. Funds under management totalled just under US$2 billion of which over US$400 million was raised in 1993.

The capital guaranteed structure remained the norm. Performance of funds was mediocre in general with blame being allocated variously to high fees, the low level of interest minimising the investable portion of the fund, optimisation of previous performance, and the state of the economy. 1994 has seen limited activity, although Marubeni raised about US$50 million in a fund with a 1 per cent yield. This meant the funds available for investing in futures markets were small.

The Japanese managed-futures industry will revive when the stock market and the economy turn and the major securities houses decide to actively promote the concept again. Although it does not make for thrilling reading, listed below are the main Japanese funds.

General partner fund	Start date co-general partner or sales agent		Co-sales agent
Ace Koeki Co. Ltd	Pentagon Futures Fund '91	7 Mar. 1991	Dai-Ichi Commodities Co. Ltd Hoxin Bussan Co. Ltd Kanetsunetsu Shoji Co. Ltd Tokio Medex Corp.
	Ace Star Futures Fund 1	1 Feb. 1993	
Aplus Co. Ltd	Aplus Commodity Fund 1	1 Apr. 1992	

Dai-Ichi Commodities Co. Ltd	Grand Harmony Futures Fund	8 Nov. 1992	Hoxin Bussan Co. Ltd Sunrise Trading Corp Taichi Shoji Co. Ltd
Diamond Lease Co.	Diamond Dynamic Futures Fund I	28 Sept. 1990	
	Diamond Dynamic Futures Fund II	22 Mar. 1991	
	Diamond Diversified Commodity Futures Fund I	15 Nov. 1991	
	Diamond Diversified Commodity Futures Fund II	18 Feb. 1993	Mitsubushi Bank Hiroshima Bank
Fuyo General Lease	FGL Futures Fund I	27 Aug. 1991	Mitsui & Co. Ltd
	Fuyo Futures Fund II	30 Mar. 1992	Mitsui & Co. Ltd
Itochu Corporation	CI and CLS Gold Linked Futures Fund I System Inc.	24 Apr. 1991	Century Leasing
	CI and CLS Gold Linked Futures Fund II System Inc.	2 Dec, 1991	Century Leasing
	CI and CLS Gold Linked Futures Fund III System Inc.	4 Dec. 1992	Century Leasing
Japan Leasing Corp	JLC Ambitious Futures I	28 Feb. 1991	
	JLC Ambitious Futures II	2 Sept. 1991	
	JOT Ambitious Futures Tokyo General Corp	1 June 1992	Okura & Co. Ltd
	JCL Ambitious Futures III	29 Mar. 1993	
Kanematsu Corp	Kanegold Futures Fund I	10 Apr. 1992	
	Kanegold Futures Fund II	26 Apr. 1993	
Kanetsu Shoji Co	Kanetsu Gold Fund I	1 July 1993	
Marubeni Corp.	Marubeni Managed Futures Fund	17 Apr. 1992	
Mitsubishi Corp.	The Allstar Commodity Futures Fund I	20 Dec. 1990	
	The Allstar Commodity Futures Fund II	23 Apr. 1991	
	The Allstar Commodity Futures Fund III	25 June 1991	
	The Polar Star Commodity Futures Fund I	2 July 1991	Yasuda Trust & Banking Co. Ltd
	The Polar Star Commodity Futures Fund II	23 Jan. 1993	Yasuda Trust & Banking Co. Ltd
Mitsui & Co. Ltd	MBK Gold Futures Fund I	31 Jan. 1991	
	MBK Gold Futures Fund II	28 Nov. 1991 5 FCMs	
	MBK Gold Futures Fund III	21 Aug. 1992 2 FCMs	
Mitsui Leasing & MLD	Futures Fund I	16 July 1991	Mitsui & Co. Ltd
	MLD Futures Fund II	19 Mar. 1992	Mitsui & Co. Ltd
	MLD Futures Fund III	18 Dec. 1992	Mitsui & Co. Ltd
	MLD Futures Fund IV	21 July 1993	Mitsui & Co. Ltd
Nichimen Corp.	NM Commodity Futures Fund	1 Jan. 1992	
	NM Futures Star Fund	17 Sept. 1992	
Nikko Securities Co.	Golden Commodity Fund Tokyo Security Co. Ltd National Security Co. Ltd	1 Dec. 1992	Tokyo General Corp
Nissho Iwai Corp.	NI & Partners' Fund I	26 Mar. 1991	Alpus Corp

Fund products

	Okato Shoji Co. Ltd		
	Hokushin Shohin Co. Ltd		
	NI & Partners' Fund II	28 Feb. 1992	Okato Shoji Co. Ltd
	Hokushin Shohin Co. Ltd		
	Santos Fund	25 Jan. 1994	Okato Shoji Co. Ltd
	Okasan Securities Co. Ltd		
Nomura Securities	Nomura Managed Futures Fund	26 Mar. 1993	Mitsui & Co. Ltd
Orient Corporation	Orico Futures Fund Ltd	16 July 1991	Sumisho Lease Co.
Orix Corporation	Orix Commodity Futures I	21 Sept. 1990	
	Orix Commodity Pool I	21 Nov. 1990	
	Orix Commodity Pool II	7 Mar. 1991	
	Orix Commodity Pool III	25 Apr. 1991	
	Orix Commodity Pool IV	21 June 1991	
	Orix Commodity Pool V	31 July 1991	
	Orix Commodity Pool VI	23 Oct. 1991	
SB Leasing Co. Ltd	SB Leasing Futures Fund	22 Jan. 1993	Mitsui & Co. Ltd
Showa Leasing Co. Ltd	SL Futures Fund I	2 Aug. 1991	Mitsui & Co. Ltd
Sumisho Lease Co. Ltd	Sumisho Lease Managed Fund I	24 Oct. 1990	
	Sumisho Lease Managed Fund II	20 Feb. 1991	
	Sumisho Lease Managed Fund II	16 July 1991	Orient Corporation
	Sumisho Lease Managed Fund IV	20 Dec. 1991	
	S & S Managed Fund I	1 Oct. 1992	SB Leasing Co. Ltd
	Sumisho Lease Managed Fund VI	1 Dec. 1993	
Sumitomo Corp.	Summit Futures Fund I	3 Jan. 1992	
Tokyo General Corp.	TGI Managed Futures Fund	1 Dec. 1993	
Tokyo Leasing Co.	TLC Futures Fund I	5 June 1991	Mitsui & Co. Ltd
	TLC Futures Fund II	9 Oct. 1991	Mitsui & Co. Ltd
	TLC Futures Fund III	11 Mar. 1992	Mitsui & Co. Ltd
	TLC Futures Fund IV	4 Aug. 1992	Mitsui & Co. Ltd
	TLC Futures Fund V	18 Feb. 1993	Mitsui & Co. Ltd
	TLC Futures Fund VI	25 June 1993	Mitsui & Co. Ltd
Tomen Corporation	Tomen Gold and Futures Fund (No. 1)	18 Mar. 1991	Central Leasing Co. Ltd
	Central Finance Co. Ltd		
	Tomen Gold and Futures Fund (No. 2)	27 Mar. 1992	Central Leasing Co. Ltd
			Central Finance Co. Ltd
	TCU Global Fund Union Trading Co. Ltd	5 Apr. 1993	Central Finance Co. Ltd
Toyota Tsusho Corp	TTC Managed Futures Fund		

At the end of March 1994 the total sales amount of Japanese commodity funds were Yen239.4 billion (US$2.4 billion). Fourteen funds had been launched in the first quarter raising about Yen30 billion. Sales continue to be slow. These results are summarised in Figure 6.2.

Some Japanese trading advisors are beginning to appear, with six companies being given Investment Fund licences in September 1994. In addition the local exchanges are considering partial liberalisation of brokerage

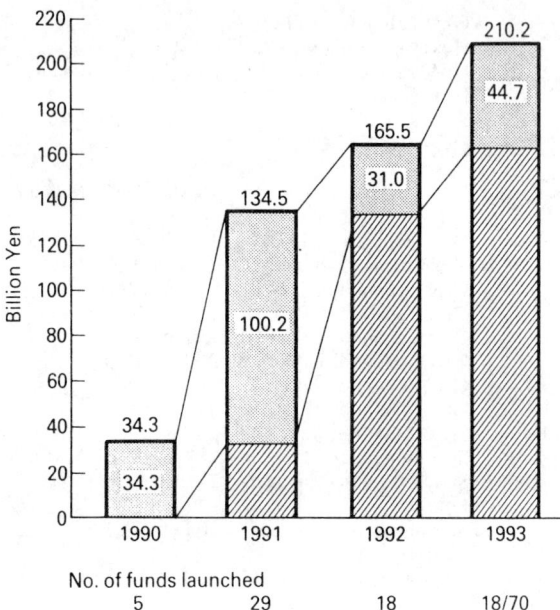

Figure 6.2 Sales amount of Japanese commodity funds (billion yen).

commissions. This means that the commission houses can fix rates at their discretion for domestic commodity funds and ordinary overseas orders, provided the rates are equal to or below the normal official rates. This is significant because one way or another Japanese funds have been very expensive for the investor.

There are obviously plenty of different variations on these themes. French banks have been noticeably successful raising money in bond-type structures. We think the new Switcher design, using the markets as a kind of global investment toolbox, will be one of the big product-development areas in the next few years (see Chapter 9).

7
OTC derivatives and investment management

The July 1993 report by the Washington-based Group of Thirty produced by the Global Derivatives Study Group – *Derivatives: Practices and Principles* – has made an important contribution to the demystification of both the products and the risks involved in the non-exchange-traded derivative sector. Whilst the report primarily set out to highlight the appropriate management needs for this area, there were some useful general common-sense observations.

The first is that derivatives do not, *per se*, introduce risks that are fundamentally different from the risks already present for participants in the financial community. Like any other business you need a solid set of established operating procedures and risk-management practices for both producers and consumers.

The second is that the ingredients of risk – whether market, credit, operational or legal – can be clearly defined and dealt with. As the report put it, 'What makes derivatives important is not so much the size of the activity as the role it plays in fostering new ways to identify, measure and manage financial risk. Through derivatives the complex risks that are bound together can be treated apart and managed independently.'

The third interesting observation was one relating to the 'zero-sum game' argument. The report argued that even though the pay-offs from a derivatives transaction are a zero-sum in the sense that the gain to one party equals the loss the other, derivatives transactions can create 'social' value. Hedging allows risk to be reduced or transferred which benefits all those associated with the hedge.

The Group of Thirty Report provides the most comprehensive summary to date of the derivatives market-place. As stated above, its objective is to outline a definitive framework of management practices for both the dealers and the end-users. Twenty-four recommendations are put forward under the general heading 'practices and principles'. For the benefit of those of you who have not read the report, these recommendations are listed below:

1. **The role of senior management**
   Dealers and end-users should use derivatives in a manner consistent with the overall risk management and capital policies approved by their boards of directors. These policies should be reviewed as business and market circumstances change. Policies for governing derivatives use should be clearly defined, including the purposes for which these transactions are to be undertaken. Senior management should approve procedures and controls to implement these policies, and management at all levels should enforce them.
2. **Marking to market**
   Dealers should mark their derivatives positions to market, on at least a daily basis, for risk management purposes.
3. **Market valuation methods**
   Derivatives portfolios of dealers should be valued based on mid-market levels less specific adjustments, or on appropriate bid or offer levels. Mid-market valuation adjustments should allow for expected future costs such as unearned credit spread, close-out costs, investing and funding costs, and administrative costs.
4. **Identifying revenue sources**
   Dealers should measure the component of revenue regularly and in sufficient detail to understand the sources of risk.
5. **Measuring market risk**
   Dealers should use a consistent measure to calculate daily the market risk of their derivatives positions and compare it to market risk limits.
   - Market risk is best measured as 'value at risk' using probability analysis based upon a common confidence interval (e.g. two standard deviations) and time horizon (e.g. one day exposure).
   - Components of market risk that should be considered across the term structure include: absolute price or rate change (delta); convexity (gamma); volatility (vega); time decay (theta); basis or correlation; and discount rate (rho).
6. **Stress simulations**
   Dealers should regularly perform simulations to determine how their portfolios would perform under stress conditions.
7. **Investing and funding forecasts**
   Dealers should periodically forecast the cash investing and funding requirements arising from their derivatives portfolios.
8. **Independent market risk management**
   Dealers should have a market risk management function, with clear independence and authority, to ensure that the following responsibilities are carried out:
   - The development of risk limit policies and the monitoring or transactions and positions for adherence to these policies.
   - The design of stress scenarios to measure the impact of market conditions, however improbable, that might cause market gaps, volatility

swings, or disruptions of major relationships, or might reduce the liquidity in the face of unfavourable market linkages, concentrated market making, or credit exhaustion.
- The design of revenue reports quantifying the contribution of various risk components, and/or market risk measures such as value at risk.
- The monitoring of variance between the actual volatility of portfolio and that predicted by the measure of market risk.
- The review and approval of pricing models and valuation systems used by front and back office personnel, and the development of reconciliation procedures if different systems are used.

9. **Practices by end-users**
As appropriate to the nature, size and complexity of their derivatives activities, end-users should adopt the same valuation and market risk management practices that are recommended for dealers. Specifically, they should consider: regularly marking to market their derivatives transactions for risk management purposes; periodically forecasting the cash investing and funding requirements arising from their derivatives transactions; and establishing a clearly independent and authoritative function to design and assure adherence to prudent risk limits.

10. **Measuring credit exposure**
Dealers and end-users should measure credit exposure on derivatives in two ways:
- Current exposure, which is the replacement cost of derivatives transactions, i.e. their market value.
- Potential exposure which is an estimate of the future replacement cost of derivatives transactions. It should be calculated using probability analysis based upon broad confidence intervals (e.g. two standard deviations) over the remaining terms of the transactions.

11. **Aggregating credit exposures**
Credit exposures on derivatives, and all other credit exposures to a counterparty, should be aggregated taking into consideration enforceable netting arrangements. Credit exposures should be calculated regularly and compared to credit limits.

12. **Independent credit risk management**
Dealers and end-users should have a credit risk management function with clear independence and authority, and with analytical capabilities in derivatives, responsible for:
- Approving credit exposure measurement standards.
- Setting credit limits and monitoring their use.
- Reviewing credits an concentrations of credit risk.
- Reviewing and monitoring risk reduction arrangements.

13. **Master agreements**
Dealers and end-users are encouraged to use one master agreement as widely as possible with each counterparty to document existing and future

derivatives transactions, including foreign exchange forward and options. Master agreements should provide for payments netting and close-out netting, using a full two-way payments approach.

14. **Credit enhancement**

    Dealers and end-users should assess both the benefits and costs of credit enhancement and related risk-reduction arrangements. Where it is proposed that credit downgrades would trigger early termination or collateral requirements, participants should carefully consider their own capacity and that of their counterparties to meet the potentially substantial funding needs that might result.

15. **Promoting enforceability**

    Dealers and end-users should work together on a continuing basis to identify and recommend solutions for issues of legal enforceability, both within and across jurisdictions, as activities evolve and new types of transactions are developed.

16. **Professional expertise**

    Dealers and end-users must ensure that their derivatives activities are undertaken by professionals in sufficient number and with the appropriate experience, skill levels, and degrees of specialisation. These professionals include specialists who transact and manage the risks involved, their supervisors, and those responsible for processing, reporting, controlling and auditing the activities.

17. **Systems**

    Dealers and end-users must ensure that adequate systems for data capture, processing, settlement and management reporting and in place so that derivatives transactions are conducted in an orderly and efficient manner in compliance with management policies. Dealers should have risk management systems that measure risks incurred in their derivatives activities including market and credit risks. End-users should have risk management systems that measure the risks incurred in their derivatives activities based upon their nature, size and complexity.

18. **Authority**

    Management of dealers and end-users should designate who is authorised to commit their institutions to derivatives transactions.

19. **Accounting practices**

    Internal harmonisation of accounting standards for derivatives is desirable. Pending the adoption of harmonised standards, the following accounting practices are recommended:
    - Dealers should account for derivatives transactions by marking them to market, taking changes in value to income each period.
    - End-users should account for derivatives used to manage risks so as to achieve a consistency of income recognition treatment between those instruments and the risks being managed. Thus, if the risk being managed is account for at cost (or, in the case of an anticipatory hedge, not

yet recognised), changes in the value of a qualifying risk management instrument should be deferred until a gain or loss is recognised on the risk being managed. Or, if the risk being managed is marked-to-market with changes in value being taken into income, a qualifying risk management instrument should be treated in a comparable fashion.
- End-users should account for derivatives not qualifying for risk management treatment on a marked-to-market basis.
- Amounts due to and from counterparties should only be offset when there is a legal right to set off or when enforceable netting arrangements are in place.

Where local regulations prevent adoption of these practices, disclosure along these lines is nevertheless recommended.

20. **Disclosures**

    Financial statements of dealers and end-users should contain sufficient information about their use of derivatives to provide an understanding of the purposes for which transactions are undertaken, the extent of the transactions, the degree of risk involved, and how the transactions have been accounted for. Pending the adoption of harmonised accounting standards, the following disclosures are recommended:
    - Information about management's attitude to financial risks, how instruments are used and how risks are monitored and controlled.
    - Accounting policies.
    - Analysis of positions at the balance sheet date.
    - Analysis of the credit risk inherent in those positions.
    - For dealers only, additional information about the extent of their activities in financial instruments.

21. **Recognising netting**

    Regulators and supervisors should recognise the benefits of netting arrangements where and to the full extent that they are enforceable, and encourage their use by reflecting these arrangements in capital adequacy standards. Specifically, they should promptly implement the recognition of the effectiveness of bilateral close-out netting in bank capital regulations.

22. **Legal and regulatory uncertainties**

    Legislators, regulators and supervisors, including central banks, should work in concert with dealers and end-users to identify and remove any remaining legal and regulatory uncertainties with respect to:
    - The form of documentation required to create legally enforceable agreements (statute of frauds).
    - The capacity of parties, such as governmental entities, insurance companies, pension funds and building societies, to enter into transactions (*ultra vires*).
    - The enforceability of bilateral close-out netting and collateral arrangements in bankruptcy.

- The enforceability of multibrance netting arrangements in bankruptcy.
- The legality/enforceability of derivatives transactions.

23. **Tax treatment**

    Legislators and tax authorities are encouraged to review and, where appropriate, amend tax laws and regulations that disadvantage the use of derivatives in risk management strategies. Tax impediments include the inconsistent or uncertain tax treatment of gains and losses on the derivatives, in comparison with the gains and losses that arise from the risks being managed.

24. **Accounting standards**

    Accounting standard-setting bodies in each country should, as a matter of priority, provide comprehensive guidance on accounting and reporting of transactions in financial instruments, including derivatives, and should work towards international harmonisation of standards on this subject. Also, the International Accounting Standards Committee should finalise its accounting standard on Financial Instruments.

The astonishing collapse of Baring Brothers Bank as a result of huge mismatching positions in the Japanese equity index markets in Osaka and Singapore has really brought home to everybody the necessity of implementing, not only the recommended G30 controls, but no doubt others to be required by the regulators. Even though the full facts are not available at the time of writing, it is obvious that at the very least there were the following failures:

1. By the trader himself in allowing the positions to become so massive, based on such an inappropriate strategy.
2. Permitting the role of the trader as both the market participant and the prime settlement controller.
3. Either the approval or the neglect of both the above by both Singapore and London Bank management.
4. The failure to implement internal audit recommendations.
5. The cash management of the margin payments.
6. Possibly the Exchanges in failing to highlight the positions to senior bank management. To be fair, if a member is fully margined and there are no position limit regulations it is hard to see exactly what exchanges can do given the apparent quality of the member firm. The same is true of the clearing houses.

It is a fascinating story and its full history will bear close examination. It will also give international regulators a good cause for tightening their own policies and procedures for market participants. The liquidation process at the Bank caused problems for other market participants in the futures and derivatives business, but not the much feared and anticipated 'domino' effect.

Table 7.1 Swap activity to the end of 1993 (notional principal $ million)

TOTAL OUTSTANDING AT YEAR-END

Year	Interest rate	% change	Currency	% change	Swaptions	% change	Totals	% change
1989	1,502,600	na	434,849	na	547,308	na	2,474,757	na
1990	2,311,544	+54%	577,535	+33%	561,261	+4%	3,450,340	+39%
1991	3,065,065	+32%	807,166	+40%	577,189	+3%	4,449,420	+30%
1992	3,850,806	+26%	860,387	+6%	634,473	+10%	5,345,666	+20%
1993	6,177,352	+60%	899,618	+4%	1,397,608	+120%	8,474,578	+58%

TOTAL REPORTED ACTIVITY

Year	Interest rate	% change	Currency	% change	Swaptions	% change	Totals	% change
1989	833,534	na	169,631	na	335,524	1,338,689	na	
1990	1,229,241	+47%	212,763	+25%	292,398	−13%	1,734,402	+29%
1991	1,621,779	+32%	328,394	+55%	382,689	+31%	2,332,862	+34%
1992	2,822,635	+74%	301,858	−8%	592,454	+54%	3,716,947	+59%
1993	4,104,666	+45%	295,191	−2%	1,116,982	+89%	5,518,839	+48%

Overview of derivatives activity

Today's financial market-place bears little resemblance to the market-place that existed twenty years ago. Most of this change has been brought about by the creation and increasing use of global derivatives and the revolution in the communications systems and software industry. The development of derivatives has occurred in response to a search for increased flexibility, higher yields, lower funding costs and a demand for tools to manage risk (see Table 7.1). The broad demand for derivatives arises from the diverse and changing financial needs of a wide range of users. Some of these may be hedging current or future risks, some may be taking directional positions in the market, and others may be exploiting the inefficiencies between markets. One area in which their use has expanded substantially over the last decade is in asset allocation.

Derivatives markets and asset allocation

Derivatives provide a particularly effective way of implementing asset allocation decisions. They offer cheap, efficient and speedy execution, facilitate cashflow management and allow the separation of currency and equity investment decisions.

Index Options and Warrants are useful tools in the asset-allocation process, although they have somewhat different properties to stock-index futures. Index options have limited risk to either the downside or upside depending on whether they are calls or puts, while stock-index futures have risk profiles identical to a basket of the underlying constituent stocks. For this reason index options are often used by asset allocators as an insurance tool. For example, a fund with exposure to the French equity market may purchase CAC40 index put options to reduce his downside risk. He still maintains exposure to any market upside. Alternatively, an investor who has no exposure to a particular market may, rather than buy index futures, purchase index call options. In doing so the investor gains positive exposure to the market, but again limits his or her downside risk.

The primary (and probably the most efficient) tool for implementing a change in asset allocation between countries is the index future. To switch country exposure from, say, France to Germany, one need only short CAC index futures and go long DAX index futures. This allows for:

quick, efficient execution – index futures are traded in liquid markets which allow investment decisions to be implemented quickly;
efficient cashflow management – margined transactions again allow for easier execution, without the need to liquidate and then reinvest in physical assets;
lower transaction charges – due to greater liquidity, typical dealing charges are much lower than for cash transactions.

Index futures offer a further benefit for asset-allocation strategies which involve *both* currency and equity investment decisions, namely:

index futures provide only equity market exposure;
equities provide both currency and equity market exposure.

A similar tool to the index future is the Equity Index Swap. Such an instrument is traded over the counter, and like the index future, offers significant cashflow, execution and cost benefits. Index-swaps are available on a wider range of indices than index futures and with their variable maturity and bespoke construction offer greater flexibility.

Of particular use for asset allocation are Quanto Equity Index Swaps (or differential swaps, to use the terminology of the interest-rate swap markets). In addition to offering currency-protected underlying equity exposure, such instruments also offer currency protection on any market movement.

The Basket Swap is a close relative of the equity index swap but with extra flexibility, based as it is on a basket of stocks selected by the client. The basket swap can be used in markets where no recognised benchmark is available and in strategies where asset allocation is sectorally based.

Although not strictly derivatives, Programme Trades are an efficient tool for switching between large numbers of international equity holdings rather than selling and subsequently buying individual equity holdings, the investor can execute all the individual trades at once on an agreed net or gross basis. This will tend to reduce transaction costs and eliminate timing risks involved in switching between markets.

Index futures, swaps and programme trades are the most direct forms of implementing asset-allocation decisions. A further class of instruments which add greater flexibility in asset allocation are Options and Warrants, and their bond counterparts, Guaranteed Return Bonds (GRBs) and Convertibles. These instruments are particularly useful for asset-allocation strategies set up to enhance absolute performance rather than simply relative performance. Such instruments allow for greater control of risk with facilities for both aggressive gearing (warrants) and defensive protection (GRBs, put options).

The final class of instruments are the cross-currency OTC equity options which enable specific currency and equity views to be implemented. The Quanto Option, as with the quanto swap, pays out the intrinsic value (calculated in domestic currency) at a fixed foreign exchange rate. A directional view on the equity (in local currency) can be separated from a currency view. The Compo(site) Option, on the other hand, is an option on the total asset value (in a foreign currency) and allows option strategies to be implemented on the basis of total asset value.

Such options add to the flexibility of asset-allocation strategies and provide one-shot implementation for the full range of currency and equity views.

Implementation with options

The one simple objective is to deliver over time significantly higher absolute returns than those achievable by traditional index-bond institutional investors. Index options enable the investor to achieve this in several ways:

1. the ability to leverage exposure, either up or down;
2. the risk profile may be altered, and to a certain degree customised to suit the exact requirements of the investor;
3. the separation of equity and currency decisions, either through the implicit nature of a vanilla option or explicitly through a quarter option.

Implementation via options facilitates these objectives:

1. by allowing leverage in both directions;
2. by allowing flexibility in controlling the risk profile;
3. by allowing independent control of equity and currency exposure.

The futures specifications for the main index futures and options are listed in Appendix B towards the end of this book.

Risk management

1994 saw its fair share of very negative investment performance supposedly because of the use of derivatives. Askin Capital, Vairocana, the Rockefeller

Foundation and Orange County are just a few of the entities pilloried by the press for their supposed reckless investment management strategies employing derivatives.

'Derivatives often get a bad rap. A frequent message we hear is that anyone who is involved in derivative transactions is tempting fate, and that sooner or later major losses will be suffered as derivatives positions inevitably go wrong. Such messages are misleading. Properly used, derivatives have been and will continue to be a source of risk reduction and enhanced investment performance for many participants. Therefore, any manager who is not looking at how derivatives can be employed to manage financial and economic risks, or to enhance yields, is doing his or her investors a disservice.' So said Moody's Investor Service, Global Credit Research, *Derivatives Risk: A Growing Credit Concern*, in April 1994.

'Properly used' is probably one of the key phrases in the above quotation, and this leads us into the maze of risk management issues when using derivative instruments in investment management activity. It is generally assumed that because derivatives can increase the gearing of a position they by definition also increase the risk. This is not necessarily the case. Furthermore, to paraphrase Robert C. Merton, George Fisher Baker Professor of Business.

> Administration at the Harvard Business School, there are at least 10 ways to take a leveraged position in the US stock market, and not all of them involve the use of derivatives. One, you can buy on margin in the cash stock market; two, you can go long futures contracts; three, you can go long OTC forward contracts; four, you can enter into a swap contract to receive the total return on the S&P500 and pay LIBOR; five, you can go long exchange-traded calls or short exchange-traded puts on the S&P500; six, you can go long OTC calls or short OTC puts; seven, you can repo finance for a purchase of an equity-linked note which pays based on the S&P500 return; eight, you can purchase a certificate of deposit which has payments linked to the S&P500 return; nine, you can either buy on margin or purchase the capital-appreciation component of unit investment trusts; and ten, you can borrow to buy a variable-rate annuity contract whose return is linked to the S&P500.

Risk and good investment management are not, contrary to most press commentators' perceptions, mutually exclusive. The key is to understand truly the risk that is being taken on whenever a derivatives instrument is bought or sold. The manager might be heavily invested in G7 government bonds via either cash or derivatives. Seemingly low risk on the surface. But when the Fed raises rates unexpectedly, as they did last February and have done several times since, and you try to hedge out the risk, you may find that there is no market in which to get your cover. A portfolio which yesterday looked sensible, innocous and low-risk, is now classified at a different end of the risk spectrum – and the reward does not look so hot.

From 1991 to the beginning of 1994 playing the leveraged fixed income game was almost a one way bet. It has been said that you had to be very unlucky not to make money and it made many fund managers in this market look like heros. Last year, of course, changed all that. The result of spectacular losses by fund managers and proprietary traders alike, forced both players and investors in the industry to look much more carefully at the various risk issues.

Liquidity, transparency and valuation are to us the three most important areas. These apply equally to fund managers looking to buy or sell any derivative instruments, and investors who are looking to invest in managers who themselves may invest in derivative instruments. You will find more on the investor issues in the next chapter.

On the subject of liquidity, how easy is it to get in or out of a particular position? What happens if numerous other market participants want to do the same thing?

When it comes to transparency, what are you buying or selling? As many investors in the macro hedge funds found out last year, they really had no idea just what they had invested in. Total transparency is crucial if you want or need to be able to value your portfolio at any given time, no matter how frequently. And if you cannot value your portfolio quickly and frequently, are you breaching any fiduciary responsibilities?

You may know that there are a number of peculiar accounting anomalies in many jurisdictions around the globe which almost encourage opaque reporting and infrequent portfolio valuation. It is perfectly acceptable in many areas for highly sophisticated and esoteric derivative instruments, which may fluctuate wildly in price, to sit on the books at the purchase price, and be marked to market only when the position is undone. Marking to market only at purchase and sale is an unusual activity for a manager with a serious concern for risk management. If the manager does not know what risk is in the portfolio, how can he/she possibly control the risk?

8
Investor considerations and fund selection

Although they may not seem to fit that comfortably together, this chapter covers investor considerations and fund selection with marketing. This chapter is the only one which remains virtually unchanged from our last book. If it helps to show how the process of creating, selling and investing in derivatives products is not that complicated it will achieve its purpose in demystifying and clarifying something which has, in the past, been used to charge high prices!

Investor considerations

Risk management

Although in many quarters derivatives still enjoy the reputation as a maverick investment medium, the truth is that they are becoming increasingly well regarded as effective tools in the management of portfolio risk. The hiatus and furore in the financial media in the spring of 1994 mainly reflected journalistic ambulance-chasing. Diversification is the essential stratagem in the portfolio manager's approach to macro-risk management. The objective is to reduce risk by selecting investments that tend to perform differently from one another over time. While the method is eminently sound, many an expensive mistake has been made by concentrating too closely on the choice of the 'macro' components and thereby neglecting the risks inherent in the individual elements themselves. As we are concerned here with derivatives, we will now take a closer look at some of the issues that should be addressed regarding effective management of their associated risk.

Basic elements of associated risk

The risks associated with derivatives and fund management fall into two categories – the risks associated with developing a portfolio and the ongoing management risks. Many of the issues have been either briefly referred to, or in some cases more extensively considered, elsewhere in this volume. Some of the issues are substantial enough to merit the dedication of entire books to their discussion. Our objective here is to highlight a few of the specific risks associated with both the development and the management of a derivatives portfolio – be it a fund or an individual account. Decisions have to be made regarding the investment managers – whether to use one manager or a group of them; which managers to use; how to select them. Other considerations include the investment approach and the market sectors. How important is the investment approach? How do you decide whether to opt for a single sector or fully diversified fund? Are there any liquidity constraints on using certain markets? A more mundane but none the less crucial consideration is the brokerage house; which company should be used to clear the transactions and provide the necessary reports? Finally, there is the issue of currency exposure. Is there a risk to the fund and its investors? Should anything be done about this risk?

The investment managers

Whether you choose to use one or more investment manager, you are looking generally at the ability of the individual or the group to produce consistent, positive returns over an agreed period of time for a specified level of risk. Such a simple requirement; the difficulties start with deciding which manager(s) should be selected.

The current wisdom in the derivatives industry is that multi-manager funds will tend to be less risky than funds using a single investment manager. Although it is interesting to note that of the 750 funds tracked by TASS, less that 25 per cent are multi-manager or fund of fund products. The practice derives straight from the precepts of portfolio diversification: in a volatile industry spreading the risk across different investment styles and different markets should improve overall performance by smoothing out the inconsistency of returns.

Extensive mathematical analysis, indicates that the ideal multi-manager derivatives portfolios are comprised of eight to fourteen specialist investment managers. While portfolios with fewer managers may yield higher absolute returns, their higher risk characteristics result in lower risk-adjusted performance. According to the study, risk-adjusted performance peaks in the range of eight to fourteen managers, then gradually turns down as more managers are added (see Figure 8.1).

Deciding how to evaluate and select investment managers is the subject of much powerful debate in the industry with all participants seeking to find (and in some cases claiming to have found) the perfect crystal ball to put together the optimum portfolio which will ensure continuous positive returns for minimal risk. Despite this common objective, most of these involved in the selection process fall into one of the following three categories. First, there are the

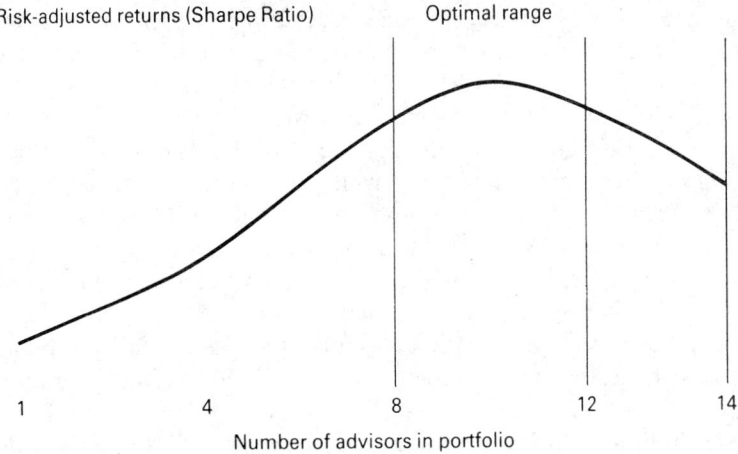

Figure 8.1 Optimal portfolio size for fund structure, based on averages of random portfolio sampling.

'quants' whose evaluation of investment managers is based solely on statistical analysis. Second, there are those for whom quantitative analysis is relatively unimportant and who believe in the superior value of diligent qualitative analysis. Third, there are those who employ both quantitative and qualitative analytical methods to review and select managers.

Consider briefly one of the 'hottest' issues in the business, namely, whether statistical analysis is a valuable component of the evaluation of investment managers and their track records. The measures of risk and reward used in this analysis are numerous. The relative value of using one over and above another is a matter of subjective judgement. What the analyst has to decide is which measures are good and which are bad; which are useful and which are not useful.

Possibly the most widely used yardstick for measuring risk is standard deviation. Standard deviation is a commonly used measure of dispersion. It is the square root of the variance and is based on the deviation of observations from the mean. More simply, it measures the average distribution of returns around the mean and is therefore a statistical indicator of the variability of returns. While standard deviation is one of the more valuable risk measures it does, however, have a major weakness; it does not tell you whether there may be upside skew or downside skew in the performance record where there is any pull away from the mean. If you use the measure blindly as a screening tool and are not fully aware of the numbers that comprise the statistic, you may be inadvertently giving up good upside performance because you have chosen to ignore managers with a seemingly high standard deviation.

Another statistical measure that is widely used in measuring performance is the Sharpe Ratio. This ratio endeavours to quantify the relationship between reward and risk by removing the risk-free rate of return. To arrive at the ratio you take the average monthly rate of return, subtract from this the risk-free rate of return (i.e. the return that could be achieved if the money allocated to investment in derivatives was instead allocated to investment in risk-free instruments such as United States Treasury Bills) and divide this by the standard deviation of the monthly rates of return. What you are left with is the reward for pure risk-taking. The higher the ratio, the better the performance and vice versa. However, there are two weaknesses to using the Sharpe Ratio as a screening tool and measure of risk. First, it is essential to have faith in all components of the equation. Second, we are aware of several different methods which can be used to compute the ratio. If you are comparing different Sharpe ratios, make sure that they have been computed using the same formula.

Sophisticated computer technology can produce statistics to support or disprove almost any particular viewpoint ('lies, lies and damned statistics'). Of the many measures used in the statistical analysis of historic performance records, some are useful and others redundant. We recommend that you leave the convoluted mathematics to the quants and focus on familiarising yourself sufficiently well with each measure to know why you should accept or reject either the measure itself or the figure that it generates.

Qualitative analytical procedures will vary from fund manager to fund manager and from company to company depending, among other things, on internal policy and requirements. As a minimum it should incorporate the following: an overall assessment of the company and its key personnel; an assessment of the investment and trading programme, the objectives and strategy; a review and analysis of the money management, risk management and administrative practices; and a review of the performance record. Such analysis is conducted generally with two objectives in mind: to assist the selection process or to justify decisions already taken.

Whichever evaluation method is used, and however sophisticated the analytical tools employed, it is worth remembering that all fund managers and investors alike are restricted to using yesterday's news to select today's portfolio which they hope will produce the same (or better) returns tomorrow. No single method is foolproof, and there are certainly no guarantees.

Investment approach

Any manager, when asked, will stress the uniqueness of his or her investment style. However, there are a number of categories which purport to define the investment approach. When selecting a portfolio of managers beware of choosing an exclusive group using identical or even similar investment approaches. What on the surface can look like the ultimate in effective diversification, might just turn out to be as diverse and effective as using a single manager. A recent example is the performance of the technical trend-followers in the month of January 1991 or, more particularly, on 15 and 16 January. As we are sure you will recall, the United Nations deadline to Iraq to withdraw peacefully from Kuwait ended on 15 January 1991. During the previous few weeks and as we got close to this deadline, the dollar, gold and oil markets were trending up in a way that would have encouraged even the most hardened contrarian to go long. Most trend-followers were long of at least one of these markets. However, few of them made profits in the month. When the markets corrected themselves sharply on 16 January, most of these managers, following the signals of their trading systems, were still long: an unfortunate situation for investors using one trend-follower; a potentially disastrous situation for investors using a number of trend-followers.

A slightly alarming development for the supporters of the non-correlation argument was the poor performance of the derivatives-investment industry in early 1994. After a good run with the bulls in 1993 on the stock and bond rallies there were substantial losses when markets collapsed in early 1994 (see also the details in Chapter 5). In theory these traders should have been making money on the short side – which by the second quarter they had begun to do. We look at the convergence point in the next chapter.

Market sectors

An investment manager's performance is only as good as his or her ability to interpret and take advantage of potential market movements. Some advisors invest across a diverse range of markets; other specialise in a particular market sector. Selecting a manager based on historic performance presupposes that the manager will continue to use the same markets, that market conditions will be repeated and that the manager will have no difficulty moving in and out of the markets despite the increase in money under management. None of these factors can be guaranteed.

As the amount of money that an advisor manages increases so too can the difficulty of moving in and out of the markets efficiently unless leverage is reduced. A manager specialising in the currency and the United States financial markets which are exceedingly deep will be in a stronger position than a manager using some of the more traditional commodity markets or the newer financial-derivatives markets which are less liquid and therefore more volatile.

We are not suggesting that the less liquid markets should be avoided; we are simply suggesting that when assessing the risk profile of either a current or future fund, and in particular a fund which envisages adding substantial business to the markets, serious consideration should be given to the historic and prevailing market conditions and volumes and the manager's skill in handling increases in equity. Some of the hedge-fund problems arose from illiquidity in their positions and an inability to mark positions to any realistic price.

The brokerage house

All too often the fund-processing, accounting and reporting issues are neglected; a situation which endangers the potential of even the most carefully researched and developed portfolio. Choosing the right brokerage house to execute and clear the transactions can make a critical difference to the overall management and administration of a fund.

The past few years have not produced the rosiest image of the brokerage community. We have witnessed a number of spectacular and not so spectacular closures and mergers, some of these as a result of fraudulent practice and others as a result of mismanagement. In 1988 Shearson American Express took over E. F. Hutton; in 1989 Thompson McKinnon went into Chapter 11 in the United States; in early 1990 Drexel Burnham Lambert went into Chapter 11 in the United States and administration in the United Kingdom; later in 1990 Stotler closed down and at the end of 1990 Balfour MacLaine withdrew from the business. Regulators have made considerable improvements in the monitoring of these groups. Even so investors should make sure they are dealing with reputable and well-capitalised groups. Even then there can be uncertainties as with Kidder Peabody in 1994.

Deciding what makes a good brokerage house and whether or not to use it is ultimately, like most things, a subjective decision; although a sound capital base is an essential start. That old adage 'People buy from people' is probably as true today as it was when first exclaimed; however, no harm ever befell anyone for conducting some thorough due diligence. The better, stronger brokerage houses are often subsidiaries of banks.

The broker should have a good relationship with both the management of the fund and with the investment managers. The investment managers should be able to rely not only on prompt executions, but also on timely and efficient delivery of daily equity runs and other required statements. The fund manager should be able to receive daily, weekly, monthly and any other reports as and when required and requested. If you are being charged more than US$20 per round turn transaction for the overall service, we suggest that you discuss the terms.

Fund administration

The fund administrator plays an important role and a few special considerations are worth bearing in mind. Location and time zone are vital for regulatory and operational purposes. Exchange control and tax regulations need to be checked. Efficient communication and language compatability are obvious prerequisites.

The fund administrator can do the following:

In the set-up phase:
1. help set up the right fund professionally;
2. help arrange the legal incorporation;
3. introduce auditors, legal advisors, directors, etc.;
4. print the fund's documentation-offering document, shares, etc.

During the fund's life:
1. calculate the funds value as required;
2. prepare necessary financial reports;
3. provide registrar services;
4. pay dividends;
5. provide facilities for the fund's meetings;
6. maintain corporate documents.

Currency risk

Some of the following will be self-evident, however currency exposure can be an important investment-risk consideration in derivatives usage, even if it generally less than that of traditional international market exposures. The investor's exposure always depends on his starting point! Any fund denominated in a currency other than US dollars and engaging investment managers using the United States derivatives markets is obviously exposed to exchange rate risk during the period when open positions are being held. Therefore profits in dollars could be significantly less healthy once converted back into the base currency. Similarly, what might appear to be small losses in dollars could become much greater losses as a result of conversation into the base currency. Very elementary stuff. What is not always so elementary is what to do about this possible situation. You can, of course, ignore the problem in the hope that on balance over time any currency movements will equal out on a net basis. However, for trustees who prefer a more disciplined approach, there are other options.

Let us take the example of a sterling denominated fund. Margin can be deposited in sterling. The cash balance can remain in sterling. So far, no real exposure. Open positions, however, might be valued in US dollars. Any variation margin required for these open positions will be valued in dollars but can be deposited in sterling. When the open positions are closed the dollar profit or loss can be converted into sterling immediately. The effect of this conversion will be to increase or decrease either the profit or the loss.

Hedging a fund against currency risk is rather like trying to hit a constantly moving target which erratically changes direction. Not only can the markets in which the fund holds open positions go up and down, and not only can the exchange rate fluctuate, there is, in addition, no way of knowing the length of time over which a position will be held open. A position might be held for a few hours; alternatively, it might be held for a few months.

The fund manager seeking to reduce the risk has quite a few options from which to choose. Depending on the desired length of the hedge, the first step is to decide the average monthly, quarterly, semi-annual or annual dollar exposure likely to be incurred by the fund and hedge this using currency forward or options. Currency overlay techniques are increasingly sophisticated.

Precision hedging is virtually impossible to execute; there are too many variables. Imperfect hedging should be considered, provided of course the cost of such protection does not outweigh the benefits. Hedging can be irritating, and time consuming, but none the less essential if you want to be protected against downpours; just as when you take out your umbrella because you think it is going to rain and the sun shines all day, so when you protect the fund against adverse currency fluctuations, the markets continually move in its favour. Murphy's Law states, however, that the day you forget the umbrella you can be almost guaranteed to get soaked.

Other general investor risks

1. Credit risks with the institution or fund's credibility.
2. Clearing and settlement risk.
3. Market risk – but that is what you are investing in – the opportunity part of the risk.
4. Market liquidity risk.
5. Market complexity and interdependency – that is, potential systemic risk.
6. Investors' authority to make the investment.
7. Appropriateness of the investment.
8. Adequate understanding of the risks.

Marketing and fund selection

The promoter's viewpoint

A derivatives fund, like insurance, has to be sold. No matter how appealing you think the fund is to potential investors, they are unlikely to beat a path to your door to hand over their money. Any and all marketing activity must be conducted within the regulatory framework (you could say restrictions) of the jurisdiction in which the fund is being promoted. Chapter 2 has already outlined the dos and don'ts with regard to fund promotion in the United Kingdom, the United States, Japan and Europe as a whole. We do not intend to stimulate you with a repetition of that scintillating information; here we will focus on the key issue of how to achieve your objectives by raising the expected amount of money within the given offer period.

Wherever they are domiciled and however they are structured, most funds require a minimum level of investment before the investment activity can begin. This is not so much for strictly legal or regulatory reasons, but more to ensure that the promoter can recover the initial costs of developing and launching the fund.

There are really three questions to be asked before deciding to market a fund. First, who is the target audience? Second, where do you find these potential investors and what are they likely to want to buy from your particular organisation? Third, how do you sell to them?

One should start by establishing a profile of the potential investor. It is obvious to assume that a fund with a minimum investment of a million dollars is unlikely to be particularly successful in attracting retail investors. On the other hand, a fund with a minimum investment of US$20,000 will have a broader appeal to the traditional retail market. Substantial institutional investors may find that the overall profile of the fund fits their specific requirements. Before even considering how to approach the investor, it is essential to define the potential audience. While there are a number of funds that appeal to both the retail and the institutional market, in the main they are directed at either one or the other. This is partly a function of fee-level acceptability and partly due to large investors tailoring their requirements.

The retail fund

Having decided to launch a fund aimed at the retail market, you now must decide on the particular sector. If the minimum investment is US$5,000, you will have a broader potential audience to sell to than if the minimum investment is US$50,000.

Once you have identified the target audience, the next step is to contact them and persuade them to part with their hard-earned or inherited cash. So how do you make the investors aware of your fund? Should you advertise it in the press, organise a direct-mail or telephone sales campaign, market through seminars, exhibit at conferences and trade shows or rely on your PR agency to do the job? There are no hard and fast rules about what works and what does not work. Your choice will probably be determined by the regulatory environment, the marketing budget, the placing power of your group, and previous experience. Whichever method you select, spreading the news and signing up the investors will be made much easier if you have a well-designed fund which has an edge on the market and genuine potential for performance.

It is also essential to have a strong network, whether large or small, of educated and well-trained sales personnel or agents. Although these points, along with much of what is being said in this chapter, are nothing more than common sense, they should not be treated lightly; to do so could add an unwelcome layer of risk to the fund as a whole.

Most funds, be they derivative funds, equity funds, property funds or any other form of collective investment, are generally promoted on the basis of the fact that in the past they have achieved (or would have achieved) good returns for the investors. To comply with regulatory requirements the promoters also point out that there are no guarantees that this healthy performance will continue. In our experience investors rarely take into account these disclaimers and focus instead solely on the upside potential. Knowing that successful derivatives funds are likely to show stronger performance than some of their equity counterparts, and that therefore the more ambitious (you could say greedy) investor will undoubtedly express interest, it is important that the point-of-sale representative genuinely understands the type of fund that he or she is selling and is able to explain fully the downside risk as well as the upside potential. The last eventuality any fund manager wants is a mass of clients who withdraw their investment because the fund takes a nosedive which is acceptable in the context of the overall investment strategy, but for which the investor is not adequately prepared.

The institutional fund

As the derivatives fund industry has matured, an increasing number of fund promoters have sought to attract the institutional investor. The term 'institutional investor' is used in many ways. It can mean pension funds, commercial banks, investment banks, portfolio managers, fund of fund managers, securities houses and insurance companies to name but a few. The attraction of offering a fund solely to the institutional market-place is obvious. Money under management objectives can be achieved with relatively fewer clients, and the administration need not be so daunting a prospect. The charges will, however, almost certainly have to be lower.

Institutional funds can be marketed far more freely than their retail counterparts – at least from a regulatory point of view. However, this does not necessarily make them any easier to sell. Unlike their retail counterparts, many institutional fund managers have specific investment objectives to achieve by a certain date in order for committed financial obligations to be met. What they do not need is a wild card added to the overall portfolio in the form of a poorly managed derivatives fund. There is also often a conflict in their giving funds to third-party managers.

Marketing to institutional investors requires patience, dedication, commitment and, of course, a strong product. Despite the great strides that have been made over the past five or six years, most potential investors still regard the whole sector with a substantial degree of suspicion, and long-standing attitudes are not easily changed. Anyone offering a fund to the institutional market-place should be prepared to engage in a slow moving and lengthy education process before coming close to achieving the objectives.

The main problems institutions have with investing are:

1. high fees;
2. difficult to monitor investment strategies;
3. tax issues;
4. illiquidity concerns/leverage concerns;
5. job risk if the investment goes wrong!

The main reasons institutions are given for investing are:

1. non-traditional strategies for diversification;
2. low or non-correlation with performance of other investments;
3. less volatility than equities/higher returns than bonds;

4. incentivised fees (pay for performance);
5. co-investment with the specialist (his money is at risk with yours);
6. access to proprietary traders in institutions.

The purchaser's viewpoint

Selecting a derivatives fund

If you or one of your clients is considering investing in a derivatives fund, how do you decide which one to select? Should it be onshore or offshore? Should it be high yield or low risk? Should the fund offer any form of 'guarantee'? How much should be invested? What historic performance should the fund show? Should the fund be limited to a certain market sector or should it be fully diversified?

Should the fund be single or multi-advisor? How easy should it be to add to the investment? How easy should it be to redeem or switch? Should profits be reinvested or paid out? What are the fee and commission levels? What is the tax position? What is the maximum liability to the investor? The relative importance of each of these questions will naturally vary from investor to investor. We can offer some guidelines that may help to simplify the process of fund evaluation and selection.

Onshore or offshore?

The issues that should be considered with regard to investing in either an onshore or an offshore fund are not exclusive to the derivatives-fund market. They apply to funds in general. Apart from the tax considerations, the key issue is investor protection. How well are the investors' interests protected (if at all) in the event that the fund self-destructs as a result of poor management or questionable practice? Some offshore centres have significantly more stringent requirements than others regarding which companies they will welcome as fund sponsors. Investors should get professional clarification.

Risk/reward profile?

It is important for all investors to understand and accept the inevitable trade-off between reward and risk. In general, derivatives-fund risk is assessed by the percentage of money under management actually allocated to outright, unhedged derivatives investment. In the United Kingdom, for example, a non-geared, or unleveraged, futures and options fund (FOF) is not considered a high-risk vehicle. FOFs may invest in futures and options provided they are fully covered by other fund assets or they may invest in these instruments for the purpose of efficient portfolio management.

Internationally, 'guaranteed funds' are the most prevalent form of low-risk funds. These are funds which provide a return of capital guarantee at the end of a specific investment period. They offer the investors the opportunity to invest in the derivatives markets safe in the knowledge that even if the trading activity of the fund is unsuccessful, they will at least get their initial investment back. There is, however, one snag; to benefit from the guarantee investors may not redeem before the maturity date, which could be anything from five to ten years. Substantial funds have recently been raised internationally using the bond type structure (especially by Citibank). Greater flexibility on the redemption side has been developing. A low interest rate does not help the guarantee type product so more funds with yields have been created and sold, especially by French banks such as Socgen.

High-yield investments can also be classified as those which are higher risk. Typically, they are neither curtailed by investment restrictions nor do they offer return of capital guarantees. They do offer the potential for substantially greater returns, but with a corresponding increase in the level of risk – as a result of the leverage potential in the derivatives market.

The investors' objectives and requirements will dictate whether they choose a high-yield or a low-risk fund. It is worth remembering that although the level of gearing is the most common way to define a high-yield or a low-risk fund, there are plenty of other risk factors to consider before opening an account.

How much to invest?

Opinions in the industry differ regarding the percentage of an investor's portfolio that should be invested in a derivatives fund. The general rule of thumb is that only pure risk capital should be invested. Depending on your means and objectives and your definition of risk capital, this might be anything from 1 per cent to 20 per cent of your total investment portfolio. Naturally, the lower the expected level of risk, the greater the portion that can safely be allocated.

Whatever the amount an investor decides to commit, he or she is almost certain to be disappointed. The allocation of a very small percentage of the portfolio to a derivatives fund will doubtless be regarded as too cautious when the fund produces stupendous returns; on the other hand, the allocation of a larger percentage of the portfolio will likely be regarded as irresponsible when the fund produces lacklustre returns!

Performance

Most funds are sold on the basis of their historic performance. The figures that the fund sponsors usually advertise are either the average monthly or the average annual rates of return. While these numbers are useful, they do not give the whole picture and can gloss over some crucial historic performance information. It is very easy to select the 'best' performing fund or the top ten funds by simply comparing rates of return. Those with the highest numbers go to the top of the pile. What these numbers do not show is the volatility experienced in the course of achieving these returns, nor do they show the overall balance between risk and reward. Although the historic performance of a fund is unlikely to be repeated exactly, being aware of the relationship between return and risk is essential to shortlisting and ultimately selecting the fund which dovetails best with the investors' expectations and risk parameters. Investors should be sure they are buying 'real' performance not simulated maximisations.

Single sector or diversified?

The current vogue among product sponsors is to offer two types of fund. Those which invest solely in a single-market sector, such as a currency fund, and those which invest in a cross-section of financial and commodity derivatives markets. The decision to opt for either one or the other is, in most cases, simply a matter of personal choice. If you are looking to establish a diversified derivatives investment it is well to remember that you can do so by assembling one or more diversified fund, or by constructing a portfolio using a number of different single-sector funds.

Single-advisor or multi-advisor funds?

A single-advisor fund is one which uses a sole derivatives fund manager to develop and implement the investment strategy. A multi-advisor fund is one which uses a number of derivative fund managers. Is one type of fund better than the other?

Most fund sponsors currently prefer multi-advisor funds. With good reason: the products generally are easier to sell. Well-constructed multi-adviser funds should, in theory, offer the investor a better balance between risk and reward than a single-advisor fund. While the single-advisor fund might produce higher absolute returns, multi-advisor funds often can offer more consistent overall performance. It is critical, however, that the individual investment managers who make up the multi-manager team, complement one another and do not correlate closely with one another. It is easier to change managers in a multi-advisor mix.

Redemption's and additions

The more flexible the structure, the more attractive the investment will seem to the investor. The ease with which additions and withdrawals can be made will depend upon how the fund is structured and where it is based. Most funds specify particular dealing dates on which investors may increase or decrease their holdings. The frequency of these dates might differ from fund to fund but should be clearly stated in the fund documentation. The investment dealing date may be monthly, but the redemption dealing date quarterly or even annual. Make sure you read the small print and know the terms. In some situations, the investor will be charged for the privilege, in others he or she will not. Guaranteed funds generally allow the investor to redeem in advance of the maturity date, but by so doing, the investor forfeits the right to benefit from the return of capital guarantee. Closed-ended funds (usually structured as closed-ended investment companies) lock in the investor until the maturity date. Closed-entry funds let the investor redeem on the appropriate dealing dates, but do not allow for additional investment.

Profits paid out or reinvested?

Most of the derivatives funds that have been launched in the last ten years have the power to pay out profits to the investors. However, the majority do not do so and prefer to reinvest the profits instead. Many of the larger, more successful managers choose to make distributions of profits from time to time. The potential to recoup initial commitment and the promise of profit distributions may well enhance the fund's appeal to potential investors.

Fees and commissions

Fee and commission levels have a direct effect on the ability of the fund to perform. Most funds (excluding those located in the United Kingdom where the concept of basing compensation on performance has yet to be introduced) have at least four potential fee levels. These are the following:

1. introductory fees;
2. management fees;
3. incentive performance fees;
4. transaction fees (brokerage commissions).

Introductory fees

Introductory fees, which can range from 1 per cent to 7 per cent, are paid to sales agents for introducing the business to the fund sponsors. These fees take two forms. They can be in the form of a one-off payment when the investment is first introduced, or they can be paid on an ongoing basis with the sales agent receiving compensation either monthly, quarterly or annually for the duration of the investment in fund. Money to pay the introducers generally comes from one of the following sources: first, it can come straight from the investors' initial investment; alternatively, it can be paid out of the management fees; lastly, it can be paid out of the brokerage commission in the form of a 'trailing' compensation generated by the ongoing transactions of the fund. Sales fees are a standard cost – although not one (generally) paid by institutions.

Management fees

Management fees currently range from 1 per cent to 6 per cent of assets under management per annum. Although the average today is 1.5 per cent to 2 per cent. There are usually two beneficiaries – the fund sponsor and the fund managers. Each investment manager is remunerated only on the basis of the precise amount he or she is managing. The fund sponsor, however, is remunerated on the assets of the whole fund. There is not currently a hard and fast international standard indicating, for example, whether interest income should be included in total asset calculation or not. As a result, practices vary from fund to fund. Investors should note that fees are paid on traded assets in many cases, which is the total value of the accounts the managers can trade.

While this may not be in itself a bad thing, it can make it difficult to compare one fund with another precisely. Investors should be aware that there is usually no spread on the purchase price of a fund. They trade at net asset value. To this extent derivatives fund charges are generally more transparent than other products.

Incentive fees

As with the management fee, there can be two beneficiaries of the incentive, or the performance, fee. The bulk of the fee goes to the derivatives investment managers; a small percentage will sometimes be distributed to the fund sponsor (who is effectively rewarded for selecting both the well- and poorly-performing managers). No performance; no incentive fee. Although a number of methods can be used to calculate incentive fees, the fee is in essence a percentage of net new high profits earned for the fund. How these 'new high profits' are defined and when the fee is calculated can vary. Some managers calculate the figures monthly or annually; most do them quarterly. Timing, however, is a relatively minor concern. Others are much more prickly indeed. Should the interest income earned on assets not allocated to trading be included in 'net new' profits for example? Some industry participants argue that it is outrageous for an investment manager to earn an incentive fee on interest income. Others argue that the manager who makes a deliberate decision to stay out of the markets for a time, has made a responsible investment decision and has every right to charge an incentive fee on interest income.

In multi-advisor products a major issue can arise from the fact that some managers might make profits and receive incentive fees whilst others might lose, with a net result of no absolute performance for the investor. This seems very inequitable given the dilution of investor funds. Some fund sponsors now promote products which have netted (i.e. absolute) incentive fees and make the investment advisor take the netting risk. An example is Derivative Market Holdings launched by Mees Pierson Derivatives in August 1994.

Fees vary widely in practice, from 12 per cent to 33 per cent (fees as high as 50 per cent have been known), although the average is around 20 per cent. As a rule of thumb, the lower the management fee the higher the incentive fee and vice versa. In some instances, although they are rare, management fees are not charged and incentive fees are substantially higher than the norm.

Brokerage commissions and transaction costs

Unlike management and incentive fees, brokerage commissions are a relatively straightforward issue. Discussion centres on how high or low the commission levels should be, and not how they should be calculated. They represent the cost of getting in and out of the markets. These fees will vary from fund to fund and generally range from 2 per cent to 25 per cent per annum as a percentage of equity under management. The per-contract cost should be below US$20.00 to be reasonable. Very roughly speaking every extra 5 US dollar per round turn charge over cost (15 US is about the cost level) is the equivalent of a 1 per cent annual charge to the fund/account.

Naturally, the lower the overall fee structure, the greater the opportunity for the fund to perform. Cheapest, however, does not necessarily mean best. Unlike that delightful phrase that bad taste does not always come cheap; bad fund management can definitely come cheap.

Maximum liability

In the event that the performance of the fund moves drastically against expectations, what is the maximum that an investor can lose? Almost all funds limit the investors' losses to the amount initially invested. Any exposure in the markets which is beyond the capacity of the fund's assets is the responsibility of the fund manager. Under no circumstances should the investors be called upon to invest additional capital in such a situation. Make certain the small print confirms that this is the case.

Another danger may be an overlap of liability between different funds or products in a series issues by a common sponsor. Investors should establish that their product cannot suffer from such third-party claims. Many products have an automatic 'close-out' policy at 25 to 30 per cent loss levels as an extra layer of insurance.

General derivatives risk considerations

1. Profitability tends to occur in moments of sharp price movement. In static or ranging markets the managers usually trade unsuccessfully.
2. Derivatives markets are leveraged and volatile – any changes in the levels of leverage affect both the fund's historic performance calculations and the likely future results.
3. Derivatives markets can become illiquid – either due to artificial price and trading limits imposed by exchanges or other 'act of God' type events.
4. The fees and commissions charged for derivatives are considered high. This is partly because equally high fees in other investment vehicles are more cunningly concealed – but the combination of different parties involved in the public funds and the 'ground-breaking' nature of some of the product design tend to create high overall costs. There is some argument that if the fees are taken against the face value of the market exposures

they are not that much higher than traditional fund-management areas. It is also relevant these funds tend to trade at net asset value with no spread and that the fees are generally very transparent.
5. In a worse-case scenario there can be counterparty, broker, exchange and clearing-house risk for positions taken in the derivative markets. In our view, the off-exchange and over-the-counter contracts are considerably more exposed to this danger than exchange-traded products. Liquidity and price transparency may also be worse for these markets.
6. The international nature and contract mixture does mean that unless the investment managers have effective hedging mechanisms there is currency exposure as well as market exposure for investors.
7. Due to the nature and timing of the available opportunities derivatives traders may become over concentrated in particular markets. This works to the investor's advantage (the wall of money) until everyone decides to try to get out at once (the fixed-interest and government-bond markets in February/March 1994)
8. The number of specialist derivative managers is quite limited – at least in terms of those with long-established reputations, good performance and significant funds under management.
9. Most public-fund vehicles have significant (usually disclosed) conflicts of interest between the different parties. These arise because all the parties are undertaking similar activities on behalf of other funds or investors, possibly at different fee rates.

With improved regulation and the involvement of the main international financial institutions in this business there has been a general improvement in the quality and pricing of the recent derivative-market-orientated funds. We expect to see continuing cost reductions for the investor and less differentiation of the product from other investment mediums.

9
Where to from here?

Few reading this book will remember the time when investment in equities was considered highly unusual. Fund management has evolved during the twentieth century as investors' acceptance and management of risk has developed. From the 1920s to the 1950s bonds were all the rage and the idea of investing an a stock was regarded as anything from innovative to rash. It definitely was not a mainstream thing to do. Then in the 1950s the so-called equities cult started. People started to have surplus money to invest – the home was covered, the children's education covered (whether public or private) and there was more than one change of clothing in the wardrobe.

Are we now, in the 1990s, in the derivatives cult? And, if so, is this going to be a passing phase?

Unlikely.

When it comes to fund management, derivatives have a range of applications which greatly increase the choice and flexibility of managers. The focus can still be on the stock and bond markets, but investors now have the option (no pun intended) to operate in either the cash or the derivative markets. The speed at which information is disseminated via increasingly powerful computer and telecommunications systems means that decisions to increase or decrease exposure to a particular market can be executed using derivatives in minutes rather than days. Valuations can be market to market almost on a real time basis. Fund management is becoming more and more competitive. Two key factors keep the 'best' ahead of the rest of the pack: first, knowledge and information; and second, the ability to interpret and act on this information wisely and speedily.

Managed derivatives are also unlikely to go away. Over the next decade or two managed derivatives will converge with the traditional fund-management industry to become just one of a series of alternatives from which the investor can choose to build and maintain the required portfolio mix. Contrary to being regarded as a maverick investment sector from another solar system, investments employing managed derivatives will become an acceptable and ordinary component of mainstream fund management.

You do not have to be either a die-hard or a born-again derivatives fan to spot the more obvious reasons why their varying applications in fund management is unlikely to be a passing phase. First, the knowledge base is growing. And it is doing so through a process of osmosis. Every year over the past 15 to 20 years more and more individuals have become involved in the derivatives markets and a high percentage of them have stayed. Ten years ago it is estimated that there were some 2,500 floor brokers and traders on the Chicago exchanges. Liffe sported approximately 500. Today those numbers have increased to 15,000 in Chicago and 4,000 on Liffe. The Matif, which is less than ten years old, currently has 2,200 traders and brokers on the floor.

The floor participants are relatively easy to keep count of because the exchanges require each individual to be accounted for through some form of permit. The desk traders, fund managers and salesmen, however, are not so easy to count but they have been growing consistently in number over the past decade. And as for the operations and back-office staff, you only have to look at the situations-vacant pages in the newspapers to see that demand is steady.

The exchange floors along with the corporate and institutional trading desks have been the spawning ground for many of the independent fund-management boutiques that have been established to date. As these players leave their jobs to build their own businesses, so their positions will probably be filled and somewhere down the chain *ingénues* will be introduced to the derivatives markets who should contribute to the continuing expansion of the knowledge base.

On the managed-money side of the derivatives industry, the growth in the number of independent or boutique fund-management operations has been startling over the past five years, particularly in Europe. As mentioned in Chapter 4, there are currently approximately 135 such organisations in Europe (and over 1,000 around the globe). Three years ago there were less than 30 in Europe. The individuals who set up these companies cite a number of different reasons for so doing. Among the more common are the desire to provide a highly flexible and superior fund-management service by freely being able to use derivatives, use leverage and short the market. Furthermore, to be compensated by being paid a percentage of the profits that are made for the investors. No profit, no pay.

Still the most difficult aspect of any fund-management business, be it in an established house or in a new boutique, is raising the money to manage. No funds under management, no fees to earn. Furthermore, the newer independent boutiques which are set up by both the excellent and indifferent managers, have a host of other issues to concern themselves with which, some might argue, have little to do with calling the markets correctly. Somebody has to deal with the compliance, administration, operations and personnel issues. In a nutshell, run the business so that the fund managers can get on with doing what they are supposed to be good at. In a number of cases these responsibilities have to be taken on by the investment managers (let's keep the overhead down, at least to start with) distracting them from the job of effectively managing the money.

Over the next decade or two we are likely to witness the convergence of the absolute return and traditional ends of the fund-management industry. For many of the reasons outlined above, the pace at which the independent boutiques are established will slow down. Furthermore, as the more traditional institutions start to incorporate practices long offered by the boutiques, there will be more incentive for the talented managers to stay put. Only those with a burning desire to run their own businesses will risk leaving the relative security of an established house and jump ship.

A number of the banks and investment banks have already responded to the fact that they are in danger of losing (and in a number of cases have in fact lost) some of their best trading talent to the 'boutique' end of the market. What they have done is to launch internal so-called hedge funds, managed by the banks' proprietary traders and offered to the banks' clients. The 'arrangement' with the traders varies from company to company. Suffice to say that in certain circumstances the trader's lot is almost as good as being independent without the hassle of having to run his or her own business. He only has to concern himself with managing the money. The compliance, administration, money raising and customer service are all handled by the bank. Among those who have done this are Bankers Trust, Salomon Brothers, Swiss Bank Corp, Paribas, CSFB, Citibank, First Chicago and, outside the banking world, Providence Capital.

Another reason for the future convergence of the traditional and managed-derivatives ends of the fund market is the steady convergence of the listed and OTC markets. The growth in EFP (exchange for physical) business, particularly in currencies, is but one example of this. Another is the inception in May 1994 of trading of futures and options contracts on individual stocks. Volumes might be relatively thin at the moment, the concept might not work, but around the world the initiative is being watched very closely.

We also expect to see the increased globalisation and convergence of regulation. We are operating in a world in which information can be disseminated in nano-seconds and transactions executed in seconds.

Assets under management will increase driven by new products, new investors and performance. The managed-derivatives and absolute-return industry will also be helped by more flexible regulations in countries which currently make it extremely difficult for banks and fund managers to offer anything other than a traditional bond or equity fund. Since the early 1990s, many new funds have been structured in two particular ways in order to greatly increase the distribution capability. Crédit Agricole and Moore Capital launched one of the first funds to be structured as a bond. Since then there have been a number of successful imitators including Citibank and Société General. The bond structure enables the fund sponsors to market the fund to institutions who are interested in investing in a managed-derivatives or absolute-return product but who might have difficulty getting such an investment through the usual investment committee red tape, unless of course the fund is packaged as an instrument with which they are more than familiar.

For the same reason (increased marketability) a growing number of funds are listing on either the Dublin or the Luxemburg stock exchange. Investors can take part by purchasing a listed security and doing so is relatively easy. They should, however, be aware that just because a fund is listed does not necessarily mean that it is a better investment than unlisted funds in the market. Furthermore, they should note who the fund's market-makers are, and how easy (or not) it will be to get out when they wish to do so.

Switcher funds are also becoming increasingly popular amongst the product developers. To date the market is dominated by certain UK houses and the focus has been almost exclusively on equities. Mercury Asset Management, John Govett and Foreign & Colonial are among the few who have bull and bear stock-index futures funds which the investors can switch in and out of. These funds have not been aimed solely at the institutional market-place, but have been offered to an audience which may never have been near a futures, derivatives, hedge or absolute-return fund.

One of the more interesting switcher funds to hit the market is the Global Manager Fund offered Bank of Bermuda. The master fund offers 31 separate funds providing the investor with access to most of the world's financial and commodity markets via futures. They can choose from the UK, United States, Japanese, European and Hong Kong equities markets; the UK, United States and German bond markets; the major currencies; gold; and the commodity markets. See Table 9.1.

What Bank of Bermuda are offering investors is a 'tool box' so that they can implement their own global asset-allocation and portfolio-management decisions. It is too early to tell whether this new product design will succeed and start a new trend for the industry. Investors can of course implement any of the above strategies without having to invest in such a fund; however, the size of the required investment and the overall cost to do so on an individual basis will be substantially higher.

As new futures and options exchanges are established around the world so the derivatives industry will continue to expand. The ever-increasing globalisation of markets will provide opportunities and pitfalls for both corporate and institutional participants. The so-called emerging markets, currently lacking in established and sophisticated derivative products, will develop both listed and OTC derivative instruments providing opportunities for players (the internal and the external) in their markets both to hedge and to invest without having to use the cash market. At the moment there are some 600 emerging markets funds which investors to choose from. Of these less than 5 per cent are so-called hedge funds. The main reasons for this are the difficulty

Table 9.1 The complete range of funds in the Global Manager umbrella

EQUITY FUNDS

	Index	Bear	Geared
UK (FTSE 100)	•	•	•
US (S&P 500)	•	•	•
JAPAN (NIKKEI DOW JONES 225)	•	•	•
GERMANY (DAX)	•	•	•
HONG KONG (HANG SENG)	•	•	•

BOND FUNDS

	Index	Bear
US TREASURY	•	•
UK GILT	•	•
GERMAN BUND	•	•

CURRENCY FUNDS

	Bull	Bear
POUND STERLING	•	•
DEUTSCHMARK	•	•
JAPANESE YEN	•	•

GOLD/CASH FUNDS

	Index
GOLD	•
US DOLLAR CASH	•

MANAGED FUNDS*

	Conservative	Active	Aggressive
	•	•	•

* to be launched

of shorting the market, and the difficulty of managing risk because there are comparatively few derivatives instruments to use.

We have now swung full circle to the fundamental reason for the development of derivatives during the past few centuries, and particularly during the latter half of the twentieth century. *Risk management.* Derivatives were originally developed to manage cash flow and profit and loss risk. Few corporates who understand how derivatives should be applied to do this, will predict anything other than the persistent expansion of their use.

Investment management should be no different. Intelligent and knowledgeable use of derivatives can provide extremely effective, cost-effective and flexible risk management. The derivatives market can also be considered an investment sector (some would argue asset class) in its own right enhancing and extending the range of investment opportunities. The innovative and creative fund managers, and the more demanding investors, are already aware of this. It is a matter of time before the rest understand the potential benefits to both investor and manager and follow suit.

The collapse of Baring Brothers Bank as a result of massive over exposure to exchange traded Japanese index futures contracts will be seen as a dampener on the development of this industry and the use of these markets.

It must be said that this is not an entirely logical reaction, given the apparent facts and circumstances of Baring's difficulties. However, adjustments will be made by some, if not all, users. The problem cases inevitably receive the largely negative, media attention, but the vast majority of users achieve their aims to a greater or lesser extent – but good news is no news.

After the dust has settled, depending on what the full circumstances turn out to have been, there is no reason why there should not continue to be serious use made of these markets for investment management purposes, as well as the more traditional uses.

1994 may have seen a return to more normal liquidity in the markets with the excess capital apparent at the end of 1993 having been reduced through a combination of losses, hedge fund liquidations and greater prudence on the part of users. Short term volatility may become less exaggerated which will enable better investment returns to be made.

The Barings story will no doubt make a successful book and film and it is certainly a thrilling, if tragic, morality tale of our times.

The publicised problems in 1994 reflect a minute part of the overall usage and activity and we believe represent no real hindrance to massive future growth in this field.

Appendices

These are a selection of general summary information on various aspects of the derivatives business. They are intended to assist the general reader with their understanding of the book.

Appendix A: The futures, derivatives and options markets
The basic ingredients!

Futures contracts

A futures contract is a standardised contract made on a domestic or foreign commodity exchange that calls for the future delivery of a specified quantity of a commodity, such as an agricultural, tropical or industrial commodity, currency, financial instrument or metal at a specified time and place. The size and terms of futures contracts on a particular item are identical and are not subject to any negotiation between the buyer and seller, except as to date of delivery, quantity and price.

The contractual obligations of a buyer/seller may be satisfied by taking/making physical delivery of an approved grade of the commodity or instrument or by making an offsetting sale/purchase of an identical futures contract prior to the designated date of delivery. The difference between the price at which the futures contract is purchased/sold and the price paid for the offsetting sale/purchase, after allowance for brokerage commissions, constitutes the profit or loss to the trader. Certain futures contracts, such as stock-index or other financial- or economic-index contracts, settle in cash (irrespective of whether any attempt is made to offset such contracts) rather than with delivery of any physical item.

In market terminology, a trader who purchases a futures contract is *long* in the market and a trader who sells a futures contract is *short* in the market. Before a trader closes out his long or short position by an offsetting sale or purchase, his outstanding contracts are known as *open trades* or *open positions*. The aggregate amount of open positions held by traders in a particular contract is referred to as the *open interest* in such contract.

Forward contracts

A forward contract is a contractual obligation to purchase or sell a specified quantity of a commodity or financial instrument at or before a specified date in the future at a specified price and, therefore, is similar to a futures contract. Unlike futures contracts, however, forward contracts are not standardised contracts; rather, forward contracts for a given commodity are generally available in any size and maturity and are subject to individual negotiation between the parties involved. Moreover, generally there is no direct means of offsetting or closing out a forward contract by taking an offsetting position as one would a futures contract on an exchange.

If a trader desires to close out a forward-contract position, he will generally establish an opposite position in the contract but will settle and recognise the profit or loss on both positions simultaneously on the 'prompt' date (i.e. the delivery date). Thus, unlike in the futures-contract market where a trader who has offset positions will recognise profit or loss immediately, in the forward market a trader with a position that has been offset at a profit will generally not receive such profit until the prompt date, and likewise a trader with a position that has been offset at a loss will generally not have to pay money until the prompt date.

In recent years, however, the terms of forward contracts have become more standardised, and in some instances such contracts now provide a right of offset or cash settlement as an alternative to making or taking delivery of the underlying commodity. Although forward contracts in commodities and financial instruments can be illiquid, the forward markets do provide what has typically been a highly liquid market for currency trading, and in certain cases the prices quoted for currency forward contracts may be more favourable than the prices for currency futures contracts traded on exchanges.

Options

An option on a futures contract, physical commodity, currency, financial instrument or other item gives the buyer of the options the right, but not the obligation, to take a position at a specified price (the 'strike', or 'exercise' price) in the underlying contract. The buyer of a 'call' option acquires the right, but not the obligation, to purchase or take a long position in the underlying contract, and the buyer of a 'put' option acquires the right, but not the obligation, to sell or take a short position in the underlying contract.

The seller (or 'writer') of an option is obliged to take a position in the underlying contract at a specified price opposite to the option buyer if the option is exercised. Thus, the seller of a call option must stand ready to take a short position in the underlying contract at the strike price if the buyer should exercise the option. The seller of a put option, on the other hand, must stand ready to take a long position in the underlying contract at the strike price.

A call option is said to be 'in-the-money' if the strike price is below current market levels, and 'out of the money' if the strike price is above current market levels. Conversely, a put option is said to be 'in the money' if the strike price is above the current market levels, and 'out of the money' if the strike price is below current market levels.

Options have limited lifespans, usually tied to the delivery or settlement date of the underlying contract. Some options, however, expire significantly in advance of such date. The purchase price of an option is referred to as its 'premium', which consists of its intrinsic value plus its 'time value'. As an option nears its expiration date, the time value shrinks and the market and intrinsic values move towards parity. An option that is out-of-the-money and not offset by the time it expires becomes worthless. On certain exchanges, in-the-money options are automatically exercised on their expiration date, but on others unexercised options become worthless after their expiration date.

The use of interrelated options and positions in the underlying contract can provide an additional means of risk management and permit a trader to retain a position in the underlying contract in hope of additional appreciation in that position, while at the same time allowing the trader to limit the effects of a move against the trader's position.

Selling options creates different and greater risks than buying options. The seller of a call option who does not have a long position in the underlying contract is subject to risk of loss should the price of the underlying contract be higher than the strike price prior to expiration of the option by an amount greater than the premium received for selling the option.

The seller of a call option who has a long position in the underlying contract is subject to the full risk of a decline in price of the underlying contract reduced by the premium received for selling the option. In exchange for the premium received for selling a call option, the option seller gives up all of the potential gain resulting from an increase in the price of the underlying contract above the strike price prior to the expiration of the option.

The seller of a put option who does not have a short position in the underlying contract is subject to risk of loss should the price of the underlying contract decrease below the strike price prior to expiration of the option by an amount in excess of the premium received for selling the option.

The seller of a put option who has a short position in the underlying contract is subject to the full risk of a rise in the price in the underlying contract reduced by the premium received for selling the option. In exchange for the premium received for selling a put option, the option seller gives up all of the potential gain resulting from a decrease in the price of the underlying contract below the strike price prior to expiration of the option.

Interest-rate and currency swaps

An interest-rate swap is a transaction in which two parties agree to make to each other periodic payments calculated on the basis of specified interest rates on a notional amount. It can be used to exchange one type of interest obligation for another and thereby enable a swap participant to tailor its interest obligations to meet its needs in a given interest rate environment. Typically, the payment to be made by one party is calculated using a floating rate of interest (such as the London Inter Bank Offer Rate (LIBOR), the Bank Bill Rate (BBR), etc.) while the payment to be made by the other party is determined on the basis of a fixed rate of interest or a different floating rate.

In its most common form, an interest-rate swap can be accomplished by two parties: the first, for example, may be a borrower which wants to pay interest at a fixed rate but which has already borrowed at a floating rate. The borrower wanting to pay a fixed rate borrows the principal amount that it needs, but on a floating rate basis. The borrower wanting to pay a floating rate borrows an identical amount at fixed rates. If a borrower was entering into the swap with respect to an existing debt, it would not undertake a new borrowing.

The two then enter into an agreement in which each undertakes to make periodic payments to the other in amounts equal to, or determined on the same basis as, the other's interest cost. Only payments calculated in the form of interest are made; payments corresponding to principal amounts are not made by either party. The net result of this exchange is that each party is able to obtain the type of interest rate, fixed or floating, which it wants and on acceptable terms.

In a currency swap, the counterparties do not lend currencies to each other but sell them to each other with a concomitant agreement to reverse the exchange of currencies at a determined rate and date in the future. The amount to be swapped is established in one currency, and the prevailing spot-exchange rate is used to establish the amount in the other currency. Currency swaps entail interest payments which take the form of a periodic (usually annual) payment by each counterparty to the other in the appropriate currency. The interest rates can be either fixed or floating.

Participants

The two broad classes of persons who trade Futures Interests are *hedgers* and *speculators*. Hedgers include financial institutions that manage or deal in interest-rate-sensitive instruments, foreign currencies or stock portfolios, and commercial interests, such as farmers and manufacturers, that market or process commodities. Hedging is a protective procedure designed to lock in profits that could otherwise be lost due to an adverse movement in the underlying commodity, for example, the adverse price movement between the time the merchandiser or processor makes a contract to buy or sell a raw or processed commodity at a certain price and the time he or she must perform the contract.

In such a case, at the time the hedger contracts to buy the commodity at a future date he or she will simultaneously sell a futures or forward contract for the necessary equivalent quantity of the commodity. At the time for performance of the contract, the hedger can offset the price change, if any, in the Underlying Interest, thus eliminating his or her original risk of price fluctuations between the date of purchase and the date of delivery.

Unlike the hedger, the speculator generally expects neither to make nor take delivery of the Underlying Interest. Instead, the speculator risks his or her capital with the hope of making profits from price fluctuations in the Futures Interests. The speculator is, in effect, the risk-bearer who assumes the risks that the hedger seeks to avoid. Speculators rarely make or take delivery of the Underlying Interest; rather they close out their positions prior to the delivery date. Since the speculator may take either a long or short position in Futures Interests, it is possible for him or her to make profits or incur losses regardless of whether prices go up or down. All trades made by the borrower will be for speculative rather than for hedging purposes.

Exchanges

Exchanges provide centralised market facilities for trading futures contracts and options (but not forward and swap contracts) relating to specified commodities. Members of a particular exchange and trades executed thereon are subject to the rules of that exchange.

Most exchanges have an associated 'clearing house'. Once trades between members of an exchange have been confirmed, the clearing house becomes substituted for each buyer and each seller of contracts traded on the exchange and in effect becomes the other party to each trader's open position in the market. Thereafter, each party to a trade looks only to the clearing house for performance. The clearing house generally establishes some sort of security or guarantee fund which acts as an emergency buffer that enables the clearing house, at least to a large degree, to meet its obligations with regard to the 'other side' of an insolvent clearing member's contracts. Furthermore, clearing houses require margin deposits and continuously mark positions to market to provide some assurance that their members will be able to fulfil their contractual obligations. Thus, a central function of the clearing houses is to ensure the integrity of trades, so that members effecting futures transactions on an organised exchange need not worry about the solvency of the party on the opposite side of the trade; their only remaining concerns are the respective solvency's of their commodity broker and the clearing house. Some exchanges also impose speculative position limits and other restrictions on customer positions to help ensure that no single trader can amass a position that would have a major impact on market prices.

Non-United States exchanges can differ significantly from their United States counterparts. In contrast to the United States exchanges, many non-

United States exchanges are *principals' markets*, where trades remain the liability of the traders involved, and the exchange or an affiliated clearing house, if any, does not become substituted for any party. Due to the absence of a clearing-house system, such exchanges are significantly more susceptible to disruptions. The results of default on such a market include the loss of substantial amounts, including profits which would otherwise be realised on a cleared exchange.

Also in contrast to United States exchanges, banks and other forward-contract participants must often satisfy themselves as to the individual credit-worthiness of each entity with which they enter into a forward contract. Commercial banks usually do not require any sort of margin deposit, but rely upon internal credit limitations, and their judgements regarding the credit-worthiness of their counterparts. Recently, certain forward-market participants have begun to require that their counterparts post margin.

Exchanges in the United States and their clearing houses are given reasonable latitude in promulgating rules and regulations to control and regulate their members. Examples of regulations by exchanges and clearing houses include the establishment of initial margin levels, size of trading units, contract specifications, speculative positions limits, and daily price-fluctuations limits. The CFTC reviews all such rules for United States exchanges (other than those relating to specific margin levels) and can disapprove, or with respect to certain of such rules, require the amendment or modification thereof. The extent to which non-United States exchanges regulate their members and trading activity varies widely. For example, on the London International Financial Futures and Options Exchange there are no speculative position limits on futures contracts.

Margins

Original or *Initial* margin is the minimum amount of funds that must be deposited by a trader with his or her broker to initiate and maintain an open position in futures and some options contracts. *Maintenance* or *variation* margin is the amount (generally less than the original margin) to which a trader's account may decline before he or she must deliver additional margin. A margin deposit is like a cash performance bond. It helps assure the trader's performance of the futures contracts that he or she purchases or sells. Futures contracts are customarily bought and sold on margins that represent a very small percentage (ranging upward from less than 2 per cent) of the aggregate purchase or sales price thereof. Because of such low margins, price fluctuations occurring in the futures markets may create profits and losses that, in relation to the amount invested, are greater than are customary in other forms of investment or speculation. The amount of margin required in connection with a particular futures contract is set from time to time by the exchange on which such contract is traded and may be modified from time to time by the exchange during the term of the contract.

Brokerage firms, carrying accounts for traders in Futures Interests may not accept lower, and generally require higher, amounts of margin as a matter of policy to further protect themselves.

Trading in the currency forward market, swaps and interbank currency markets does not require margin but generally does require the extension of credit by a bank to those with whom the bank trades. Effectively, traders still participate on a margin basis.

When a trader purchases an option, there is no margin requirement. However, the option premium must be paid in full. When a trader sells an option, on the other hand, he or she is required to deposit margin in an amount determined by the margin requirements established for the Underlying Interest and, in addition, an amount substantially equal to the current premium for the option. The margin requirements imposed on the selling of options, although adjusted to reflect the probability that out-of-the-money options will not be exercised, can in fact be higher than those imposed in dealing in the futures markets directly. Complicated margin requirements apply to *spreads* and *conversions* which are complex trading strategies in which a trader acquires a mixture of options positions and positions in the Underlying Interest.

Margin requirements are computed each day by a trader's broker. When the market value of a particular open position changes to a point where the margin on deposit does not satisfy maintenance margin requirements, a margin call is made by the broker. If the margin call is not met within a reasonable time, the broker may close out the trader's position.

Several major exchanges have recently established certain combined margining arrangements involving procedures pursuant to which the futures and options positions held in certain accounts will be aggregated and margin requirements assessed on a portfolio basis, measuring the total risk of the combined positions. Several overseas exchanges and clearing houses, such as those in London, margin brokers on a *net* basis offsetting profitable and unprofitable positions in a given account. This reduces the amount of margin which must be posted but increased the risks to the trader if the broker becomes insolvent.

Appendix B: Glossary of some frequent derivative terms

Basket: a portfolio of stocks
compo option: an option on an overseas asset valued, and with strike set, in the domestic currency (e.g. an ADR option, or an option on the sterling value of the S&P-500 index). The effective underlying is a compo(site) of the currency and domestic equity values.
CPEN: capital protected equity note – also known as a GRB.

equity index swap: a contract under which floating rate interest payments are 'swapped' for the performance of an equity index. Similar contracts can be set up for individual equities (equity swaps) and portfolios of stocks (basket swaps).

future: the obligation to buy (long) or sell (short) an underlying index.

GRB: guaranteed return bond, a combination of bond and equity, equity-basket or equity-index options, which provide protection of capital, but with upside equity exposure. All also known as a CPEN.

index future: a listed futures contract on an equity index.

option: the right to buy (call) or sell (put) an index or a stock at a set price.

OTC: a contract traded over-the-counter, i.e. directly with a counterparty and not through an open market.

programme trade: an agreement to execute a series of equity trades on a set basis.

quanto option: an option on an overseas asset which pays out at a fixed exchange rate.

quanto index swap: an index swap in which payouts calculated against local index values) are made at a fixed exchange rate. Also known as a differential swap.

spread option: an option on the difference between the prices of two assets.

warrant: a listed security with the right to buy (call) or sell (put) a stock at a set price.

Appendix C

We are listing a very brief outline of the various option strategies usable for portfolio protection purposes.

Most major bank members of the London Stock Exchange in the United Kingdom can provide better and more complete details. Exchange-traded options are recommended for short term trades, but the OTC sector is more flexible. These are put options – similar arrangements can be made for call option strategies – as always get professional advice!

Regular put option

Strategy

- Investor pays set premium today.
- Portfolio protected below strike level.

Key advantages

- Cheaper than alternative more flexible protection.
- Upside potential remains unlimited.

Key disadvantages

- Premium due in full today.

Collar

Strategy

- Investor buys put option with strike at or below market level.
- Investor sells a call option with strike at or above market level.

Key advantages

- Can be priced at zero net cost.

Key disadvantages

- Gains capped above strike of call option.

Barrier put options

Strategy

- Investor buys put option today.
- The put has an outstrike – a market level above spot at which the option expires.

Key advantages

- Premium less than regular put option.
- If the market does not trade above outstrike then the option behaves exactly like a regular put.
- Upside potential remains unlimited.

Key disadvantages

- If market trades above outstrike during life, option expires.

Contingent option

Strategy

- A put option is purchased today.
- The investor pays nothing today.
- The investor pays premium:
    only on the exercise date; and
    only if the option is in-the-money.
  This premium is referred to as the contingent premium.

Key advantages

- No premium due today.
- Premium only due if option expires in-the-money.
- Upside potential remains unlimited.

Key disadvantages

- Contingent put premium is more expensive than regular put premium (approximately regular call option price/delta).

Premium trigger option

Strategy

- The investor buys a put option today.
- The investor pays nothing today.
- Premium is only paid if the market trades down to a pre-agreed level, below strike, at any time during the life of the option.

Key advantages

- No premium due today.
- Investor receives protection at strike but only pays if market trades down to the pre-agreed trigger level.
- Upside potential remains unlimited.

Key disadvantages

- Trigger option premium, if paid, is more expensive than a regular put option.

Step-down trigger put option

Strategy

- A put option is purchased today.
- The investor pays fixed amounts at pre-defined market levels.

Key advantages

- No premium due today.
- Premium only due as protection becomes more likely to have value at expiry.
- Upside potential remains unlimited.

Key disadvantages

- If market trades all the way down to strike and total premium paid, then this amount is greater than premium due on a regular put option.

Extendible put option

Strategy

- A put option with a short life is purchased and paid for today.
- At the end of the initial term the option will either pay out parity or continue for a further pre-agreed term.

Key advantages

- Upside potential remains unlimited.
- If market drifts sideways, option can be extended for no additional premium.

Key disadvantages

- Option may pay out parity and additional protection may be required for a further term.

Variable life option

Strategy

- A put option with a short life is purchased and paid for today.
- At the end of the initial term the option can be abandoned or extended for a further premium payment.
- The option only pays out parity if it is extended to the full maximum term.

Key advantages

- Upside potential remains unlimited.
- If market drifts sideways, option can be abandoned for no additional premium.
- Allows flexibility and low initial outlay.
- Investor can give consideration as to whether the strategy should be further employed.

Key disadvantages

- Option outlay will be higher if full term taken up.

Instalment option

Strategy

- A put option is purchased today.
- The option is paid for in instalments at regular intervals.
- All instalments must be paid for in full.

Key advantages

- Premium can be spread over time.
- Upside potential remains unlimited.

Key disadvantages

- Total premium is more expensive than if it is received in full up front (simply by financing costs).

Pay as you go put option

Strategy

- A put option is purchased today.
- The option is paid for in instalments at regular intervals.
- If at any time the option is no longer required, it may be terminated and no further instalments are due.

Key advantages

- Where protection is required but the view is that the market is also likely to rally, this protection can be terminated early before full payment has been made. (At this point a regular put option would be very out-of-the-money and therefore not worth much to an investor who sells it back.)
- If in a bull market, the intention is to roll up protection to a higher market level, then this alternative is likely to be cheaper than purchasing a regular put option, depending on when the PAYG option is terminated.
- Upside potential remains unlimited.

Key disadvantages

- If all instalments are paid, the total premium will be greater than that for a regular put option.

Roll-up put option

Strategy

- The investor buys a roll-up put option today for the same price as a regular put. The roll-up put automatically switches into a higher strike put if the market trades up to a certain barrier level above spot. Therefore protecting portfolio at higher level.
- If the market further appreciates to a second barrier then the options expires.

Key advantages

- Protects portfolio at a higher level if market trades up, for the same price as a regular put option.

Key disadvantages

- If the market further appreciates, then the second barrier is hit and the protection is lost. (However, if the investor had bought the 100% put initially, then with the market at the higher level, this original put would have little value.)

In-the-money knockout put option

Strategy

- A put option is purchased and paid for today.
- The option expires worthless if the market trades down to a pre-defined level below strike.

Key advantages

- Option is cheaper than regular put option.
- Upside potential remains unlimited.

Key disadvantages

- Option will expire worthless if market trades down to knock-out level, below strike.

Appendix D

This is a simple description of the main investment trading techniques.

Systematic and discretionary trading approaches

Traders may generally be classified as either systematic or discretionary. A systematic trader may use a degree of judgemental decisions concerning, for example, what markets to follow and contracts to trade, when to liquidate a position in a contract which is about to expire and how large a position to take in a particular sector. However, although these judgemental decisions may have a substantial effect on a systematic trading advisor's performance, his primary reliance is on trading programmes or models which generate trading signals. The systems utilised to generate trading signals are changed from time to time (although generally infrequently), but the trading instructions generated by the systems being used are followed without significant additional analysis or interpretation. Discretionary traders, on the other hand, while they may utilise market charts, computer programs and compilations of quantifiable fundamental information to assist them in making trading decisions, make trading decisions on the basis of their own judgement and 'trading instinct', not on the basis of trading signals generated by any programme or model.

Each approach involves certain inherent risks. Systematic traders may fail to capitalise on market trends which their systems would otherwise have exploited due to judgemental decisions made by them in the context of applying their generally mechanical trading systems. Discretionary traders, on the other hand, may decide to make trades which would not have been signalled by a trading system and which result in substantial losses. Furthermore, any trading system or trader may suffer substantial losses by misjudging the market. Systematic traders tend to rely more on computerised programs than do discretionary traders, and some consider the prospect of disciplined trading, which largely removes the emotion of the individual trader from the trading process, advantageous. In addition, due to their use of computers, systematic traders are generally able to incorporate more data into a particular trading decision than can discretionary traders. However, when fundamental factors dominate the market, trading systems may suffer rapid and severe losses due to their inability to respond to such factors until such factors have had a sufficient effect on the market to create a trend of enough magnitude to generate a reversal of trading signals, by which time a precipitous price change may already be in progress, preventing liquidation at anything but substantial losses.

Technical and fundamental analysis

In addition to being distinguished from one another by the criterion of whether they trade systematically or on the basis of their discretionary evaluations of the markets, managers are also distinguished by whether they use 'technical' or 'fundamental' analysis, or a combination of the two. Systematic traders tend to rely on technical analysis, because the data relevant to such analysis is more susceptible to being isolated and quantified to the extent necessary to be successfully incorporated into a programme or mathematical model than is most 'fundamental' information, but there is no inconsistency in attempting to trade systematically on the basis of fundamental analysis. The fundamental information which can be evaluated by a formalised trading system is, however, limited to some extent in that it generally must be quantifiable in order to be processed by such a system.

Technical analysis is not based on anticipated supply and demand factors; instead, it is based on the theory that the study of the commodities markets themselves will provide a means of anticipating future prices. Technical analysis operates on the theory that market prices at any given point in time reflect all known factors affecting the supply and demand for a particular commodity. Consequently, technical analysis focuses not on evaluating those factors directly but on an analysis of market prices themselves, theorising that a detailed analysis of, among other things, actual daily, weekly and monthly price fluctuations, volume variations and changes in open interest is the most effective means of attempting to predict the future course of price movements.

Fundamental analysis, in contrast, is based on the study of factors external to the trading markets that affect the supply and demand of a particular commodity in an attempt to predict future price levels. Such factors might include weather, the economy of a particular country, government policies, domestic and foreign political and economic events, and changing trade prospects. Fundamental analysis theorises that by monitoring relevant supply and demand factors for a particular commodity, a state of current or potential disequilibrium of market conditions may be identified that has yet to be reflected in the price level of that commodity. Fundamental analysis assumes that markets are imperfect, that information is not instantaneously assimilated or disseminated and that econometric models can be constructed that generate equilibrium prices that may indicate that current prices are inconsistent with underlying economic conditions and will, accordingly, change in the future.

Trend following

'Trend-following' managers gear their trading approaches towards positioning themselves to take advantage of major price movements, as opposed to traders who seek to achieve overall profitability by making numerous small profits on short-term trades, or through arbitrage techniques. Trend-following traders assume that most of their trades will be unprofitable. Their objective is to make a few large profits, more than offsetting their more numerous but smaller losses, from capitalising on major trends. Consequently, during periods when no major price trends develop in a market, a trend-following trading advisor is likely to incur substantial losses.

Risk-control techniques

An important aspect of any speculative futures strategy relates to the control of losses, and not only the ability to identify profitable trades. Unless it is possible to avoid major drawdowns, it is very difficult to achieve long-term profitability.

Traders often adopt fairly rigid *risk management* or *money management* principles. Such principles typically restrict the size of positions which will be taken as well as establishing *stop-loss* points at which losing positions must be liquidated. It is important for prospective investors to recognise that none of the various risk control techniques is *fail safe* and none can, in fact, assure that major drawdowns will be avoided. Not only do estimates of market volatility themselves require judgemental input, but also market illiquidity can make it impossible for an account to liquidate a position against which the market is moving strongly, whatever risk-management principles are utilised. Similarly, irrespective of how small the initial *probing* positions taken by an advisor, unless he trades profitably, the innumerable small losses incurred in the course of such *probing* can quickly cumulate into a major drawdown. Advisors' risk-management principles should, accordingly, be seen more as a discipline applied to their trading in highly speculative markets than as effective protection against loss. The markets are always changing.

Appendix E: Hedge fund types

There has been a lot of media coverage about hedge funds; here is a summary of what they do. Hedge funds fall into a variety of different categories and types. The most straightforward of which are as follows.

Arbitrage

Purchase a security at one price and the simultaneous or nearly simultaneous sale of its equivalent at a higher price.

Bottom up

Methodically select specific stocks using traditional securities analysis techniques.

Emerging markets

Invest in any country where the economy and market is generally considered to be emerging or developing, e.g. Chile, Israel, Thailand.

Macro

Take a broad top-down approach to the selection of both countries, asset classes and sectors in which to invest.

Market neutral

Primary goal is to neutralise market risk by matching as closely as possible the correlation of its long and short positions. For example, a manager may be long and short United States equities.

Opportunistic

Employ a wide variety of trading strategies to capitalise on different profit-making opportunities as trading shifts among the markets.

Short selling

Attempt to profit from the greater pricing inefficiencies believed to exist on the short side of the securities market. Used by those who perceive the market as becoming bearish or as a hedge for long-only portfolios.

Smallcap

Focus on common stock of companies whose market capitalisation's and/or total revenues are less than US$600 million. The premise is these companies are well positioned to provide greater growth than what is available for over-all economy.

Special situations

Invest primarily in special situations including the purchase of securities of bankrupt or near-bankrupt companies.

Value

Purchase securities that are trading at a substantial discount to net asset value, that is, selling at a price well below the intrinsic value of the business with the hope that capital appreciation will result. Holding period is generally long term.

Yield-curve arbitrage

Buy or sell treasury securities of one maturity and simultaneously sell or buy weighted amounts of securities or either shorter or longer maturities.

This is approximately US$75 billion under management in these hedge fund categories in about 900 funds, 30 per cent of the money is held by the largest four funds. After excellent, indeed exceptional performance in 1993, 1994 saw some large reversals and losses. These attracted negative media attention and served to highlight the potential dangers. In the most extreme cases investors lost all their money.

Postscript
The collapse of Barings Bank

This book was already in the final stages of production at the time of the collapse of Barings as a result of losses on its proprietary exchange traded futures positions carried out in its subsidiary, Barings Futures Singapore.

The losses from the futures positions were £610 million in Tokyo, £90 million in Osaka and £160 million in Singapore. The Bank was put into Administration (the UK equivalent of Chapter 11) under the administrative control of Ernst & Young on Sunday, February 26th 1995. This was once it had become clear that any unquantifiable losses arising from outstanding open positions in Far Eastern futures contracts made a rescue attempt unrealistic. After a frantic week of analysis, liquidation of positions and realisation of losses, on Monday, March 6th 1995 the Dutch bank Internationale Nederlanden Groep NV (ING) acquired the operations of Barings.

ING took on £860 million of losses and injected £660 million into the securities, corporate finance and asset management arms. After taking into account original shareholders' funds of £440 million, the new business had net assets of £240 million.

Although not strictly a case of the use of derivatives for fund management purposes, this situation clearly merits attention. Inevitably there is considerable conjecture in the following analysis given that the full facts are not openly available and the official reports on the affair have not yet been prepared. In addition, a number of matters remain *sub judice*. This is not therefore a case study with the full benefit of hindsight, but an attempt to report on the general situation and the lessons to be learnt from it.

Barings' Singapore futures activity had been noticed in the market in late 1994 and early 1995. It was obvious that large futures positions were being accumulated in Tokyo, Osaka and Singapore. The belief internally and externally was that the positions were arbitrage positions partly on behalf of customers, whereby Barings was holding short Singapore Nikkei 225 contracts and long Osaka equivalents.

By the numbers		
Internationale Nederlanden Group and Barings PLC		
	ING	Barings
Total assets	$214.8bln	$9.56bln
Assets under mgmt.	$6.8bln	$46bln
First-half 1994 profit*	$658mln	$80mln
Employees (at home)	30,000	1,866
Employees (abroad)	17,000	2,134
Countries present (licensed bank)	48	38
Countries present (rep. office)	23	13
*net profit for ING, pretax profit for Barings		
Source: Company reports		

Figure P.1 By the numbers: Internationale Nederlanden Group and Barings PLC.

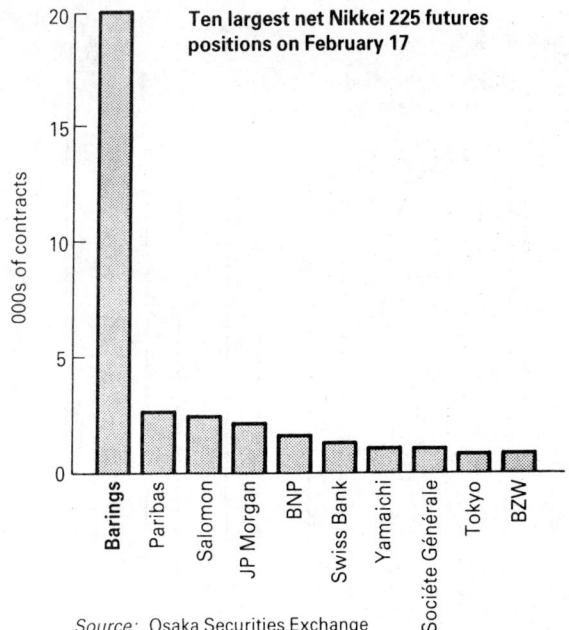

Figure P.2 Ten largest net Nikkei 225 futures positions on February 17.

Barings' bullish view of the market was general knowledge and a number of houses amongst the Japanese brokerage companies, as well as the major American traders such as Morgan Stanley, Goldman Sachs and Lehman Brothers had been happy to sell futures contracts to Barings whilst buying the stocks in the index.

Barings' position in the Osaka Securities Exchange was six times its nearest participant's, and this information was published weekly.

On January 26th Barings crossed 16,000 contracts on Simex, the Singapore Exchange, five minutes after Osaka had closed. This assisted the market impression that positions had been hedged. In fact Barings had an exposed long position in all the markets and as the Nikkei 225 price declined during January and February, compounded by the effect of the Kobe earthquake on January 17th, Barings' problems and losses grew. 16,000 of the contracts crossed were placed into an error account, number 88888; a number presumably chosen somewhat tongue-in-cheek since eight is a lucky number in Chinese culture. This account had 61,039 long futures contracts at the close of business on February 24th 1995. The crunch finally came.

Initially, it was thought that the Singapore trader was solely to blame. However, the payment of the margin call deposits required by the different exchanges had led to some 1.3 billion Singapore dollars (US$900 million)

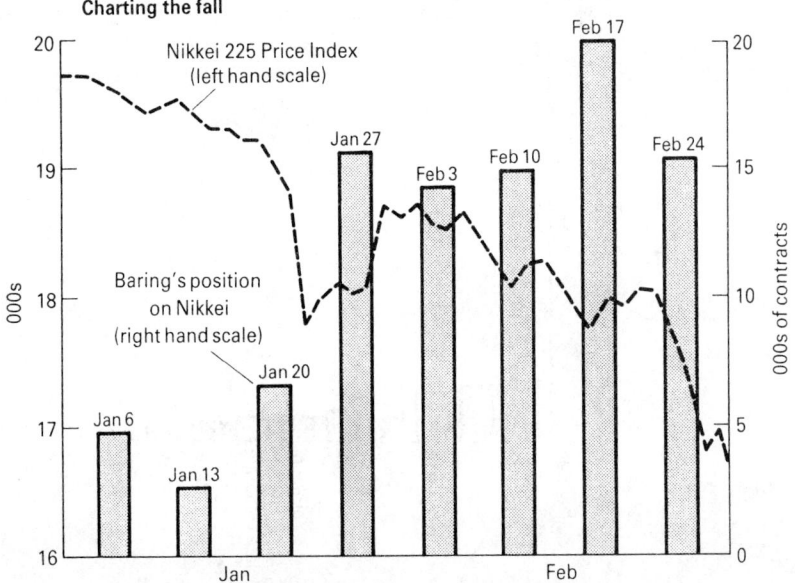

Figure P.3 Charting the fall.

being sent to Barings in Singapore during January and February to pay margin calls.

It has also transpired that the exchanges (both in Osaka and Simex) had discussed Barings' positions with senior managers, that market participants had spoken at various levels with Barings managers and directors outside Singapore. On February 8th the Barings Group Treasurer had reassured officials of Simex, the Singapore exchange, that Barings was aware of its exposures and had credit facilities in place to accommodate them. It transpired that three out of the four accounts Barings Futures held were Baring company accounts.

The operational structure of Barings Futures Singapore gave rise to the first failure in the long list of checks and balances which exist to control the risks of participants in these markets. The Singapore trader was also manager of the back office, a situation which, given the size and level of activity, must be unique as well as extremely foolish. Because of the reorganisation taking place within Barings generally, the trader reported to three different bosses for his three activities (futures, sales and settlements), all of them, because of office politics, based in London. Managers appear to have had responsibilities they either could not, or did not, fulfill. Indeed, Barings' internal auditors and the Barings General Manager in Singapore had raised the issue with the appropriate internal authorities. Apparently, because of the profitability being demonstrated by the Singapore operation, management failed to restructure the department to remove operational control from the actual trader. This is a classic example of the cultural mis-match which has caused so much difficulty within the financial service community in the reconciliation between the traditional conservative banking culture and the more aggressive free-wheeling approach of the new market areas. The expansion of the US dealing room culture with its concentration of power in the large business producers or profitable traders has proved time and again to be very difficult to manage because everyone in the organisation becomes mesmerised by the profit contribution. Barings had already experienced similar difficulties in the United States where the Securities and Exchange Commission found the Bank to be in breach of reporting rules on its financial position. The trader in Singapore responsible for Barings' collapse was 28 years old and managed to destroy a 233 year old merchant bank in two months. The fact is, however, that no-one stopped him.

Apart from the inappropriate internal structure and responsibility in Barings Futures, and the problems arising from Barings' internal territorial battles, there are some external considerations which contributed to the disaster. The Simex market has experienced tremendous growth in recent years and it has done so partly out of its success with the Nikkei 225 futures contract which started in 1986. Because of the competition between Simex and Osaka on this contract, communication between the exchanges has been limited and somewhat frosty. Indeed the Osaka Exchange department

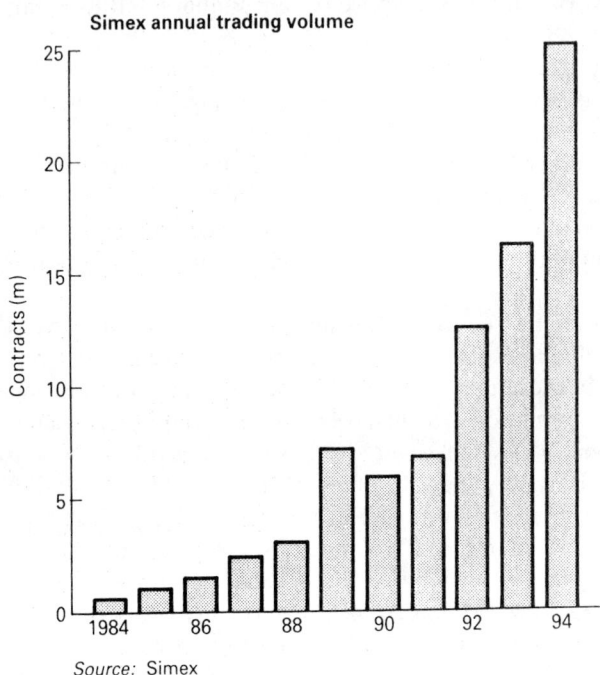

Figure P.4 Simex annual trading volume.

assigned to communicate with Simex apparently had no employees who spoke English. Because the positions were conducted through different exchanges with different clearing houses and because Barings was paying its margin calls in both places (it remains unclear exactly how the Singapore office was able to persuade Barings' London treasury to pay so much money), it would seem possible that both exchanges were just pleased to have such good business.

Ironically, regulation in its general sense may also have played a part in the situation escalating and running through so many theoretical road blocks and red warning lights. The development of regulations internationally has not always been either parallel, communal or well co-ordinated and authorities in Singapore and Japan almost certainly took comfort from the role they believed to be played by both the so called self-regulatory authorities in the UK such as the Securities and Futures Authority and the Bank of England itself with its responsibility for the regulatory supervision of the banking sector. In the very week of the collapse, the Organisation for Economic Co-operation and Development hosted a meeting between its financial market committee and representatives from the financial services industry to review the management of risk in the new financial environment. Everybody has been concerned about their information and risk management systems in this field for some time.

The fifteen Japanese banks which had lent nearly 70 billion Yen (US$715 million) had done so on the basis that the loans were to cover increases in margin on securities hedged in other markets. The proof of such hedging almost certainly came via Barings' head office in London, and presumably there must have been some capital adequacy analysis which would have rung alarm bells. However, the overall sense of complacency relating to Barings itself as very much a blue chip, blue-blooded member of the UK financial establishment, must have encouraged everyone in their belief that the Bank not only knew what it was doing, but also was being supervised in such a way which allowed it to do what it was doing.

The UK 1987 Banking Act requires auditors to produce a management report of management systems and controls and any internal audit concerns should have been noted. In addition, Section 3 of the Act requires that no bank should have a credit exposure of more than 25 per cent of its capital, without an exemption. This applies to loans and intra-company funding. The payments for the margin calls by Barings well exceeded the capital of the Bank. Banks have to submit a monthly liquidity report from the treasury to its supervisors.

Early claims by the Bank of conspiracy and fraud seem hollow given the disclosure of subsequent information and were presumably markers laid down at the suggestion of the London administrators in order to justify claims under insurance policies held by the Bank in the sum of £205 million, of which £75 million was for criminal related losses, £100 million was for professional indemnity and the balance for directors and officers. The report of the Board of Banking Supervision will be fascinating reading, provided that it is not a whitewash, it is aimed at drawing practical operational lessons for the future and that it really is an independent report.

As mentioned elsewhere in the book, there have been concerns raised by regulators and market participants about the effect of a major collapse in these markets. The expansion in this industry is clearly seen, and has given rise to fears of so called 'systemic risk'. This is a risk that the failure of one financial institution will trigger a chain reaction and global knock-on effect.

The Barings case, however, has shown the resilience of the exchange traded contracts and the success of the Clearing Houses role in London, Singapore and Japan. The London Clearing House had closed out Barings' positions early on Monday, 27th February, and although there was market weakness in the Japanese stock market arising from the liquidation, the systems implementing the liquidation proved to be robust and effective. The Monetary Authority of Singapore which supervises Simex was quick to demonstrate the essential integrity of its management as well as discovering the evidence of Barings' internal communications about its business. There were some problems with clients of Barings persuading the Japanese authorities to free up frozen collateral in the sum of US$200 million in margin payments for trades on the Japanese markets. There was considerable liaison between Japanese

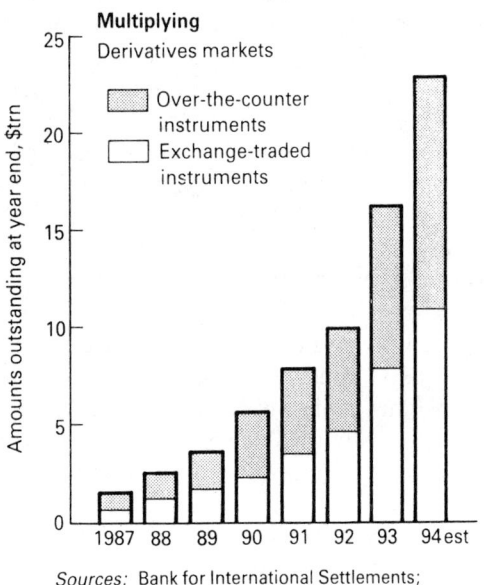

Figure P.5 Derivatives markets, amounts outstanding at end year.

authorities, the Commodities Futures Trading Commission in the United States and the Securities and Futures Authority in the UK. As a result, the liquidation process itself was clinical and effective. The speed of the collapse reminded everybody of their responsibilities and obligations to control this business effectively.

There is as yet no final conclusion to this sorry saga. The most obvious general conclusions however are:

1. Market participants must have an independent and powerful middle office/back office function over which sales traders have no influence.
2. Market participants must have effective information and risk management systems.
3. Regulators of exchanges must have constructive open channels of communication.
4. Whilst the dealing room culture of individualism, competition and security can be highly rewarding and creative, a management structure of co-operation must reduce the room for rogue traders to operate. There needs to be a reality check.
5. The case highlighted the breakdown between the political and financial links in the UK and showed how global markets have reduced the effectiveness of domestic regulatory operators.

It must be noted, however, that this is not a case where derivatives themselves have been blamed or not understood by the users, but a case where the trader was not understood by his employers. Time will tell, but on the face of it, ING got a bargin as a result of its being able to purchase Barings due to these events.

It should also be noted that certain derivative fund managers, not least George Soros with his Quantum Fund, have been able to profit hugely from being on the other side of the market. Barings was a big loser, but there were also some big winners.

Index

absolute return managers 84
accounting practices 128–129
advisors, question of number 148, 150
agreements, master, and G30 recommendations 127–128
annual reports, responsibility to file 23
arbitrage, as hedge fund function 174
Argentina, place in rankings 3
Arkansas Best Corp (US) 55, 56–57
asset allocation 131–133
Australia, place in rankings 2
Austria, place in rankings 3
Authorised Futures and Options Funds (AFOFs) (UK) 25–27
Authorised Unit Trusts (AUTs) (UK) 44, 47, 48
authority, and G30 recommendations 128

back office, potential conflict of interest in 179
Bahamas, as low-tax jurisdiction 31, 32
Bank of England, question of regulation of Barings 180
Barings Bank
    collapse 176–183
    lessons 17, 130, 158, 182–183
    contrasted with ING 177
    question of breach of SEC reporting rules in US 179
Barran and Partners, profile 90–92
barrier put options, principles 167
basket, defined 165
basket swaps, and asset allocation 132, 133
Belgium 3, 14
benchmarks 64–81
    scope 64
    and skill-based Market Performance Indices 72

Bermuda 25, 29
bias
    and DFMs' track record 80
    in market indices 74, 75
Board of Banking Supervision (UK) 181
Brazil 2, 4
British Virgin Islands (BVI) 31, 32
brokers 37, 140–141
    commissions 77, 151–152
    firms' margins 165
Buchanan, profile 88–90

Canada, exchanges' places in rankings 2
Capital Futures Management 103, 107
capital gains, and UK taxation 42, 44, 45, 46
Capital Protected Futures and Options Funds, scope of IFSC 33–34
Cayman Islands 31, 32–33
Chescor 102, 105
Chicago, exchanges 2, 4, 5, 154
Cohn, Michael 104
collars, principles outlined 167
commissions
    and retail fund selection 151–152
    see also fees
commodities dealers, US taxation 58–60
commodity funds, regulation of 36, 37
Commodity Futures Trading Commission (CFTC) (US) 20, 61–62, 164, 181–182
    rules 21, 22
commodity indices 66–72
Commodity Pool Operators (CPOs) 20, 21, 22
Commodity Research Bureau Future Prices Index 66–67
Commodity Training Advisors (CTAs) 11, 19, 25, 82, 83

Index

American criteria 20–21, 22
contingent options, outlined 167–168
conversions, defined 165
convertibles, and asset allocation 133
Corn Products (US) 55–56, 57
credit enhancement 128
credit exposure 127
currency, as asset 41
currency risk 142–143
    and UK taxation 43–44, 45–47, 51–52
currency swaps 40, 133, 162

dealers, securities and commodities, US taxation 58–60
Denmark, place in rankings 3
derivatives
    emergence 7–9
    exchanges' rankings 2–3
    markets compared 5–6
    market trends 1, 3
    object of fund management 6
    overview 131–133
Derivatives Fund Managers (DFMs) 19, 82, 83
    and construction of MPIs 79–80
    scope 24, 84–85
deviation, standard 138
differential swaps 132, 133
disclosure documents 20
disclosures, and G30 recommendations 129
discretionary trading approach 171–172

effective portfolio management (EPM) 51
employment, growth 154
end-users, question of valuation and market risk management practices 127
enforcement, promotion of 128
equity, addition and withdrawals, and construction of MPIs 75–76
equity index swaps 132, 133, 166
equity options, US taxation 61–62
Europe
    development of derivative markets 11–17
    fund products 119–121
European Community 11–12, 25
    Investment Services Directive (ISD), scope 36
    Undertakings for Collective Investments in Transferable Securities (UCITS) Directive 12–13, 28, 35–36
exchange control regulations 141
exchanges, scope 163–164
exempt unit trusts, unauthorised *see* unauthorised exempt unit trusts (UK)

extendible put options, principles 169

Federal National Mortgage Association (Fannie Mae) (US) 55, 57
fees, and retail fund selection 149–152
financial instruments 47–48
Financial Intermediaries Managers and Brokers Regulatory Association (FIMBRA) (UK) 24
Financial Services Act (FSA) (UK), scope 24
foreign futures and options 21
forward contracts, defined 160
forward currency contracts, defined 40
France 2, 4, 5, 13–14, 154
FT-Actuaries World Indices Consortium 65–66
fund administration 141–142
fundamental analysis 172–173
fund of funds 50, 53, 137
fund management 9–11, 153–158, 176
fund managers 82
fund products 109–124
    Europe, Citibank Keynoted Bonds, profile 119–121
    Japan, main funds listed 121–123
    United Kingdom, Hypo Foreign and Colonial's Reserve Asset Fund Higher Income Plan, profile 115–119
    United States, Merrill Lynch Global Horizons LP, profile 109–115
fund selection
    and marketing
    promoter's viewpoint 143–146
    purchaser's viewpoint 146–152
futures
    and Barings' collapse 179
    contrasted with options 41
    defined 166
    history 6–7
    role in fund management 9–11
futures brokers, relationship with Commodity Training Advisors 20
Futures Commissions Merchants (FCMs), relationship with Commodity Training Advisors 20
futures contracts 41
    defined 40, 159–160
futures funds 10, 15–16
    management 19, 21
Futures and Options Funds (FOFs) (UK) 15, 50, 52, 53

Geared Futures and Options Funds (GFOFs) (UK) 15, 26–27, 50, 52, 53

186 Index

Germany 2, 4, 5, 16–17
Gillis, Simon, profile 94, 96
Global Asset Management 94
Goldman Sachs Commodity Index 68–72
Gottex Fund Management, profile 92, 94
guaranteed return bonds (GRBs) 133, 166
Guernsey 25, 29, 30–31

Hasenbichler Trading Services Ltd 107–108
hedged fund managers, object in life 82
hedge funds 155, 156–157, 174–175
    background 83–86, 88
hedging 125, 142–143, 162
hedging transactions, and US taxation 53–57
Hong Kong, place in rankings 2

IFM Asset Management Limited 88
incentive fees 150
income, and UK taxation 42, 44–45, 46
index futures 132, 133, 166
index options, scope 133
initial margins, defined 164
instalment options, principles 169–170
institutional investors 60, 144, 145–146
insurance companies (UK) 48
interest income, and construction of MPIs 77–78
interest-rate swaps 93–94, 162
Internationale Nederlanden Groep NV (ING), and Barings 176, 177, 183
in-the-money knockabout put options 171
investment, size of, and retail fund selection 147
investment approaches 84, 139–140
investment limits, for personal equity plans, and UK taxation 52
investment management 82, 125–135, 137–139, 150, 157–158
Investment Managers Regulatory Organisation (IMRO) (UK) 24
investments, pooled 20
investment terms 148–150
investment trusts (UK) 48, 49–50
investor considerations 136–143
    see also risk management
investors, and fund selection 143–145
Ireland 3, 14, 156
    Dublin International Financial Services Centre (IFSC) 31, 33–34
Isle of Man 25, 29, 31
Italy, place in rankings 2

Japan 2, 36–37, 121–123

and Barings 178, 179, 180, 181–182
TIFFE 4, 5
Jersey 25, 29–30

leveraged fund managers 82, 83
Leveraged Protected Futures and Options Funds 33, 34
liquidity, as risk issue 135
London International Financial Futures and Options Exchange (Liffe) 2, 4, 5, 154, 164
long, defined 159–160
losses
    application of legislation 48–49
    treatment under proposed regime 47–48
Luxemburg 14–15, 31, 34–35, 156

maintenance margins, defined 164
Malaysia, place in rankings 3
managed futures, see derivatives
management, senior, role 126
margins, defined 164–165
marketing
    and fund selection 143–152
    see also fund selection
Market Performance Indices (MPIs), skill-based, construction 72–81
Merrill Lynch Global Horizons LP, profile 109–115
mixed-investment vehicles 22
Monetary Authority of Singapore 181
money market funds 50, 53
multi-manager funds 137

National Futures Authority (NFA) (US) 20
Netherlands 3, 15
Netherlands Antilles 31, 35
netting, recognition of 129
New Zealand, place in rankings 3
Nikkei 225 contracts, and Barings collapse 176, 177, 178, 179–180
non-actual equity, and MPIs 76
non-regulated contracts, US taxation 63
Norway, place in rankings 3

offshore funds 22, 23, 146
on-balance-sheet positions, defined 40
open interest, defined 160
open positions, defined 159–160
open trades, defined 159–160
options 6–7, 41, 133
    defined 40, 160–161, 166
Orange County (US) 5, 133–134

original margins, defined 164
OTC (over the counter), defined 166
OTC (over the counter) derivatives 125–135
OTC (over the counter) options 22

Panther Capital Management, profile 104–105
pay as you go options, principles 170
pension funds, taxation 44–45, 60
performance 82, 147–148
   fees 150
   indices 64–81
      construction 72–81
      Goldman Sachs Commodity Index 68–72
personal equity plans (PEPs) (UK) 52–53
Personal Investments Authority (PIA) (UK), scope 24
Philippines, place in rankings 2
premium trigger options, principles 168
principals' markets, outside US 163–164
private investors 10
private placement 27–28
profits 47–49, 149
programme trades 132, 133, 166
promoter, view of marketing and fund selection 143–152
property funds 50, 53

Qualified Eligible Participants (QEPs) 21

rate of return, computation 78–79
redemptions, and retail fund selection 148–149
regular put options, principles 166–167
regulated contracts 61–63
regulators, and G30 recommendations 129–130
revenue sources, and G30 recommendations 126
risk 125, 134, 151–152
risk-control techniques 173–174
risk-disclosure statements 25
risk management 126–127, 133–135, 157, 180
   as investor consideration 136–143
risk/reward profile 146–147
risk warnings 27
Robertson, Julian 84, 86
roll-up put options, principles 170–171

Sabre Fund Management 97, 99, 101
securities, issuer's duty to register 23
securities dealers, US taxation 58–60
securities funds, and UK taxation 50–52
Securities and Futures Authority (SFA) (UK) 24
   and Barings 180, 181–182
Securities and Investments Board (SIB) (UK) 24, 25, 50
Security and Exchange Commission (SEC) 21, 22
   and Barings 179
self-regulatory authorities (SROs) (UK) 24
Sharpe Ratio, as yardstick 138–139
short, defined 159–160
Silver Knight, profile 101, 104
Singapore 5
   and Barings 180, 181
   Simex 2, 5
   and Barings 176, 179–180
Soros, George 84, 86, 183
South Africa, place in rankings 2
Spain, place in rankings 2
speculators, defined 162, 163
spreads, defined 165
standard deviation, as yardstick 138
Steinhardt, Michael 84, 86
step-down trigger options, principles 168
sterling, status in UK tax system 40
stock indices, scope 64–66
straddles, and US taxation 63
stress simulations 126
supervisors, responsibilities 129–130
swaps, as investment/futures fund permitted by SEC 22
Sweden, place in rankings 2
switcher funds 156
Switzerland 2, 5
systematic trading approach 171–172
system risk, and Barings 181
systems, and G30 recommendations 128

TASS Management, and new performance benchmark 72, 79
taxation 39–63
   United Kingdom *see* United Kingdom, taxation
   United States *see* United States, taxation
tax regulations, as investor consideration 141
tax treatment, and G30 recommendations 130
technical analysis 172–173
Thirty, Group of (G30), *Derivatives: Practices and Principles* 125–130
transaction costs 151–152
transparency, as risk issue 135
trend-following 139–140, 173

unauthorised unit trusts (UK) 45–46, 53
United Kingdom

development of derivatives markets
  15–16
draft legislation on financial instruments
  39
exchanges' place in rankings 2, 4, 5
Hypo Foreign and Colonial's Reserve
  Asset Fund Higher Income Plan,
  profile 115–119
marketing in 26–35
  AFOFs and GFOFs 26–27
  non-public funds, scope 27–28
  and recognised low-tax jurisdictions
    28–35
  public funds, scope of Financial Services
    Act 25
regulation of DFMs 13
requirements 24–26
taxation 39–53
  application of proposed regimes 47–49
  Authorised Unit Trusts 44
  capital 41–42
  insurance companies 46–47
  investment trusts 42–44
  miscellaneous income 42
  pension funds 44–45
  personal equity plans 52–53
  tax-exempt bodies 42
  trading 41
  unauthorised exempt unit trusts 45–46

unit trusts 51–52
see also Barings Bank
United States 7, 73, 83
  and Barings Bank 179, 181–182
  exchanges
    place in rankings 2, 3, 4, 5
    scope 163–164
  Orange County collapse 5, 133–134
  requirements
    derivatives funds 20–21
    non-US operations 21–24
  taxation
    capital gains 57–60
    and gains arising from derivative
      instruments 60–63
    and hedging transactions 53–55
unit trusts, unauthorised exempt *see*
  unauthorised unit trusts (UK)

valuation, as risk issue 135
Value Management and Research (VMR),
  profile 99
variable life options, principles 169
variation margins, defined 164

warrant funds 50, 53
warrants 40, 133, 166
weightings, and construction of MPIs 79–80
World Index Policy Committee 65–66